Urban Planning in a Multicultural Society

Edited by
Michael A. Burayidi

PRAEGER

Westport, Connecticut
London

Library of Congress Cataloging-in-Publication Data

Urban planning in a multicultural society / edited by Michael A.
Burayidi.
    p.   cm.
  Includes bibliographical references and index.
  ISBN 0–275–96125–7 (alk. paper)
  1. City planning.   2. Community development, Urban.   3.
Multiculturalism.   4. Ethnicity.   I. Burayidi, Michael A.
  HT165.5 .U75   2000
  307.1′216—dc21   99–18013

British Library Cataloguing in Publication Data is available.

Library of Congress Catalog Card Number: 99–18013
ISBN: 0–275–96125–7

First published in 2000

Praeger Publishers, 88 Post Road West, Westport, CT 06881
An imprint of Greenwood Publishing Group, Inc.
www.praeger.com

Printed in the United States of America

The paper used in this book complies with the
Permanent Paper Standard issued by the National
Information Standards Organization (Z39.48–1984).

10 9 8 7 6 5 4 3 2 1

The Neighborhood

In this new neighborhood
there isn't a God-damned rummy.
Families are a rainbow, hearts roomy.
When you see me walking my dog
there is no misgiving, come along.
In this haven, you're my neighbor,
closer to the bone, not a burden to bear.

Along this new trail come join the jog.
I won't run you down because you're small
or change lanes to avoid you because you're tall.
I'll say "Hi!" to you, light or dark.
In this neighborhood, buzzards of hate
no more cast their talons or decide our fate.
A whiff of sameness pervades the air.

At the club house, come be jovial
You and I on the stage in the limelight,
singing limericks of our ethnicity,
sharing hugs of diversity,
tossing mugs,
to each other's health.

In your backyard and mine,
we're the rose and the lily
waving to our neighbors in green,
the runics and the orchids.

Alfred Kisubi

Contents

Illustrations

TABLES

FIGURES

Acknowledgments

A project of this measure could not have been undertaken without the loving support of several people. To paraphrase an African proverb, it took a village to get this project to maturity. Space will not permit the acknowledgment of all who contributed in no small measure to the completion of the project, but I am confident that even without personal acknowledgment, all who shared in this project will rejoice and take pride in the final product.

I wish to thank the following individuals for reading preliminary drafts of some chapters in this volume and giving their incisive comments: Howell Baum, Robert Beauregard, Richard Smith, David Jones, Alfred Kisubi, and David Varady. I am also grateful to Mary Bleser for help in the preparation and formatting of the manuscripts. Mary's sense of humor and her tireless devotion to the project are incommensurable.

To all my friends, colleagues, and family who put up with me during this project, many thanks.

CHAPTER 1

Urban Planning as a Multicultural Canon

Michael A. Burayidi

Planning is a democratic process through which communities, with the help of planners, are able to determine their felt needs and find ways to address these needs through a deliberative and reflective process. While planners bring their expertise to bear on the deliberations, it is ultimately the community that determines the final outcome of the decisions reached. Since communities differ in their needs and socio-cultural groups within communities seek different ends, it necessarily follows that effective planning would result in a plurality of plans to suit the needs of the diverse public. Planning therefore is a multidimensional and multifaceted profession with sensitivity toward class, race, sex, and culture. This makes planning a multicultural canon.

Given this conclusion, it is puzzling that what constitutes much of the tangible outcomes of plans, the urban physical environment, reflects less of a variation of the diverse cultures in the country. One is hard pressed to find the stamp of Chinese, Japanese, Ukrainian, Italian, or Greek architecture and built forms in U.S. cities where many of these groups reside. This implies that either planners have done a good job in creating a consensus among the diverse ethno-cultural groups in the country or that through coercion, lack of representation, or the muzzling of the voices of nondominant socio-cultural groups, the urban landscape failed to articulate their culture[1] and needs.

Modernist planning in the postwar years did a good job of eliminating the vestiges of cultural identity in urban form and architecture as ethnic enclaves were bulldozed to make way for new development. The current attraction of neo-traditional planning is in part a reflection of the rejection of the homogeneity in urban form and architecture that modernist planning produced over the years. In a sense, it is a way of injecting culture back into the built environment and into planning.

THE NEED FOR A MULTICULTURAL SENSITIVITY IN PLANNING

The central argument of this book is that culture matters in planning and that it matters in a number of significant ways. For one thing, there has been a shift from a modernist to a postmodern conception of the world. Planning, like the other social sciences, came into existence during the Enlightenment (modern) era. As such, the methods, approaches, assumptions, and concepts of the profession were shaped by the thinking of the time. Thus, the use of the scientific method as a research procedure and a means for understanding human behavior, the reliance on reason, the belief in objectivity and value neutrality, all became a part of the planning dictum.

In the Enlightenment era there was a belief that only a society based on science and universal values is truly free, and that truth, knowledge, and rationality were more important than anything else. Today many of these tenets of the Enlightenment and modernism have been called into question. Nietzsche (1967), for example, has criticized the principles of modernism. He argued that what may be of most value to a community or group may be something that cannot be proven such as culture, traditions, myths, and customs. Postmodernists also argue against modernist suggestions of a universal value system. For postmodern scholars (see for example Foucault 1986; Habermas 1981; and Lyotard 1992), society and world cultures are fragmented and particularistic. Hence, one cannot attribute normative values to all societies. Doing so amounts to paternalism and domination. Instead, Postmodernists argue for acknowledgment of diversity, difference, and cultural fragmentation. For planners working in a postmodern era, this necessitates that we jettison, or at the very least, modify the assumptions, methods, and procedures that have in the past been the mainstay of modernist planning in order to better understand and plan for communities of the twenty-first century.

The second reason why culture matters in planning is that multiculturalism has become practically necessary. Put differently, different groups insist on being treated differently. Traditional minority groups in the United States, such as African Americans and Native Americans argue, and rightly so, that the plight of these groups in society today cannot be understood aside from the historical context of the groups in the country. Thus, inner city poverty and high unemployment rates among African Americans can only be understood in the context of a history of slavery and segregation laws to which this group was subjugated. In the same vein, Native-American land-use laws can only be understood in reference to Treaty Rights signed between the federal government and Indian tribes. Hence, in addressing problems of cities, it is well for planners to take these concerns into consideration. This way, planning can become one means for righting past injustices.

Third, culture matters in planning because it is morally and ethically incumbent on planners to treat different groups differently. People have different needs, come from different social and cultural backgrounds, and are exposed to different experiences. Understanding how these backgrounds and experiences help to shape people's view of the world will help ensure better planning.

To be sure, planners have not been entirely oblivious to the importance of culture in their work. It was simply viewed as a problem of planning in third-world countries whose value systems, social organization, and political culture were different from those of the West. Thus, as early as the 1960s, planners working in third world countries cautioned against the wholesale transfer of planning techniques and procedures from the West to the third world without modification to suit these countries' unique conditions (see for example, Oberlander 1962; Gullick 1967). However, while the tensions between culture and modernist planning were obvious in the third-world environment, in the western countries little attention was given to the accommodation of the pluralist cultural groups within their midst. This was due in part to the expectation that cultural and ethnic minorities would assimilate into mainstream culture. If any value differences existed between the cultural and ethnic minorities and the mainstream culture, it was thought, it must be because the assimilation process had not occurred fast enough.

As we have seen, persuasive arguments by Postmodernists, at least since the 1970s, have identified the shortcomings of Enlightenment doctrines. These scholars have questioned power relations between dominated and subordinated groups in the construction of knowledge, the applicability and relevance of universals to minority cultures and women, the reductionist and hegemonic tendencies of scientific deductive reasoning, and the role of culture in identity politics and difference.

As Smart acknowledged:

In societies such as ours truth is centered on the forms of scientific discourse and the institutions which produce it and to a substantial degree all forms of discourse lie in its shadow and remain subject to its measure. But the "truth" of our (western) societies is not reducible to scientific rationality alone. The post Enlightenment world-view evokes particular notions of the individual, material interests, rights and responsibilities, as well as universal goals and values which are being challenged by a complex combination of reconstituted traditional forms of life and "postmodern" reflections on both persisting and emerging forms of cultural difference and diversity. (Smart 1993, 117)

Western modernity and its values can no longer be presented as universal in contrast to other forms of knowledge. Hence, the need to broaden our understanding of the knowledge construction process and to embrace other ways of knowing that had been marginalized in the process of modernity.

These postmodern views have helped us to better understand the development of urban form and structure that resulted from modernist planning. For planners, the practical imperative is no longer whether planning ought to be culturally sensitive, but how? How do planners accommodate one group's view of the physical environment when it conflicts with that of another group? More importantly, the question remains whether it is possible for planning to be sensitive to diverse cultures and yet maintain a unified public realm?

THE PUBLIC REALM OF PLANNING

The public realm is where the various interests in a community collide and vie for attention. In the public realm it is often impossible to accommodate all group interests. Where there is conflict between group interests, as there often is, then a resolution must be found through the political process. While all groups may not be satisfied with the outcome of the decision arrived at through the political process, they usually go along with it if they feel that they have been given due process to be heard before the decision was made. Perceptions of fairness in the political process hinges on whether there is a balanced representation of the interests of the groups in the decision-making body, and the openness of the body to diverse opinions, even if these opinions are different from mainstream views and norms. It is in this sense that minority groups have sought increased political representation on decision-making bodies to make their interests and views heard.

Among the many issues that planners have to address in the public realm is the clash of interests resulting from cultural differences. This may erupt from identity claims from ethnic and cultural groups or it may result from differences in opinions regarding the built environment. In 1998, for example, the Saudi Arabian government proposed to build an Islamic Academy for Muslim children in Poolesville, Maryland, but the project was successfully blocked under the veil of limiting growth in the city and a claim that the project did not conform to the existing zoning regulations. However, the clash of cultures was made obvious when the Saudi government found an alternate site for the school in Loudon County.

The county board had to approve zoning changes to allow the school to be built. The proposed school, which will cost about $75 million and house a projected 3,500 student population, would, under normal circumstances, be welcomed in the community with open arms given the employment and incomes that the project would generate. The plan was, however, resisted by some community groups with protests and threats of violence because of fears that the school would become a breeding ground for Islamic terrorists. An unsigned flier warned that Middle East strangers would roam the streets while real Virginians are away at work. One couple expressed fear that bullets fired from within the compound would kill local children. In plain language, community residents resisted what they perceived to be an influx of a new cultural group into this predominantly White middle- and upper-middle-class community. All Arabs were portrayed by some of the community members as terrorists, and Muslims were not viewed as real Virginians, which also implies that they are not real Americans. It was only after intense negotiation and intervention by General Norman Schwarzkopf that the county approved the proposal.

This example of cultural misunderstanding is one way in which planning outcomes may be biased or planning's effectiveness compromised because of the xenophobic attitudes of a community. In this particular case, planners would be caught in a quandary between upholding zoning laws, which are supposed to be fair, versus the strong sentiments of a community, which, for the most part, are unfounded. Resolving the conflict between cultures in the public realm, therefore, requires planners to be tolerant, sensitive to the needs of all groups in the community, and willing to give each group due process to be heard.

There are six ways in which cultural misunderstanding between planners and ethno-cultural groups on the one hand, and between different community groups on the other could occur. To be culturally sensitive means that planners must become conscious of these pitfalls and guard against them. These cultural differences relate to (i) communication style (cultural differences affect the outcomes of the transactive and social learning process in planning); (ii) attitude toward disclosure (cultural differences influence the types of information people are willing to share with planners); (iii) attitude toward conflict (this has implications for the role that the planner plays as mediator in community conflicts); (iv) approaches to accomplishing task (this may affect the way in which planners and other professionals undertake teamwork in planning projects); (v) styles of decision making (different cultural groups have different decision-making procedures); and (vi) approaches to knowing (this affects the procedural approach to planning). Each of these are discussed in turn below.

Transactive Planning and Social Learning in Planning

Planners are often urged to engage in a communicative discourse with community groups so that they can share their professional knowledge with these groups and in turn learn from the experiential knowledge of community residents. This requires that the discourse medium be understandable to both agencies. Where there is a communication gap either due to differences in meaning attached to words or actions by either group, then the benefits of social learning and transactive planning are lost. Cultures differ in their communication styles. The form of communication could be verbal or nonverbal. Across cultures, words may have different meanings. For example, when a Japanese responds by saying "yes, yes" to a comment, she is not necessarily agreeing with what is being said but merely acknowledging that she has heard you.

In nonverbal communication, facial expression, gestures, seating arrangements, personal distance, and sense of time also differ. Africans use time to interpret and describe, while Europeans use time to predict and control. There are also different cultural norms regarding the degree of assertiveness in communicating. In western democratic discourse a reasonable degree of assertiveness is often associated with confidence and passion for a subject or issue. Eastern cultures on the other hand, frown upon people who are assertive and regard it as rude behavior.

In planning deliberations the style of communication by different groups making representation before a planning commission or planning staff could lead to different outcomes if there is a bias in what is considered to be the appropriate communication style. Worse still, the different communication styles between groups could lead to miscues and wrong interpretations that may adversely affect decision outcomes.

Information and Data Gathering

Planners need to be sensitive to ways in which they solicit information from community groups. Planners often collect information from communities as a part of the planning process. But different groups have different beliefs about what is information, what information matters, how one collects and tests it, and what one should disclose. The amount and type of information that people are willing and comfortable to reveal to planners may vary according to their socio-cultural background. Questions that may seem natural to planners may be viewed as intrusive by some groups. When members of a cultural group find questions to be intrusive, they may not readily offer this information, especially if it is being asked for by an outside agent. The unwillingness to disclose information by community groups could hinder planning's effectiveness. Planners would do well to explore other ways of gathering information from cultural groups that may be disinclined to provide this information through traditional means such as opinion surveys. Some alternative ways of gathering information that need to be explored by planners include ethnographic studies, narration and description, storytelling, talking circles, and role acting.

The Mediating Role of the Planner

Differences arise in how cultures respond to conflict. While western democracies regard confrontational dialogue as necessary and desirable for resolving disputes, Eastern cultures generally regard this as demeaning and embarrassing. In these cultures it is preferred that differences be worked out quietly before a face-to-face encounter takes place between the parties.

In the United States many Native-American tribes, such as the Navajo, have now established alternative dispute resolution mechanisms that are more suitable to the cultures of these tribes and that provide alternatives to the court system. These legal systems rely on traditional authority figures and communal pressure to resolve disputes rather than using the non-Indian legal system (Zioni 1983).

This implies that planners must offer several options to aggrieved parties for resolving their differences, especially where ethno-cultural groups are involved. Arranging for separate meetings between planners and the individuals or groups involved could help identify the preferred mediation options to be used. This also provides a way to reach a middle ground without confrontation and to build consensus among the groups.

Teamwork in Planning

Planners often work in teams to address planning problems. Frequently, planners have to work with engineers, architects and landscape architects, sociologists, economists, and politicians. Each of these professionals brings to the table their professional expertise but also their values, which may be ingrained by their culture.

While European Americans typically focus on the task at hand, Hispanic, African, and Asian cultures attach greater value to developing relationships at the beginning of the group project, with emphasis on task completion at the end. This helps to build trust among group members and allows them to later share their views on the project without fear of offending group members. Such value differences to the accomplishment of tasks could have a debilitating effect on the group if they are not recognized and addressed at the onset of the project.

Community Participation in Planning Deliberations

Perceptions that individuals hold about their role in decision making is influenced by their culture. In African and Asian cultures, decision making by consensus is often the norm. Reaching agreement with ones neighbors, coworkers, or group, even if one is not completely satisfied with the decision, is expected in these cultures. By stressing consensus rather than conflict and majority rule, group members are able to reach amicable solutions and thus avoid perceptions of "losers" and "winners" in a decision. By contrast, in western democracies majority rule is used to resolve differences and in making group decisions.

These differences in decision making may create problems for planners working with ethno-cultural groups. An aggrieved party may not necessarily be satisfied with a planning decision that is made through majority rule. Thus, cooperation from him/her may not be forthcoming in the pursuit of the public good.

The Knowledge Development Process

Ethno-cultural groups also differ in their approaches to knowing, that is, how they acquire knowledge. African cultures prefer affective ways of knowing involving touching, seeing, and feeling. Asian cultures, on the other hand, emphasize knowledge gained through striving toward transcendence. European cultures prefer knowledge and information gained through cognitive means, such as counting and measuring.

These various ways of knowing could affect how planners address community problems. While some planners may want to do research in the library to obtain the data needed for making a decision, others may prefer to visit the places and people experiencing these problems in order to better comprehend the scope and nature of the problem. A combination of affective and cognitive methods of knowledge acquisition may be necessary to satisfy planners from different cultures.

These differences between cultures require planners to approach planning differently in the twenty-first century. The planning process must be seen as fair and just to all ethno-cultural groups. If planning is to be perceived by these groups as fair and impartial, planners must demonstrate their sensitivity to the cultures of these groups. While the representation of diverse community groups on planning boards, citizen committees, and local legislative bodies is important, there is also a need for planners to demonstrate that they are sensitive to and are willing to accommodate the different world views of minority cultural groups in the country.

The essays in this volume indicate that planners have begun to recognize the challenge that multiculturalism poses for the profession, and have begun the search for appropriate responses. These responses have taken root in the critical dialogue among planning professionals, in the approaches to planning with ethnic and minority communities, and in planning institutions. The book is organized along these three broad areas.

PART I: CRITICAL PERSPECTIVES IN PLANNING

Through self-reflection and introspection, members of a profession are able to assess how well their practice is meeting the desired goals of the profession and society's needs. This process of self-reflection often leads to changes in professional practice as new knowledge becomes available, and in response to changing circumstances. Over the years the urban planning profession has grown and changed through this process of critical self-reflection.

Largely through the works of planning theorists, a number of criticisms have been and continue to be leveled against the profession. From an earlier criticism that the planning profession was too narrowly focused on physical development of cities to the neglect of socio-economic concerns, to one of equity and sexism in the physical development of cities, critical pragmatism now provides yet another attack on planning practice. Critical pragmatists argue that planning is too process-driven and doesn't adequately address problems of plan implementation. This forms the subject of the collection of chapters in Part I of this volume.

James traces and discusses the demographic changes that have taken place, and continue to take place, in the United States and establishes the fact that the United States is a multicultural and multi-ethnic society. In addition to this, James cautions planners to be careful with how they interpret data they obtain with conventional data collection methods because these results may reflect outcomes of historical discrimination and bias. Thus, in chapter 2, he suggests that planners need to complement conventional data sources with much more qualitative and indepth analysis of the communities in which they plan. This will enable planners to unearth the real needs of the people and result in better programmatic planning to meet these needs.

Burayidi's essay in chapter 3 traces the metamorphosis of the planning profession since its conception to date. He critiques current planning practices for submerging cultural differences under a universalist umbrella of monistic planning. Burayidi identifies and discusses some of the problems that result from monistic and universalist planning with examples from several communities. In place of monistic planning, Burayidi proposes a more tolerant approach to planning, one that is holistic and responsive to the cultural diversity in the United States. The rationale for holistic planning and how it can be institutionalized into planning practice is then discussed.

In chapter 4 Beauregard argues that it is difficult to reconcile the ideals of critical pragmatism in planning with the requirements of multiculturalism. While critical pragmatism assumes egalitarianism and a nonembodied individual participation in planning deliberations, multiculturalism requires planners to confer special privileges on groups and to acknowledge special competence of group members.

Beauregard concludes from this that critical pragmatism is not sufficiently embedded in its social context and it also disembodies participants in the planning process by not recognizing the group belonging of participants as required of multiculturalism. Because of these limitations, critical pragmatism may be of limited usefulness to planners in a multicultural society because it fails to give guidance to practice.

Stein and Harper in chapter 5 discuss the contributions and limitations of modernist and postmodernist ideologies for planning in a liberal democratic society. For them, a pragmatic reconciliation that appeals to the critical perspectives of modernism and the conciliatory elements of postmodernism may hold the key to planning with multicultural groups. They, therefore, suggest a situational balance between Enlightenment values and traditionalism, as well as an open and noncoercive dialogue between dominant and nondominant cultures to promote cultural understanding and planning decision making.

In chapter 6, Meyer and Reaves argue, using case studies in both developed and third-world countries, that while planners have so far addressed the problem of planning with multiple constituencies—interest groups—with similar value systems, we are yet to confront the much more difficult problem of planning with multicultural groups that have different values from those of the dominant culture. The authors point out that multicultural groups differ from multiple constituencies because of differences in what these groups consider to be appropriate elements to be considered in the optimization function, in the weights they assign to different outcomes of decisions, and in the constraints and limits they impose on alternative solutions to planning problems. An even greater challenge is whether multicultural groups accept the legitimacy of the decision-making body itself since the criteria that such bodies use in making decisions may be unacceptable to these groups. In response to this the authors propose a twelve-step process for addressing planning problems in a multicultural society with the hope that this may help to reduce the conflicts that may arise.

PART II: PLANNING WITH ETHNIC AND CULTURAL COMMUNITIES

In Part II the authors discuss specific cases of their experiences with planning with ethnic and cultural communities, pointing out some cautions for planners. The authors point to the intricacies required of planners working in nondominant cultures and the limitations of current planning practice in such environments. The essays help to illuminate our understanding not only of these cultures, but also how we might better prepare planners to address the needs of ethno-cultural communities.

Ameyaw's essay in chapter 7 points to some of the qualities that ethno-cultural groups could bring to the planning process if planners reached out to them. He suggests that planners could do this through Appreciative planning. Using case studies of Canadian communities, Ameyaw discusses how Appreciative planning has been used to revitalize declining urban neighborhoods, to transform streets into active public spaces, and to increase park use by ethnic groups. Finally, he outlines and discusses a process for moving from modernist planning to Appreciative planning.

Baum's discussion sheds light on the conflicts between the culture of a planning organization and that of an ethno-cultural community. This discussion is provided in chapter 8. The Associated, a Jewish planning organization, brought together members of synagogues in Baltimore to plan for the improvement of the Jewish community. While the Associated culture was based on developing programs and projects, members of the Jewish community valued "process" over programs because of their belief that this would foster closer relations among members of the community. These differences in culture between the two groups ultimately led to conflict and the demise of the coalition. The case illustrates the failure of a planning culture to address community interests.

Baum cautions us to the fact that groups that may appear homogeneous on the outside may in fact be heterogeneous with significant internal differences. Such was the case with the Jewish community in Baltimore. As a consequence, the planners were unable to get the community to reach agreement on programs and policies for the community as a whole. In the attempt to avoid conflict and promote consensus among the diverse synagogues in Baltimore, and increase donations to The Associated, planners failed to get community members to step aside from their culture and to critically examine their values, which would necessitate change.

There are two lessons to learn from this case study: First, planners must not uncritically accept the culture of those with whom they plan, but should help community members to re-examine their culture so as to identify its shortcomings and make changes; second, planners must be aware that they bring their own values and prejudices into planning and this may be in conflict with the values of the community with whom they plan.

In chapter 9 Lapping alerts us to the diversity of America's rural population and discusses the differential impacts of planning on three ethno-cultural groups—rural African Americans, Native-American communities, and the Amish. He argues that these three communities are some of the many diverse cultural groups in rural areas with distinct needs that must be addressed *within the rural setting*. For those who choose or are forced to live in rural communities, Lapping argues, planners should help to improve their socio-economic well-being and help preserve the pluralist and rural character of their lifestyles rather than try to urbanize them.

In chapter 10 Forester narrates the mediation practices of two planners and how they addressed conflicts that arose in multicultural settings. In the case of Shirley Solomon, it is an account of her mediation and facilitator role in resolving land-use disputes between Native Americans and non-Native Americans in Skagit County, Washington. The account of Larry Sherman involves mediating differences arising from gender and power. These stories are shared, not to provide instruction on what planners should do in multicultural settings, but to offer other options besides the adversarial approach to conflict resolution to which planners are often accustomed.

Dinero's essay addresses the problem of planning in traditional communities. His discussion in chapter 11 shows that planning with traditional communities poses a far greater challenge for planners than what occurs with ethnic groups in western society. This is so because (i) the value systems between these societies and planners differ; (ii) there is a difference in their way of life; and (iii) similar to arguments made by Meyer and Reaves in chapter 6, there are differences in what traditional communities expect to be included in the optimization function of decisions. Such is the situation with the resettlement program of the Bedouin nomadic community in Israel. Dinero observes that resettlement planners did not involve the Bedouin in the planning and implementation of the program. As a result of this top-down, nonparticipatory approach to service provision planning, the Bedouin feel alienated from the decision- making process. Thus, although their socio-economic condition may have improved due to the resettlement, the Bedouin are resentful of the Israeli government and program planners. He suggests the development of traditional indigenous structures and institutions with greater Bedouin involvement in these institutions to ensure better planning effectiveness.

PART III: INSTITUTIONAL RESPONSES TO MULTICULTURALISM

Given multiculturalism's demands on the planning profession, how do we modify planning institutions to better accommodate the needs of a multicultural society? Three of the most important planning institutions to which this question may be relevant are: (i) the planning departments of local government, which are directly responsible for meeting the planning needs of their communities; (ii) local planning commissions, which must decide on the appropriateness of planning proposals and offer advice to local governments; and (iii) schools of planning, which must prepare students for work in multicultural environments. In addition to these institutions, multiculturalism also requires new thinking in the way we structure programs and policies to address problems of living in a diverse multicultural society. The essays in Part III of the book address these concerns.

With regards to local planning commissions, Allor and Spence suggest, in chapter 12, a need to broaden their composition to reflect the demographics of the community, and an openness by commission members to diversity of values held and expressed by community residents before planning commissions. The authors suggest that planning standards and requirements should not be narrowly based on Euro-American urban design guidelines, otherwise they will exclude people who hold different values about the physical environment.

Since planning schools shape the practice behaviors of future planners, Sen suggests that planning schools should incorporate multicultural issues in urban design education. In chapter 13 Sen provides several persuasive arguments why this is crucial: First, the changing demographics of the United States will result in a different use of urban space, and planners must learn how to meet this need. Second, the redevelopment of older ethnic neighborhoods will require an understanding of the cultures of these ethnic groups so that redevelopment of these neighborhoods is culturally sensitive. Third, there is a need for urban designers to understand how global restructuring is affecting derelict urban spaces in older industrial cities and how urban planners can help restore the historical character of these cities.

The other face of institutional responses to multiculturalism has to do with planning programs and policies. Marcuse examines the Enterprise Zone concept as a means for inner city redevelopment in chapter 14 and concludes that the program's merits may be outweighed by its shortcomings. He observes that the Enterprise Zone program reinforces the ghettoization of poor and minority urban residents. Because the program is spatially based, it reduces the chances for minority integration into the larger society.

Finally, in chapter 15, Smith provides us with tools for measuring the spatial distribution of ethno-cultural groups. This is important because inter-cultural understanding is shown to increase with greater interaction among the races and cultural groups. This interaction is enhanced if there is proximity between the groups. While a lot of literature exists on segregation and how this is measured, few have provided guidance on measuring integration. Smith provides two ways for identifying stable and diverse multicultural neighborhoods using census data. The first approach is the comparative approach. It compares the racial composition of a census tract to that of a larger region, usually the county. A census tract with the same racial proportion of residents as that of the county is said to be racially mixed. Tracts that do not meet this proportion are segregated. The second approach, the market approach, uses housing cost and the purchasing power of racial groups to calculate the proportion of a racial group that should reside in a given neighborhood. Smith's major contribution to this volume is his findings that integrated neighborhoods do exist and he shows us how to identify these neighborhoods in any community.

SUMMARY

In the past planners have paid attention to the impact of planning policies and programs on race, especially following the abysmal failure of the urban renewal program of the 1960s to ameliorate the conditions of African Americans in the inner city (see Thomas and Ritzdorf 1997 for the latest discussion of this issue). A lot of literature also exists on the interconnections between planning and sexism (see, for example, Beauregard 1992; Hayden 1986; Leavitt 1986; Moore 1991). To date, however, very little has been written about culture and planning. Yet, anthropologists observe that what really distinguishes people from each other is not race, but culture (Cohen 1998). People might belong to the same race but exhibit entirely different cultures. In the same vein, people of different races may share similar values and social norms. Hence, culture and race are not synonymous although the two are often portrayed that way.

The essays in this volume tell us that planners are gradually warming up to the realization of the importance of cultural considerations in planning. The objectives of the book are twofold: First, our objective is to show that culture matters in planning. We argue that planners are not value neutral but that through their professional training and in their personal upbringing they are imbued with values that they bring to their professional practice. These values may not always be congruent with those of the community groups with whom they plan. In the pursuit of their professional practice, therefore, it is important for planners to pay attention to the tensions that may arise between them and their clients, the values that might cloud their judgment, and the frustrations that may result from planning with a diverse multicultural public. Most importantly, we hope that an *a priori* sensibility to culture will aid planners to arrive at amicable solutions that are satisfactory to both planners and the public and thereby improve professional morale rather than create frustration. The case studies and examples of planning practices discussed in the book provide lessons of how cultural sensitivity in planning can be achieved.

The second objective of the book is a much more limited one. It is our hope that the book will serve as an impetus to planning educators as they begin the arduous task of incorporating culture into planning curricula. If we are to make a difference in planning practice, it must start with the way we train future planners. Hopefully, this book will make it all too clear why planning schools need to sensitize students to planning with a cultural sensibility.

The publication of this book is itself an acknowledgment that a new epoch has dawned on planning. It is a recognition that as we approach the twenty-first century, we must critically rethink planning's role in shaping our communities. Doing so requires planners to cast a wider net to embrace a multicultural, diverse, global, and postmodern perspective of the world in which we live and the communities with which we plan. Anything less is professional stagnation!

NOTE

1. Throughout this book, culture is used in both its broadest and narrowest sense. In its narrow sense, culture is used to denote the commonly held norms, beliefs, and values that a social group shares as a result of birth or socialization and that governs the group's worldview. More broadly, culture is also used in reference to all socially patterned human thought and behavior. In this sense, it includes what people think, what they do, and the artifacts they make. It also includes aesthetics, manners and customs, social institutions, religion, values and attitudes, bodily adornment, etiquette, eating customs, housing, physical infrastructure, clothing, and music. While some of the authors in this volume adhere to the

narrow definition of culture, others take the much broader definition of the word. The reader should judge the word's meaning based on the context of the argument made by individual authors in the book.

REFERENCES

Beauregard, Robert A. "Planning Theories, Feminist Theories: A Symposium." *Planning Theory Newsletter*, vol. 7/8, 1992: 9–64.

Cohen, Mark N. "Culture, Not Race, Explains Human Diversity." *The Chronicle of Higher Education*, vol. XLIV, no. 32, April 1998:B4–5.

Foucault, J. F. "What is Enlightenment?" in P. Rabinow (ed.) *The Foucault Reader*. Harmondsworth, Penguin Books. 1986.

Gullick, John. "Baghdad: Portrait of a City in Physical and Cultural Change." *Journal of the American Institute of Planners*, vol. 33, no. 4, 1967:246–55.

Habermas, J. "Modernity Versus Postmodernity." *New German Critique*, no. 22. 1981.

Hayden, Dolores. "What Would a Non Sexist City Really Be Like? Speculation on Housing, Urban Design and Human Work" in Bratt, Rachel G., Chester Hartman, and Ann Meyerson. *Critical Perspectives on Housing*. Philadelphia: Temple University Press. 1986:230–46.

Leavitt, Jacqueline. "Feminist Advocacy Planning in the 1980s" in Barry Checkoway (ed.) *Strategic Perspectives on Planning Practice*. Lexington Books. 1986:181–94.

Lyotard, J. F. *Postmodernism Explained*. Minneapolis: University of Minnesota Press. 1992.

Moore, Milroy Beth. "Taking Stock of Planning, Space, and Gender." *Journal of Planning Literature*, vol. 6, no. 1, 1991:99–106.

Nietzche, F. "What is the Meaning of Ascetic Ideals?" in W. Kaufmann (ed.) *Geneaology of Morals*. New York: Random House. 1967:97–163.

Oberlander, P. "Planning Education for Newly Independent Countries." *Journal of the American Institute of Planners*, vol. 28, 1962:116–23.

Smart, Barry. *Postmodernity*. London: Routledge. 1993.

Thomas, June M. and Marsha Ritzdorf (eds.). *Urban Planning and the African American Community: In the Shadows*. Sage Publications. 1997.

Zioni, James W. "The Navajo Peacemaker Court: Deference to the Old and Accommodation to the New." *American Indian Law Review*, vol. II, 1983:89.

PART I

Critical Perspectives on Planning in a Multicultural Society

CHAPTER 2

Demographic Shifts and the Challenge for Planners: Insights from a Practitioner

Alvin James

As the United States positions itself to embark upon a new century and a new millennium, it finds itself in a place that is at once both familiar and new. What remains conventional is the role that it has played for more than 200 years as a destination for new immigrants, many of whom were and are still seeking a different, and perhaps economically enhanced, way of life. For much of the country's early history, its immigration pattern was largely Eurocentric in composition and origin. While cultural diversity certainly existed, the relatively narrow range of countries from which individuals emigrated ensured that nearly as many common characteristics existed as differences. Today, however, the neoteric dimension confronting the nation is the fact that the breadth of immigration has expanded dramatically. As a result, its demographic composition is reflective of virtually every part of the globe.

Notwithstanding its Eurocentric orientation, the United States has always considered itself to be a pluralistic society. The country has historically struggled, however, often unsuccessfully, with the question of how to balance its stated ideals for an assimilated society (i.e., of becoming a "melting pot" in which the cultural attributes of many nationalities and ethnic minorities might fuse together into a distinctly American culture) with the reality of its experience in perpetuating segregated subcultures. John Hope Franklin, a noted African-American historian, observed that during the brief span of three and one-half centuries of colonial and national history, Americans developed traditions and prejudices that have created two worlds of race in modern America (Franklin 1989). The "two worlds of race," together with society's often expressed bias against national origin, have combined to pose a formidable challenge to the nation's capacity to successfully accommodate its newest inhabitants.

Historically, planning practitioners and policy-makers have concerned themselves with a variety of issues that affect the nation's communities. In so doing, they have developed principles and policies to guide decision making in such areas as land use, urban design, environmental protection, and historic preservation for the purpose of improving the overall quality of life. Out of their work have come valuable policy frameworks and technical standards intended to guide physical development, protect fragile ecological systems, preserve significant historical assets, and encourage long-term community sustainability. Yet, quite often such policies and requirements have worked to adversely impact new immigrant and domestic ethnic communities and have frustrated rather than enhanced the overall quality of life.

Understanding the cultural characteristics of ethnic groups specifically to determine if local land-use policy is responsive to their respective needs has rarely been of concern to planners. As a consequence, the "rules" frequently undermine the very purpose for which they were created. If citizen planners and planning professionals are committed to ensuring the most livable communities possible, it is vitally important that they recognize that such an objective can be elusive in a rapidly evolving multicultural society.

Understanding how to plan for multicultural communities requires that planning practitioners and policy-makers not only correctly assess their ethnic and cultural makeup but also properly evaluate historical factors influencing their evolution. Proper assessment of historical context is critical to identifying the basis or rationale supporting unique requirements and may assist in the formulation of responsive land-use policy and/or goals. Efforts to understand factors that have affected these groups over time, within the context of the American experience, may provide sensitivity and insight regarding how best to establish dialogue and solicit feedback. To do so, then, requires that policy-makers not just limit their inquiry to land-use policy, but also to the question of how the broader scope of public policy actions can and have factored into the lives of residents of multicultural communities. The broader perspective may also help policy-makers to better understand the tools with which they work, including the range of public policy outcomes that are possible.

HISTORICAL CONTEXT—THE IMMIGRATION PERSPECTIVE

The sovereign authority to control immigration in the United States has its roots in colonial policy. Before the American Revolution the control of immigration and naturalization was a function of the sovereign authority that governed the individual colonies. The Declaration of Independence refers to immigration and naturalization problems then existing. In the list of indictments against the King of Great Britain for his "injuries and usurpations" in the government of the Colonies, it mentions among seven charges that: "he has endeavored to prevent the population of these States; for that purpose obstructing the laws for naturalization of foreigners; refusing to pass others to encourage their migration hither, and raising the conditions of new Appropriations of Lands."

The Articles of Confederation were adopted in 1778. Article 4 of that document made the citizens of each state citizens of every other state, but every state legally controlled immigration, which in those days was practically equivalent to encouragement. Communities welcomed increases in population because it increased safety of life and property. Owners of large grants of land wanted their holdings occupied to increase their value, and local governments often provided land free or at low prices to those who would settle and work it. However, the colonists had hardly set foot in America when they sought to prevent the admission of certain types of additional immigrants. Policies varied among the Colonies with respect to selection of immigrants on the basis of religious beliefs, and their physical, mental, moral, and economic fitness. These policies would evolve over time, form the basis of a nativistic school of thought, and become even more exclusionary as greater and greater numbers of immigrants made their way to America.

Between 1790 and 1820 annual immigration into the United States averaged about 10,000 persons per year. During the decade of the 1830s, however, the immigration rate increased fivefold. The tide of immigration rose still higher during the next decade. Indeed, the total number of immigrants entering the country during the ten years beginning in 1841 exceeded the number that arrived during America's entire previous history of more than two centuries. The immigration rate continued to rise in the 1850s, reaching a peak in 1854 (Fogel 1989).

For the first century after the colonies were initially established, immigrants were largely British; however, Ireland and Germany subsequently joined England to provide, by far, the greatest number of immigrants during the first half of the nineteenth century. In fact, by the middle of the nineteenth century, the culture and customs of western Europe dominated the United States from coast to coast. Following the Civil War immigration again increased dramatically. The composition of the immigrant population had shifted, however, with most now coming from eastern and southern Europe. A notable exception to this overall European trend was the significant percentage of Chinese workers that were attracted to the United States both by California's Gold Rush in 1849, and subsequent employment opportunities associated with railroad construction.

The Chinese Exclusion Act of 1882

Many efforts had been made by various groups, for various reasons, early in the nineteenth century to restrict various immigrants from entering the United States. However, the first restrictive legislation aimed at immigrants to be passed by the United States Congress was the Act of March 3, 1875. Among other things, that law provided for inquiry by consular officers as to contracts of immigrants from China or Japan for service for lewd or "immoral" purposes. Penalties were imposed for citizens of the United States transporting subjects of China or Japan without free consent for a term of service and the legislation made contracts for such service void. Furthermore, it imposed penalties for contracting to supply unskilled oriental laborers. Seven years later, on May 6, 1882, the Chinese Exclusion Act was passed.

Because of the tremendous influx of Chinese immigrants (200,000 from 1850 to 1880) following the discovery of gold in California, Congress, in 1882, enacted the first of the Chinese Exclusion Acts. The initial Act executed certain stipulations of a treaty with China dated November 17, 1880, and provided for suspension of immigration of Chinese laborers to the United States for a period of ten years. Chinese laborers[1] who were in the United States on November 17, 1880, however, were given the privilege of departure and reentry into the country. Chinese found not to be lawfully entitled to be, or remain, in the United States were ordered deported. The Act also barred Chinese from being admitted to citizenship. The Chinese exclusion law was extended again in 1892 and 1902, and in 1904 it was extended without limitation. From 1924 to 1965 fixed quotas and other restrictions in U.S. immigration law favored immigrants from northern European countries and effectively excluded most Asians altogether (Watson 1992).

The Chinese Exclusion Act of 1882 serves as a significant reminder of the extremes to which public policy was being put during the period to exclude and/or disenfranchise members of immigrant and ethnic populations from participation in American society. It also serves as a backdrop against which to assess more recent legislative efforts[2] to the extent that both relate to legal immigrant populations.

U.S. IMMIGRATION PATTERNS DURING THE TWENTIETH CENTURY

Figure 2.1 depicts U.S. immigration patterns for the first ninety years of the twentieth century. The 1930s and 1940s experienced a dramatic drop in the rate of immigration. While the decline was largely due to the impacts of the Great Depression and World Wars I and II, some of it resulted from public policy actions originating with the Chinese Exclusion Act of 1882 and culminating with subsequent immigration legislation. The Immigration Act of 1907 enabled the President to refuse immigration to certain persons when he was satisfied that such immigration was detrimental to labor conditions in the United States This Act was a result of the growing alarm, particularly on the Pacific coast and in states adjacent to Canada and Mexico, that labor conditions would be seriously affected by a continuation of the then existing rate of increase in admission of Japanese laborers. On the basis of the 1907 law, the President issued a proclamation on March 14, 1907, excluding from the continental United States certain skilled and unskilled Japanese or Korean laborers (*U.S. Code Congressional and Administrative News*, Immigration and Nationality Act of 1952:1669).

The Immigration Act of 1917 laid down further restrictions by declaring inadmissible natives of parts of China, all of India, Burma, Siam, the Malay States, a part of Russia, part of Arabia, part of Afghanistan, most of the Polynesian Islands, and the East Indian Islands. The Act defined a geographical section called the "barren zone," described by degrees of latitude and longitude. Exempted by a box cut out of the area were natives of Persia and natives of part of Afghanistan and of part of Russia. The purpose of the "barren zone" provision was primarily to exclude immigrants from China, Japan, and Korea (Miller and Miller 1996:6). Near term, these policy actions effectively precluded some populations from entering the country for many decades. Ultimately, they reinforced many of the deeply rooted exclusionary policies and practices that have tragically distorted the social development of the nation throughout its history.

Figure 2.1
Immigration: 1901–90

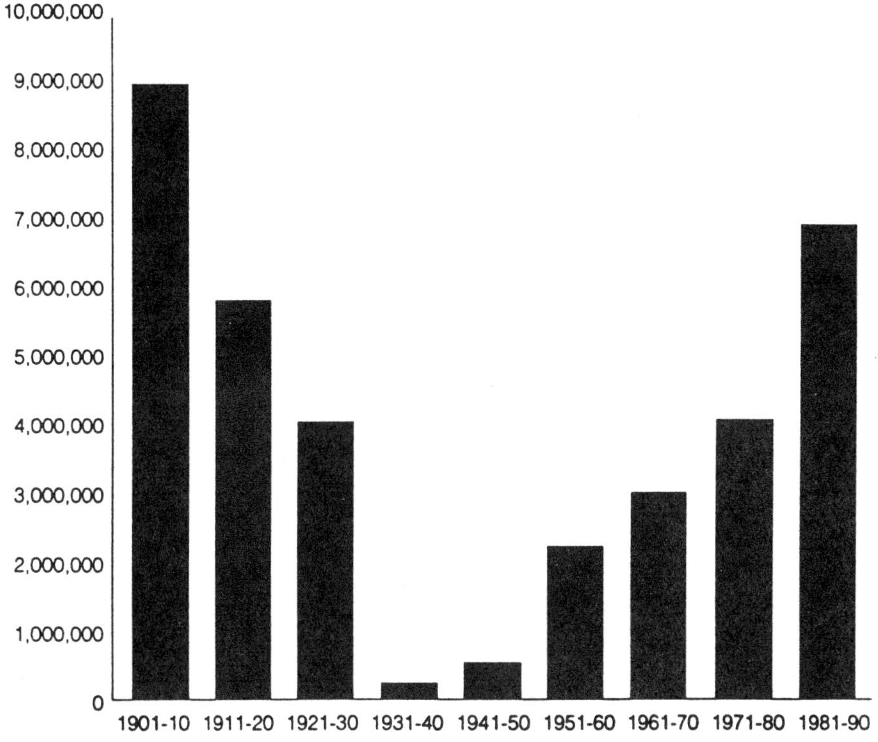

Source: U.S. Bureau of the Census. *Statistical Abstract of the United States, 1992.* Washington, DC: GPO, 1992. Table 2, p. 10. For fiscal years, ending the year shown.

Much of the high rate of immigration that characterized the early part of the century had returned by the 1980s. In fact, in 1994, 8.7 percent of the population of the United States (one in eleven Americans) were foreign-born. This statistic represented nearly double the percent foreign-born in 1970 (4.8%), almost a quarter of a century earlier.

Although the most recently calculated percentage of foreign-born is at the highest level since before World War II, much greater proportions of the United States population were foreign-born during the early part of the century. From a high of 14.7 percent in 1910, the percent of foreign-born declined to the 1970 level. Since that time, however, the percent has steadily increased. Figure 2.2 illustrates what percent of the United States population foreign-born individuals comprised between 1900 and 1994. Not surprisingly, this pattern is somewhat similar to United States immigration patterns as indicated in Figure 2.1.

A review of historical patterns reveal that changes have occurred in the overall composition of immigrants as well—particularly in recent years. Figure 2.3 reveals United States immigration by country of origin from 1820 to 1996. Of the top ten countries, seven were European and listed by immigrants as their last place of residence. Of the remaining three countries, one (Canada) has a population also largely of European origin. These figures contrast sharply with U.S. Immigration and Naturalization Service statistics, which have evidenced the extent of demographic change that has taken place in immigrant populations during the last fifteen of that 176-year period.

It is interesting to note, however, that between 1981 and 1996, not one European country was listed among the top ten identified as the place of origin of immigrant populations. As indicated in Figure 2.4, replacing significant traditional European sources of immigration are countries located in such places as Central America, the Carribean, and the Pacific Rim.

The figure also indicates that over 40 percent of all U.S. immigrants are of Hispanic origin. In fact, of the 24.6 million foreign-born persons living in the United States on March, 1996, 6.7 million (more than 25%) came from Mexico, thereby making that country by far the source of the largest number of immigrants. The second largest group was from the Philippines. Notwithstanding this significant recent change, more than two-thirds of the overall foreign-born population in the United States remain classified as White (68%). Eighteen percent are categorized as Asian or Pacific Islander, and only seven percent Black. Nearly half (46%) of all foreign-born persons were of Hispanic origin (U.S. Census 1997).

Figure 2.5 indicates the percent of foreign-born population by state of residence in 1994. Although the chart is expressed in percentages, California was home to 7.7 million foreign-born persons—more than one-third of all immigrants to the United States and nearly one-quarter of all California residents. New York ranked second with 2.9 million and Florida ranked third with 2.1 million foreign-born individuals. Three other states have more than 1 million non-native born residents—Texas, Illinois, and New Jersey. The remaining forty-four states collectively accommodate about 29 percent of the total foreign-born population.

These statistics underscore the fact that the foreign-born population is not evenly distributed geographically throughout the country. On first impression the numbers would suggest the occurrence of a rather dramatic phenomenon were it not for the fact that the historical pattern of immigrant settlement in the United States has also been uneven. In fact, even in 1850, 60 percent of the foreign-born population lived in just four states: New York, Pennsylvania, Ohio, and Massachusetts. Despite their largely peasant origins, the majority of immigrants who settled in the northern states during that period crowded into cities. About 37 percent of the population of northern cities with more than 10,000 inhabitants in 1860 was foreign born, while the corresponding figure for the rural areas was hardly 10 percent. What is

Figure 2.2
Percent Foreign-born, 1900–1994

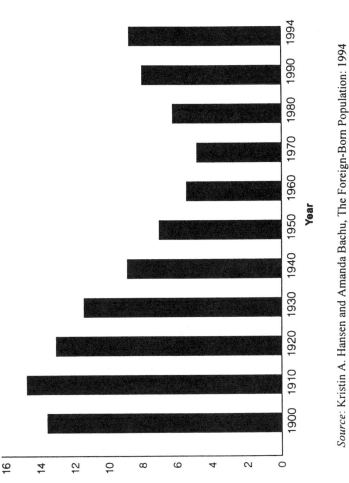

Source: Kristin A. Hansen and Amanda Bachu, The Foreign-Born Population: 1994
U.S. Bureau of the Census, Current Population Reports, p. 1

Figure 2.3
Immigration: 1820-1996

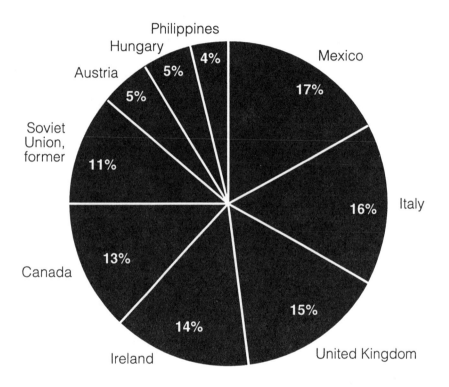

Source: U.S. Department of Justice, Immigration & Naturalization Service Statistics, October, 1997

Figure 2.4
Immigration: 1981–96

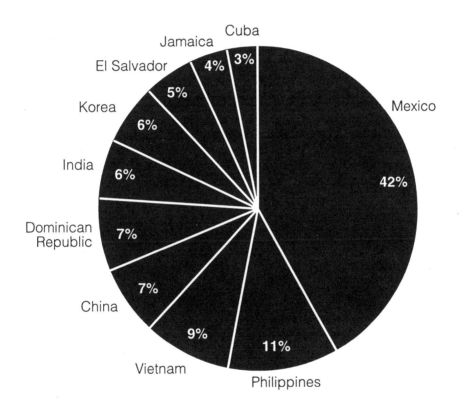

Source: U.S. Immigration & Naturalization Service

Figure 2.5
Foreign-Born Population by State of Residence

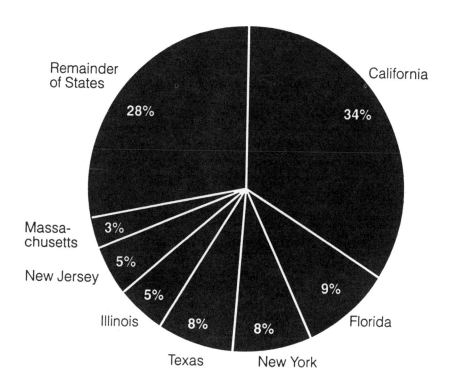

Source: Kristin A. Hansen and Amanda Bachu, The Foreign-Born Population: 1994
U.S. Bureau of the Census, Current Population Reports, p. 1

significant is the fact that the geographical focus of immigrant settlement patterns has shifted away from the northeast and/or middle Atlantic states. Currently, more than three-fourths of all immigrants to the United States reside in the three "border" states of California, Florida, and Texas.

HISTORICAL CONTEXT—THE ETHNIC PERSPECTIVE

The story of America's growth is marred by incidents of ethnic aggression as well as recurring attempts to restrict immigration. Its experience with pluralistic conflict began even before becoming a nation as the first settlers encountered Native Americans upon arrival in the new world. It did not matter to the Europeans that this New World was already inhabited. It was of no consequence that the Powhatans in Virginia, the Pequots in Massachusetts, and the Tuscaroras in the Carolinas were "civilized"—some by a future "official" designation, others by virtue of the state of their development. No serious thought was given to the possibility that Native Americans might share equally or even substantially in the social order that grew out of the dreams of Europeans. The latter simply appropriated the land of these groups with impunity and, in many instances, sought strenuously to enslave them. Later, in 1887, the United States Congress would pass the General Allotment Act that assigned 160 acres of land to each head of a family, with lesser amounts to bachelors, women, and minors, and conferred citizenship on those Indians who resided separate and apart from their tribe and "adopted the habits of civilized life" (Franklin 1989:338).

By the early part of the seventeenth century, colonialists introduced African slave labor into the Virginia colony. In 1700, some eighty years after the first group of slaves landed in Virginia, the Black population of that colony was estimated to be 16,000, or approximately 60 percent of the entire Black population present in all United States colonies at that time. By the time of George Washington's presidency, the African-born component of the Black population had shrunk to a bit over 20 percent. It hovered close to this share from 1780 to 1810 and then rapidly headed toward zero (Fogel 1989). The rapid decline in the relative share of Africans in the United States' Black population merely indicated that importation became an increasingly minor component of the latter groups' population growth. By 1720 the annual rate of natural increase in the United States colonies was greater than the annual increase due to importations. Whether by importation or natural increase, 100 years later the United States had become the leading user of slave labor in the New World (Fogel 1989).

The early free Black community also experienced hostility. Almost from the beginning, American Whites rejected the proposition that free Blacks were entitled to the same treatment as other free persons. The pronouncement of the Virginia magistrate in 1642 in sentencing a free Black indentured servant to a life of slavery for running away was a precedent that subsequent authorities seemed all too eager to follow. In 1790 Congress enacted a law limiting naturalization to White aliens. Two years later it restricted enlistment in the militia to able-bodied White men, thus declaring to the 5,000 Blacks who had fought in the War for Independence that their services were no longer required. When Congress passed laws for the operation of the government after it moved to the new capitol at Washington in 1801, it excluded free Blacks from participating in the affairs of government. In the following year Congress passed a law, signed by President Thomas Jefferson, specifically excluding Blacks from carrying the United States Mail (Franklin 1989). By the middle of the eighteenth century, laws governing Blacks denied to them certain basic rights that were conceded to others. As indicated by Franklin, "they were permitted no independence of thought, no opportunity to improve their minds or their talents, or to worship freely, no right to marry and enjoy the conventional family relationships, no right to own or dispose of property, and no protection against miscarriages of justice or cruel and unreasonable punishments" (Franklin 1989:132).

Historical inter-ethnic group aggression, as evidenced in public policy, was not confined to Native Americans, Blacks, and Whites. As mentioned earlier, Chinese laborers, initially welcomed, were banned both from immigration and citizenship in 1882. Other representative examples of public policy expressions of intergroup conflicts include:

1. In 1705 Massachusetts enacted legislation prohibiting intermarriage between Blacks and Whites (Watson 1992).

2. Rhode Island limited immigration to Britain only in 1729 (Watson 1992).

3. In 1863 a Conscription Act was passed, allowing men to avoid military service by paying $300 or by obtaining a substitute. This so infuriated the working-class Irish in New York—who could do neither—that they turned on local Blacks, whom they held responsible for the Civil War. After four days of rioting, hundreds of people had been killed (Watson 1992).

4. In October 1883 the United States Supreme Court declared unconstitutional the Civil Rights Act of 1875. The Act proposed to enact into law the principle that "all persons within the jurisdiction of the United States shall be entitled to the full and equal enjoyment of the accommodations, advantages, facilities, and privileges of inns, public conveyances on land or water, theaters, and other places of public amusement," and that such enjoyment should be subject "only to the conditions and limitations established by law, and applicable alike to citizens of every race and color, regardless of any previous condition of servitude" (Franklin 1989:116–17).

The group that the Civil Rights Act sought to enfranchise (African Americans) had only a few years earlier been granted citizenship status by the Fourteenth Amendment to the U.S. Constitution. The provisions of the Civil Rights Act were intended to extend the protections accorded by the constitutional amendment against discriminatory violations of citizens' civil rights by government to those by private individuals.[3] Another Civil Rights Act would not be enacted until 1964, nearly ninety years after the adoption of the original legislation. In 1905 the San Francisco School Board ordered Japanese, Chinese, and Korean children to be segregated in a separate Oriental school. Under the terms of a 1907 "Gentleman's Agreement," Japan was persuaded to limit emigration to the United States (Watson 1992:206).

CONTEMPORARY ETHNIC/IMMIGRATION PATTERN COMPARISONS

Table 2.1 describes the ethnic composition of the five largest United States metropolitan areas between 1980 and 1990. Even a casual comparison with Figure 2.5 reveals that not only is there a high coincidence of geographic similarity between domestic ethnic and immigrant population distributions, but also the latter is growing in representation in many of these areas at an extremely rapid pace. Table 2.2 indicates the major metropolitan areas ranked by proportion of minority group population according to the 1990 United States Census. The locations depicted by these tables, given their rapidly changing demographic characteristics, can either be interpreted as providing the most promising opportunity for multiculturalism to be experienced in its greatest dimension or, within the context of a national perspective, considered racial repositories that will ultimately result in essentially separate ethnic societies.

This observation has been affirmed by demographer William H. Frey, who noted in his research that the 1990 census suggests that international immigration to and internal migration within the United States may be resulting in a spontaneous racial self-sorting in the nation (Frey 1997). Frey, of the University of Michigan, suggests that the United States may be headed toward becoming a collection of several distinct societies, at least in terms of racial makeup. Frey's interpretation of census data reveals that much of the nation's interior has remained over 95 percent White. In addition to confirming that the overwhelming majority of new immigrants go to six states, his research indicates that of the six million legal immigrants to the United States during the 1980s, 45 percent were Asian and 38 percent were Latin American. According to Frey, internal population movements along racial lines suggest a flight from diversity.

PUBLIC POLICY AND MULTICULTURALISM

Creation of an effective planning model for serving multiculturalism first requires understanding the linkages between contemporary expressions of public policy and the context in which such policy has historically impacted pluralism in the United States. Understanding the relationship between public policy in general and its specific expression within the context of land-use planning may be a key determinant of the health and welfare of American society as a whole in the twenty-first century.

As suggested in earlier discussion, public policy has often been used over time as a device to satisfy the parochial interests of groups or individuals determined to achieve economic and other benefits. In theory, use in such a manner is not inappropriate. In fact, parochially based public policy-making is fundamental to the success of a political system, such as that of the United States, which values competitiveness among the various interest groups comprising it. It has unquestionably provided, in many instances, the incentive required for entrepreneurial risk-taking, which has resulted in unparalleled growth and prosperity for the nation as a whole. Furthermore, history has shown that parochial policy-making has not been a significant barrier to the realization of national goals when transcendence of provincialism has so required.

Table 2.1
Ethnic Composition of Five Largest Metropolitan Areas
1980 and 1990

		Total	African American	Hispanic*	Asian & Pacific Islanders
New York	1980	17,539,000	2,825,102	2,050,998	370,731
	1990	18,087,251	3,289,465	2,777,951	873,213
	% Change	3.1	16.4	35.4	135.5
Los Angeles	1980	11,498,000	1,059,124	2,755,914	561,876
	1990	14,531,529	1,229,809	4,779,118	1,339,048
	% Change	26	16.1	73.4	138.3
Chicago	1980	7,937,000	1,557,287	632,443	144,626
	1990	8,065,633	1,547,725	893,422	256,050
	% Change	1.6	-0.6	41.3	77.0
San Francisco	1980	5,368,000	468,477	660,190	454,647
	1990	6,253,311	537,753	970,403	926,961
	% Change	16	14.8	47.0	103.9
Philadelphia	1980	5,681,000	1,032,882	147,902	53,291
	1990	5,899,345	1,100,347	225,868	123,458
	% Change	3.8	6.5	52.7	131.7

* NOTE: Persons of Hispanic origin may be of any race.
Sources: U.S. Census Bureau Release 91-229; Statistical Abstract of the U.S., 1990.

Table 2.2 Major Metropolitan Areas Ranked by Proportion of Minority Group Population (in millions) 1990				
Total	African American	Hispanic*	Asians & Pacific Islanders	American Indians/et al
New York	New York	Los Angeles	Los Angeles	Los Angeles
18.1	3.3	4.8	˙ 1.3	0.087
Los Angeles	Chicago	New York	San Francisco	Tulsa
14.5	1.5	2.8	0.9	0.048
Chicago	Los Angeles	Miami	New York	New York
8.1	1.2	1.1	0.87	0.046
San Francisco	Philadelphia	San Francisco	Honolulu	Oklahoma City
6.3	1.1	0.97	0.53	0.046
Philadelphia	Washington DC	Chicago	Chicago	San Francisco
5.9	1	0.89	0.26	0.041

* NOTE: Persons of Hispanic original may be of any race.
Source: U.S. Census Bureau Release 91-229.

Centered exclusively in a Eurocentric society, or indeed, any relatively monocultural experience, parochial policy-making might perhaps be made to serve all members of society with relatively equal effectiveness. However, the reality of the American experience is not monocultural. It is a pluralistic society and all of its members, new and old, have not been served effectively by parochial policy-making. Public policies have been devised not only to promote the interests of some but often at significant, sometimes tragic, expense to others. They have been utilized to undermine the rights and privileges of various immigrant and ethnic populations in the United States; to exclude them entirely from benefits and from avenues to competitive access. Public policy, utilized in such manner, has historically been initiated at every level of government and without geographic limitation to achieve such purposes.

The middle of the twentieth century marked a turning point in the direct use of instruments of public policy for exclusionary purposes. In fact, as early as the start of the 1940s, a number of the discriminatory legislative Acts first enacted in the latter part of the nineteenth century and the early twentieth century had begun to be dismantled. For example in 1943 the Chinese Exclusion Act was repealed. In

1946 Filipinos and persons belonging to ethnic groups native of India were granted the privilege of admission to the United States and were declared eligible for naturalization. Immigration was permitted to increase after World War II. In 1952 the United States Congress expressly acknowledged its long-standing policy of using racial bars in its statutes pertaining to immigration as it moved through the Immigration and Nationality Act of that year to eliminate the legislative practice (*U.S. Code Congressional and Administrative News*, Immigration and Nationality Act of 1952:1673). Two years later the United States Supreme Court rendered its landmark decision in *Brown versus The Board of Education* that reversed its long embraced "separate but equal" doctrine in the area of education, by requiring public school desegregation (Hornsby 1997:163). New laws were passed in such areas as voting rights, immigration, and civil rights, not without significant urging and protest, to ensure that government would no longer serve directly as an instrument of exclusion to ethnic and immigrant populations. These steps, with notable exceptions, have made significant progress toward the substantial reduction, if not elimination, of legislative and regulatory enactments that sanction the direct usage of public policy to exclude and disenfranchise ethnic and immigrant populations.[4] However, public policy that results in the creation of barriers based upon racial and national origin continue to be a problem. Nowhere has that observation been more evident than in the area of planning policy.

Planning is a dimension of public policy. Therefore, it is important to evaluate it within the context of the evolution of public policy in order to understand the forces that influence planning as a public policy instrument, as well as the challenges that confront efforts to plan for multiculturalism. Such an evaluation is not possible, however, without at least setting forth a working definition of multiculturalism.

Culture Defined

Websters Dictionary defines culture as being: the ideas, customs, skills, arts, and so forth, of a given people in a given period (Guralnik 1972:345). Culture includes learned patterns of behavior, socially acquired traditions, repetitive ways of thinking and acting, attitudes, values, and morals. Cultural programming specifies rules for acquiring and transferring information. It standardizes perceptions. It also defines attitudes for intragroup relationships and for dealing with nonmembers. Furthermore, it sets the institutional parameters that condition human behavior and stabilize social systems. Culture standardizes relationships so that people need not be constantly mindful of the implications of their behavior. They can make reasonably confident assumptions about the reactions of those with whom they interact.

Throughout much of United States history, successful cultural programming has been equated with Eurocentric cultural relativism; that is, a belief that the dominant groups' culture, largely based in European traditions, is the norm and perhaps superior to others. This model has perpetually served to undermine efforts to make significant progress toward realization of a multicultural paradigm that can more effectively serve the needs of what in reality is, and always has been, a multicultural society.

The term "multiculturalism," as it is used today, is a rapidly escalating movement to bring about recognition of, sensitivity to, and appreciation for the diverse cultures that comprise American society. Where applicable, it seeks redress for the centuries-long practices of exclusion. Empowerment through legislation, inclusion in all strata of society, and the rewriting of American history to correct distortions and omissions with respect to ethnic and immigrant populations are seen as necessary steps where such has been an intentional impediment to progress.

The United States has evolved into the world's largest multicultural society. As a result of the diverse countries of origin, the immigrants possess wide cultural backgrounds. For example, Asian immigrants coming from such countries as the Philippines, South Korea, China, India, Vietnam, Cambodia, Saudi Arabia, Israel, and Japan have a richly diverse ethnic and cultural background. The native tongues include Tagalog (Filipinos), Korean, Khmer, Vietnamese, Hindi, Urdu, Gujarati, Faisi, Arabic, Yiddish, and Japanese, as well as scores of dialects (Miller and Miller 1996). Next to language, religious diversity also characterizes these immigrants and further adds to cultural complexity. The Bureau of the Census, however, for statistical reporting purposes, only has six basic racial categories, one "other race" category, and one "ethnicity" category (Hispanic) with which to classify them. While these grossly defined survey classifications may be useful for summarizing the aggregate demographic characteristics of foreign-born and ethnic populations, they are of little assistance in providing the level of insight required to develop land-use policy that will be sensitive to the specifics of their respective situations. If planning is to serve as an effective instrument of public policy for these communities, it will require more sophisticated survey tools to assist in identifying the groups to be engaged in the formulation of the policies that will affect them.

Improved demographic statistical tools can increase awareness of the broader range of cultures and groups that comprise our communities. However, planning advocates will need other levels of information to increase their effectiveness in developing responsive public policy proposals. Sources of information are required to increase sensitivity to the many ideas, customs, unique behavioral and social relationships that may be present in a multicultural community. There may be varying values, traditions, and firmly held beliefs. These attributes all contribute to the richness of the diversity that so uniquely defines these communities. However, they also can serve as basis for disharmony if improperly or not well understood.

It is important for planning practitioners and policy-makers to realize that it is not enough to simply gather "the facts" regarding these characteristics. They must also realize that the effort to truly understand does not stop with detached observation but with understanding how one's own values, attitudes, and customs affect the observers' opinions and preconceived notions. Furthermore, the attributes observed must be evaluated within an historical context to probe the question of whether they are based in the customs of the community are a result of the application of previous public policy actions. For example, planning professionals, in attempting to positively respond to a jurisdictions adopted policy for more affordable housing, may conduct studies to determine where the need exists in the community. Perhaps they may determine through census data that not only is there a need for such housing to meet the needs of large families but that a particular racial category has a significant percentage of families that meet that attribute. The planners may also determine that the geographic area of the jurisdiction that has the greatest percentage of population from that racial category also has the greatest amount of low-cost land and space available to accommodate housing for large families. Furthermore, the geographic area may already have the largest number of existing residential facilities that are designed to meet the needs of large families. The planners may have assumed that because a large percentage of the ethnic and/or immigrant population is represented in the large family category and because a large number of residential facilities designed to meet the needs of large families already exist that the addition of more such units will solve the need for more affordable housing for this population segment. They may recommend a change of land-use policy and zoning, or preservation of the same to facilitate construction of additional facilities designed to meet the needs of large families in this location of the jurisdiction.

Facts like these have often led to the assumption by planning advocates not sensitive to the traditions and needs of such communities that developing programs to build a significant amount of additional such housing in the described location will resolve both a housing problem and quality of life issue. A little more research might reveal that the broader ethnic population moved to the subject geographic location not out of market choice but due to a combination of historical factors related to exclusionary housing practices elsewhere (public and private) and affordability limitations. The cost of land may be attributable to the fact that few services and amenities exist, or the fact that it is located in proximity to other incompatible land uses. A little introspection by the researcher may reveal preconceived notions and biases about the population based upon the existing significant percentage of large families that obscures the capacity to discern that there may also be a significant percentage of others in the population who are not included in the percentages of large families whose housing needs may be different. An indiscriminate change in land use to facilitate the construction of residential facilities to meet the needs of large families could result in influencing market forces in a manner that discourages the development of housing to meet the needs of other population segments. Specifically, it could result in increased land prices that could be noncompetitive for lower density housing. Not only could such a phenomenon result in the cessation of construction of such housing but it could increase the cost of existing inventory and/or encourage the alteration of such, resulting in a reduced inventory available to meet the needs of population segments not included in the large family category. Further research might reveal that over-representation of such large family housing in the geographic location already exists relative to the rest of the jurisdiction and that additional construction could result in an over-impaction. It might reveal that local schools, parks, and other community services are already at capacity and unable to effectively serve the population. The addition of more housing for large families, without sensitivity to its overall impact on the traditions, culture, and needs of the broader community, could result in a deterioration rather than enhancement of the overall quality of life.

Another important concept for planning professionals and policy-makers to improve understanding is that of diversity itself. Planning has often occurred in relation to socio-economic considerations but largely from an orientation that evaluates the economic implications of social programs designed to serve specific populations. As a consequence, little effort has been made to understand the systemic issues related to how groups from different cultures may interact when circumstances require them to do so, even though the country's history offers an abundant supply of examples for consideration. As described earlier, immigration history, particularly in the early to mid-1800s, informs us that diversity can increase the potential for inter-group conflict. The riots of the 1960s remind us that the potential has not been diluted by time. Add to the equation the existence of tensions caused by competition for jobs and housing, exacerbated by language barriers and cultural misunderstandings, and the complications increase dramatically.

Understanding these factors may not be critical to planning for physical facilities but it may be important to social programming associated with the use of such facilities. For example, in planning a graffiti abatement strategy, planners may determine that it would be appropriate to implement a summer mural program to afford a positive alternative for youth populations residing in a particular community to express themselves. They may decide on a certain number of projects to be implemented in a limited number of locations. Knowing the diversity characteristics of the community can assist in ensuring that youth from all cultures are invited to participate in the project. Mural projects can be planned to either ensure that all cultures represented are reflected or that noncultural themes are consciously pursued so that everyone can feel included. Not being sensitive to these considerations can actually encourage cultural turfism and exacerbate the graffitti problem, as excluded groups may create their own "unauthorized" mural projects.

PLANNING WITH MULTICULTURAL COMMUNITIES

Planning advocates must strive to achieve a better understanding of the parameters of public policy and how it has been used when applied to the range of communities comprising American society. They must seek to understand those communities demographically, culturally, and historically. To do so would better position them to assess the needs of the "client," who is becoming increasingly more reflective of the global community. Not only is it important to understand these communities, it is important to engage them in the planning decision-making process. Traditional tools of citizen participation can and should be adapted for such interaction. For example, it may not be enough to simply post notices of public hearings or meetings on telephone poles or other structures in the public right-of-way to alert neighborhood residents of pending development proposals. Effective outreach may require polling prominent community representatives and others of the best way to get in contact with people. In some instances, posting of notices may be adequate. In others, contacting neighborbhood associations, religious organizations, social organizations, or other such entities may be required as well.

Ultimately, the most effective way to ensure participation of multicultural communities in public policy formulation via the planning process is to ensure balanced representation of community members on various boards and commissions that have responsibility for deciding planning issues. Ensuring that the professional and technical staffs employed to support such bodies is also reflective of the communities they collectively serve will increase the likelihood that sensitive and effective planning will take place.

Planning policy-makers, professionals, and advocates can contribute significantly toward establishing the information sources and designing the participatory processes essential to assuring that effecting planning in the twenty-first century is equated with embracing the whole of society, including its history, in establishing models to plan *with* rather than *for* the many cultures that comprise it.

NOTES

1. "Laborer" was broadly defined to include skilled and unskilled, thereby effectively precluding all but the very old and the very young from entering the country. By denying citizenship, the legislation erected a barrier to property and other forms of capital ownership to Chinese immigrants residing in the United States.

2. Recent legislative efforts such as California's Proposition 187, and the recently passed federal welfare reform legislation, to the extent that it deals with immigrant populations, have underscored the fact that the nation, and/or significant parts of it, still pursues efforts to exclude members of immigrant and ethnic populations from privileges enjoyed by other members of American society.

3. In denouncing the action of the United States Supreme Court, Frederick Douglass, a noted Abolitionist of the era, had these words to say:

It (the decision) presents the United States before the world as a nation utterly destitute of power to protect the constitutional rights of its own citizens upon its own soil.

It can claim service and allegiance, loyalty and life from them, but it cannot protect them against the most palpable violation of the rights of human nature, . . . It can tax their bread and tax their blood, but it has no protecting power for their persons. . . . It gives to the railroad conductor in South Carolina or Mississippi more power than it gives to the National Government. (Douglas 1892, revised 1962:545)

4. The recent approval of ballot initiatives dealing with illegal immigration and affirmative action (Propositions 187 and 209) in California suggest, at least to some, a disturbing trend toward reversing efforts to improve political and socio-economic access of ethnic and immigrant populations

REFERENCES

Bureau of the Census, United States Department of Commerce. *How We're Changing—Demographic State of the Nation: 1997.* Current Population Reports, Special Studies Series, March 1997:23–193.

Douglas, Frederick. *Life and Times of Frederick Douglass.* New York: Collier. 1962.

Fogel, Robert William. *Without Consent or Contract, The Rise and Fall of American Slavery,* New York: W.W. Norton & Co. 1989.

Franklin, John Hope. *The Two Worlds of Race: A Historical View, Race and History: Selected Essays 1938-1988.* Baton Rouge: Louisiana State University Press. 1989.

Frey, William H. *Emerging Demographic Balkanization: Toward One America or Two?* University of Michigan Population Studies Center Research Report No. 97–410. 1997.

Guralnik, David B., Editor in Chief. *Websters New World Dictionary of the American Language,* 2nd College Edition. New York and Cleveland: The World Publishing Company. 1972.

Hansen, Kristin A. and Amara Bachu. *The Foreign-Born Population: 1994.* U.S. Bureau of the Census, Current Population Reports, p. 1.

Hornsby, Alton Jr. *Chronology of African American History—From 1492 to the Present,* 2nd Edition. Gale Research, Detroit. 1997.

Miller, E. Willard and Ruby Miller. *United States Immigration, A Reference Handbook.* Santa Barbara: ABC CLIO Inc. 1996.

U.S. Bureau of the Census. *Statistical Abstract of the United States, 1992.* Washington, DC: GPO, 1992. Table 2, p. 10.

U.S. Census Bureau Release 91-229; Statistical Abstract of the U.S., 1990.

U.S. Code Congressional and Administrative News. *Legislative History—Immigration and Nationality Act of 1952,* P.L. 414; Ch. 477, Laws of 82nd Congress—2nd Session, June 27, 1952.

U.S. Department of Justice, Immigration & Naturalization Service Statistics, October 1997.

Watson, Bernard C. *The Demographic Revolution: Diversity in 21st Century America, The State of Black America.* New York: NAACP. 1992.

CHAPTER 3

Tracking the Planning Profession: From Monistic Planning to Holistic Planning for a Multicultural Society

Michael A. Burayidi

A study of thirty-two planning faculty by Friedmann and Kuester (1994) indicated that the ability to plan in a multicultural environment is one of the most critical skills needed of planners in North America today. This response by planners may be due to the obvious demographic shifts that have taken place in the United States at least since the 1960s, a trend that was discussed by James in the previous chapter.

Urban planners have always had to address a diverse public in their work. Whether the issue is one of land use, the location of public housing, or business attraction strategies, there are always competing interests that planners must consider since every plan impacts people differently. Among the diverse publics that planners have had to consider include the needs and the effects of plans on people of different races and ethnicities, suburbanites and inner city residents, as well as people of various socio-economic backgrounds. The need for the planner to respond to a diverse clientele is thus not new. What is new, and what holistic planning is advocating, however, differs significantly from previous planning practices.

The dominant epistemology on which current planning is based is universalist. This universalist approach is predicated on deductive logic, instrumental rationality, a hierarchical social structure, and a unidirectional causal flow. Beauregard characterized this type of planning as "a totalizing and singular vision, the quest for an all-encompassing endeavor, and a pronounced elitism" Beauregard 1991:191).

Such reasoning is "mixed with the peculiarly American world view of a unidimensionally rankable universe, competition, conquest, technocentrism and multicultural assimilation" (Maruyama 1973:349). Planning practices based on this perspective have failed in a number of instances to respond to the needs of a multicultural society with ethnic and cultural minorities whose worldview differs from that of the dominant culture. For example, many Native-American cultures such as the Navajo and Inuit believe in the balance of nature, while Asian (Japanese and Chinese) social life is based on cooperation and mutual complementarity rather than competition. The dissatisfaction with this type of planning doesn't even have to be along the racial or ethnic divide. Mormon city builders deviated from these universal planning standards by outlining principles for the design of what they perceived to be good towns based primarily on their religious beliefs and needs (Sellers 1962).

It is perhaps in this light that Maruyama asserted that "we have been misguided, by the traditional logical model based on unidirectional causality and on the classical physics to believe that generalizability, universality, homogenization, and competition are not only the rules of the universe but also the desirable goals of the society" (1973:355). Fitch also observed, with regards to this worldview, that: "The United States was built upon a faulty premise that has not served it well in the past and most assuredly will not in the future; it was the idea that there was only one valid world view or perspective, that it was not particularistic but 'universal,' that to be 'human' meant aspiring toward, and finally embracing, that world view" (Fitch 1992:48).

While some attempts have been made in the past to change planning practices to respond to the needs of a diverse society, these adjustments have been oscillations within the same epistemology. Thus, Davidoff's call for advocacy for the disadvantaged groups and minorities was viewed as inappropriate by Marcuse who felt that the lawyer's role, which advocacy planning mirrors, will not respond to the substantive problem-solving needs of minority communities because:

A lawyer "represents" his client; if the ghetto is to make decisions on its future, it must "represent" itself through its own leaders and advocates. The real issues requiring advocacy and representation are substantive rather than technical; knowledge of the rules of the game may be helpful, but it is more important that the community fight for its own self-determined needs. Technical assistance, not advocacy, is required of planners. Where planning is a process by which the total environment is increasingly brought within the conscious control of its inhabitants, outside "professional" prescription may be the opposite of good planning. (1969:116)

One can cite criticisms of other planning approaches, such as the incremental planning approach, transactive planning, and mixed scanning approaches. Kraushaar (1988) has critiqued planners for working "inside the whale" and Baum (1982) also berated planners for not pushing for changes in existing institutions. Beauregard observed that "planners' actions help to maintain the existing pattern of power and privilege" (1978:249).

In this chapter we discuss planners' orientations to the dominant epistemology and how this approach has failed to meet the needs and concerns of people whose worldview differs from that of the dominant culture. Next, we examine multiculturalism and how planning can be reoriented to be more inclusive, and to respond more realistically to a diverse multicultural public through holistic planning.

PLANNING AND CULTURE

Like other professions, planning practices reflect the socio-cultural context within which planning takes place. Therefore, an understanding of planners' responses to ethnic and cultural differences in their practice would be better understood if we examine it in relation to prevailing national policy on race and ethnicity over the years. This seems appropriate because planners function within the larger society and national policies have a bearing on the way that planning as a profession responds to national interests and priorities.

There are three phases in the evolution of urban planning practice as far as accommodation of cultural diversity is concerned. The first phase stretches from the early beginning of the profession until 1960. The second phase spanned the period from 1961 to the mid-1980s, and the third and current phase started in the mid-1980s. Each of these phases correspond roughly with changes in the prevailing national ideology on race and ethnicity. We will discuss each of these phases in turn. A summary of the discussion that follows is provided in Table 3.1.

ASSIMILATION AND MONISTIC PLANNING PRACTICE

The policy of the United States government up to the 1960s, regarding cultural and ethnic groups, was one of assimilation. Under this policy minority groups were to lose their distinctiveness and acquire the values of the dominant culture. The founding fathers were interested in preserving a common bond and a common set of values based on the Anglo-Saxon culture. All immigrants were thus required to assimilate into this culture. Writing about the immigrants from southern, eastern, and central Europe, Cubberley, a renowned educationist at the time, wrote:

Our task is to break up these groups or settlements, to assimilate and amalgamate these people as part of the American race, and to implant in their children, as far as can be done, the Anglo-Saxon conception of righteousness, law and order and popular government, and to awaken in them a reverence for our democratic institutions and for those things in our national life which we as a people hold to be of abiding worth. (1909:15–16)

For those immigrants from Europe, assimilation offered them an opportunity for both social and economic progress in the new world.[1] However, persons of non-European origin, such as Native Americans, African Americans, and Mexican Americans, could not assimilate completely into the dominant culture because of their obvious physical differences. They were denied jobs, education, and full participation in the political process. This policy would later haunt the country as minority groups see a disjuncture between the country's avowed creed of justice, fairness, and equality, and the practical reality of their daily existence.

It was within this national ideological framework that the planning profession had its early beginnings. The 1900s to 1930s are generally regarded as the formative years of the planning profession (Adams and Hodge 1965). The first conference on planning was held in 1909. It was the same year that the first course in urban planning was offered at Harvard. The assimilation ideology meant that planners did not have to worry much about how planning affected cultural and ethnic groups. The profession itself was, at the time, fighting for recognition and for its very existence. The approach to planning was monistic as planners adhered to a value-free unitary public interest, which planners were to promote. The planner's role in society was that of a technician, seeking the best way to meet the chosen ends of society, which in this case was the physical improvement of the urban environment. As the constitution of the American Institute of Planners (AIP) stated, the Institute's "particular sphere of activity shall be the planning of the unified development of urban communities and their environs and of states, regions, and the nation as expressed through determination of the comprehensive arrangement of land and land occupancy and regulation thereof" (Constitution of the AIP 1965:8).

Table 3.1 The Culture-Planning Continuum Timeline		
Approximate Time Frame	Conceptual Framework	Planners' Response
1900-1960	Assimilation Amalgamation Cultural Pluralism	Monistic Planning Rational Comprehensive Unitary Public Interest Planner as Technician City Practical
1961-1980	Integration	Pluralist Planning: Equity Planning Advocacy Planning Transactive Planning Feminist Planning Radical Planning
Since 1981	Multiculturalism	Holistic Planning Unified Diversity

Urban planning was also perceived as an instrument that would help the nation meet its goal of assimilating immigrants to the American way of life. As Webber observed with regard to planning at the time: "acculturation of ethnic, racial, and other minority groups to the American, middle-class, urban ways-of-life but awaited their introduction to the American middle class, physical environment" (1963:233).

In this assimilationist phase of the planning profession, ethnic enclaves in cities were regarded by planners as aberrations to the normal development of the urban landscape. Such neighborhoods were seen as transitional areas that would eventually be replaced through the ecological process of succession and invasion from the modern built sector. As a result, no effort was made by planners to legitimize these neighborhoods and support their sustainability over time.

Nowhere was this approach to planning more clear than in planners support of the Urban Renewal program. As Gans (1982) pointed out, the program resulted not only in the displacement of the poor, but in the destruction of ethnic neighborhoods, examples of which included Boston's Italo-American West End, Yorkville and Lincoln Square in New York, and the Valley southwest of Chicago's Loop. The ethnic character of both black and white neighborhoods was affected through the razing of immigrant quarters in urban areas. Deacon (1983) observed that these neighborhoods were seen as unattractive although they did not exhibit any physical blight or social pathologies. Thus, the primary objective was to "modernize" these neighborhoods and blend them in through modernist architecture and city design. This approach to planning has been "linked with the bureaucratic rationality of high modernism propounded by international style architect/planners such as Le Corbusier and Ludwig Mies van der Rohe" (Lin 1995:631). And as Warner also observed: "Properly understood, the many interrelated programs which go under the rubric 'urban renewal' have as their legitimate function the *modernizing of our metropolitan regions* in a way which will bring them in closer accord to the possibilities of a wealthy and expanding economy" (Warner 1972:242, emphasis added).

While planners may not have formulated the urban renewal policies, they certainly aided and abetted in their implementation. They are therefore just as guilty of the outcomes of these policies as the politicians who initiated them.

The monistic approach to planning, with its focus on assimilation came under attack, especially following the social unrests of the 1960s, for planning's failure to address the pressing problems of minority neighborhoods. This, in part, led to the paradigm shift from one of assimilation of racial and ethnic groups to that of integration and pluralist planning.

INTEGRATION AND PLURALIST PLANNING

The next phase in the culture-planning continuum may be referred to as the era of integration. The 1960s ushered in a new era of national consciousness following the race riots of the 1960s and the Civil Rights Movement. Although many immigrants were perfectly willing to assimilate into "American" culture, starting in the 1960s, there was a ground swell demand by immigrant communities for recognition of their ethnic and cultural identity. Pressure was mounted by minority groups to seek full inclusion into American society starting with demands for political representation. Besides the African-American community, other non-White groups such as Hispanic Americans and Native Americans as well as white ethnic groups, such as Irish Americans, Polish Americans and Italian Americans, all called for a redress of past injustices suffered through the years of assimilation. This led to a commission's report on the *Civil Rights Issues of Euro-Ethnic*

Americans in the United States: Opportunities and Challenges in 1979. Following these ethnic revitalization movements, a number of changes were made, especially in public institutions.

In the area of education, for example, the landmark case of *Brown vs. Board of Topeka* (1954) cleared the way for the integration of schools. A program of Intergroup Education (Banks 1986) was introduced to teach students about minority groups and to help reduce prejudice and promote intergroup understanding. In some states, such as Iowa, California, and Minnesota, legislations were enacted that required textbooks to depict the contributions of minorities to American culture and to provide training for teachers so they can learn about the history and culture of America's ethnic groups. Residential and neighborhood segregation, made possible through snob and exclusionary zoning practices since the 1920s, was also ruled unconstitutional by the courts.

The ethnic revival movements had an impact on planning. This phase, called the "pluralist phase" by Thomas (1997), had three characteristic features. One was the increase in race issues in planning in the 1960s, the second characteristic was the concern for social justice, and the third feature was the rise of the feminist movement and literature on women and planning.

The profession witnessed a steady stream of criticism for its failure to respond to the needs of minority groups, especially African Americans in the inner city. One such eloquent criticism was made by Melvin Webber at the 1963 American Institute of Planners (AIP) conference. Regarding the universalist tendencies of the rational comprehensive approach to planning, he cautioned that the outcomes of such plans,

could be especially troublesome for the minority racial and ethnic groups whose value systems and behavior differ greatly from those of the middle class professionals who design the programs intended to help them. We in the several welfare professions, have frequently assumed that our ways are best ways, that our aspirations are or should be their aspirations, that a neighborhood designed to suit us is just the type that would best suit them. (1963:239)

By the latter part of the 1960s, the urban renewal program was widely perceived as a failure primarily because the program was based on changing the physical environment of the poor with the hope that this would also trigger behavioral changes. The Model Cities program initiated by the federal government to replace the Urban Renewal program in the Demonstration Cities and Metropolitan Development Act of 1966 had a much more comprehensive focus. The program was implemented by the federal government with substantial support from planners.

The purpose of the program was not just to improve physical blight but also to address cities' social and economic problems. Included in its objectives were programs addressing housing, transportation, education, crime, health, and the provision of social services.

The Model Cities program started at about the same time that planners began to broaden the field of the profession. In the integrationist period the scope of planning was broadened from a concern for the physical attributes of the city to include a concern for the psycho-biological and socio-economic considerations of well-being. The attempt to address social issues during the period of integration quickly presented problems for planning. There was a greater recognition of the political nature of planning and the fact that different outcomes could only be achieved through political action. This realization was at the heart of Davidoff's proposal for advocacy planning. Planners were not just to provide lower income and minority groups with information and technical assistance, this information was also to be used as a powerful tool in the battle to secure outcomes that were favorable to these groups.

In reaching out to other racial, cultural, and ethnic groups, it also became apparent that these groups frequently had interests that diverged from those of mainstream practice and, therefore, planning was forced to deal with the problems of how to incorporate these alternative views into public policy and programs. It was also evident at the time that the monistic planning approach, and its proclivity toward homogenizing cultural and ethnic diversity, was inadequate for responding to the new challenge of cultural pluralism. This resulted in a plurality of planning proposals to address the diverse groups and their interests that integration now made obvious (see Davidoff, 1965; Friedmann 1973; Krumholz 1982; Alinsky 1971; and Grabow and Heskin 1973). For the most part, these proposals critiqued the rational planning process for subsuming the needs of the poor, minority, and women under the rubric of promoting the public interest.

In the trenches of planning practice, a group of planners, now called equity planners, devoted themselves to promoting social justice through community planning. Rather than using trickle down approaches to revitalizing declining neighborhoods, these planners addressed programs and policies directly to the urban poor themselves. Examples of these programs included fair share public housing, rent control, linkage fees, greater community involvement in planning, and redistribution of resources from the wealthy to the poor (Krumholz and Clavel 1994). In the City of Cleveland, where Krumholz was planning director, the planning department defined the city's policy as that of "expanding choices to those who had a few." This objective provided the framework from which planners considered all policy decisions.

While progress was made by equity planners in cities where they operated, equity planning had its limitations. As Clavel, himself an equity planner, admitted,

Equity planning is also fraught with issues of race and the problem of "handling" diversity. Here, neither the equity planners nor the traditions of local politics have given an adequate answer. Traditional politics works at access and creates an arena where, on occasion, racially defined groups can bargain for resources by contributing leadership to a system that may work systematically against them. Leadership is thus coopted, while grassroots populations remain, at best, organized in an informal planning way or outside the loop of politics. The equity planners we have known, as it happens, mostly tended to be white males or females, often representing people of color, but not drawn from these populations. (Krumholz and Clavel 1994:3)

So although the balance had shifted from assimilation as the dominant paradigm to a recognition of diversity in the integration period, the voices and stories narrated by cultural and ethnic group members continued to inhabit the margins and borderlands of the planning profession and were usually not represented in public discourse (Sandercock 1995). Also, by the 1970s ethnic groups were no longer satisfied just to share political power, and to twist the outcome of decisions in their favor, they began to demand a recognition of their cultures as distinct and legitimate parts of the American cultural tapestry. At the same time they called for a broadening of the epistemological debate so that it took cognisance of other ways of knowing that were peculiar to nondominant cultures, and the legitimation of these knowledge processes. This change in approach by ethnic and cultural groups may be explained by three developments: (i) globalization and technological improvements that shrank national borders and provided real time interface among world cultures, (ii) immigration and demographic shifts in the population, and (iii) an increase in the political clout of minority groups at both local and national levels. These developments are at the root of the paradigm shift to multiculturalism and the need for a holistic approach to planning.

MULTICULTURALISM AND HOLISTIC PLANNING

The objective of the integration period was to bring other ethnic groups into the political decision-making process and give them the resources to deal with political outcomes that would help to insure that, at least sometimes, outcomes will be favorable to these groups. In the multicultural period the argument has moved from one of "winning" in a political environment to one of mutual accommodation. The argument over what should be included in textbooks in schools is a good illustration; the multicultural perspective suggests that the contributions of all races and cultures can be included and this does not represent a zero-sum game.

Multiculturalists call for a restructuring of the dominant national epistemology so that it represents a fusion of the disparate cultures present in the United States. As Banks (1993:24) rightly observed, "the multiculturalists view *e pluribus unum* as an appropriate national goal, but they believe that the *unum* must be negotiated, discussed, and restructured to reflect the nation's ethnic and cultural diversity." Multiculturalism is an acknowledgment that culture is important and that it influences people's worldviews, perceptions, attitudes, and values. Multiculturalism strengthens rather than weakens a country's social fabric. In relation to planning, multiculturalism suggests that planners must now pay greater attention to how culture impacts, and is in turn impacted by, planning practices.

Pluralist planning was a response to the need for planners to address the differential impacts of planning on race, gender, and class. While planners must continue to address these issues, the demands for recognition by ethno-cultural groups, the changing demographics of the country, and globalization now make culture an exigent element of planning. Hence, the need exists for holistic planning.

Holistic planning is a culturally sensitive approach to planning that also recognizes planning's impact on race, class, and gender. These features of holistic planning are similar to Thomas' (1997) proposal for "Unified Diversity" in which planning becomes a means for social action based on diversity, tolerance, and cooperation.

There are several distinct and important differences between holistic planning and the universalist approaches. These differences are shown thematically in Table 3.2. First, while current planning approaches are situated within the principles of modernism and the Enlightenment, holistic planning denounces modernism and scientism as the only prescribing values of society. Holistic planning therefore searches for the meaning of actions rather than causality. As Stein and Harper discuss in chapter 5, a ritual dance in a traditional society may be a means of uniting the tribe and psyching members up for war, but a participant who thinks of the ritual in these terms loses the meaning attached to the custom and may lose his motive to dance.

Holistic planning also differs from the universalist planning approaches because it is nonfoundationalist. That is, there are no universal norms prescribed for all communities and no set standards that all communities must follow in a planning process. Holistic planning is disjointed, fragmented, and nonlinear. It enables communities to identify and build on their strengths in planning their future, with the planner interjecting his/her expertise for consideration by the community, but only does so as a partner in the planning process. Hence, the planner only acts as a facilitator, helping communities to write their own plans. Such an approach is similar to the planning practices of Shirley Solomon and Larry Sherman described in chapter 10 by Forester.

Holistic planning accepts and expects diversity among and within communities. Ethnic neighborhoods are seen as authentic and enduring, adding a rich flavor to a community's architectural and cultural fabric. Efforts are thus made to sustain these neighborhoods rather than seek their demise.

Holistic planning reflects a quantum leap in thinking beyond the narrow confines of the universalist monistic and pluralist approaches to planning. Holistic planning acknowledges that there are a multiplicity of cultures in the United States and that each culture has its own social realities that generate behavior and attitudes that are perfectly logical to that culture, even if they seem illogical to other cultures. Evans-Pritchard's account of the western anthropologist in Africa is instructive: A western anthropologist witnesses an Azande hut burn down in a Central African village and explains it from a logical empirical reasoning. "A match was struck by a child and this accidentally burnt down the hut," he said. From the western value-based reality, this makes a perfect explanation. But the Zande are interested not in the "how?" of the event but the "why?" For this, the anthropologist's explanation does not suffice. In order to answer the "why?" the Zande must consult a sorcerer. While the anthropologist might find the Zande reasoning to be illogical, it makes perfect sense to the Azande because it acts as a form of social control for deviant behavior within the society (Winch 1970).

The Azande example is one that we can infer to planning with inner city African-American communities and Latino barrios, recent immigrants from third-world countries, or even European ethnic groups. For example, Maruyama (1973) has suggested that the typical survey method used by planners to gather data lacks "relevance resonance" with Native-American and inner city African-American communities who have a distrust for outside agents and may, therefore, simply provide information they believe the researcher wants, not necessarily what the members of the community actually believe. For planners then, what this means is that we must become conversant and vigilant when planning with different cultures because each culture has its "particular language, a characteristic configuration of metaphors, historical destiny, and moral purpose—a language densely textured enough that no one who has not participated deeply in the life of the community can fully understand" (Madsen 1993:30). It also means that the traditional methods for soliciting information from ethnic and cultural groups, such as opinion surveys, are inapposite of good planning among such communities.

Table 3.2
Differences Between the Universalist Planning Approaches
and Holistic Planning

Evaluation Criteria	Monistic/Pluralist Planning	Holistic Planning
Decision Objective	Instrumental Rationality	Value Rationality
Power Structure	Hierarchical	Participatory/Mutual Accommodation
Worldview	Universalistic	Particularistic
View Towards the Ethnic Built Environment	Ecological Succession and Invasion	Re-use and Revitalization of Ethnic Enclaves
Architecture and Urban Form	Monotonous, Technical, Functionalist	Eclectic, Historical, Aesthetic

Holistic planning is responsive to a diversity of worldviews and cultures, acknowledges economic relations that allow for competition as well as sharing, social organizations predicated on individualism as well as cooperation, political decision making that is sometimes based on majority rule and sometimes based on consensus, and an economic system that is both econocentric and sociocentric. The concern for the environment and the ineffectiveness of the market system in addressing distributional issues, the marginalization of some social groups from the political process, social organizations that are built around the extended family system, and the informal trading systems in some urban communities all testify to the need for such a broader context. In order for these other views to enter the national discourse, however, they must be seen as a part of, rather than deviations from, what is considered to be the norm. Holistic planning legitimizes these different viewpoints.

THE CASE FOR HOLISTIC PLANNING

There are several reasons why holistic planning is advocated for planning in a multicultural society. First, holistic planning would foster greater cultural understanding and appreciation between planners and ethno-cultural groups. Second, holistic planning would help to legitimate planning among minority groups by making it relevant to their felt needs. Finally, holistic planning would broaden the epistemological debate to include voices from the margins. These points are discussed below in greater detail.

Holistic planning is relevant in an increasingly globalized village where greater interaction among cultural groups is likely to generate friction among people. Sensitivity to cultural diversity and the reflection of cultural and ethnic iconoclasm in the professional practice of planners offers the best chance for dampening such conflicts. In the United States, the fastest growing segment of the population are of nonwestern European origins. This implies that in the twenty-first century, planners will be faced with the making of decisions and choices that they did not have to address in the past. Pressure from ethnic and cultural groups for social inclusion and the recognition and legitimation of their religion, distinct values, beliefs and custom, in community plans, and goal setting will place planners in unfamiliar role settings. Therefore, an understanding of the cultural idiosyncrasies of the population in the community is a *sin qua non* for planners in a multicultural environment.

There is also a need to legitimate planning among cultural groups. Acceptance of planning as a fair and just process among ethnic and cultural groups will be difficult if planning decisions continue to rely solely on the planning traditions derived, for the most part, from Anglo-Saxon culture. For example, where planning and land-use regulations impose cultural biases on minority groups, such regulations are likely to be ignored or protested by these groups. The battle over regulations governing the height of trees and pollarding in Canada, for example, has pitted Anglo-Saxon values against those of Italians and Portuguese (Qadeer 1997). While Anglo-Saxons prefer their trees to be tall and leafy, Italians and Portuguese prefer shorter trees to provide for a better view of the neighbors. Chinese, on the other hand, believe that trees in front of houses bring bad luck. The planning regulations seem to favor the Anglo-Saxons and, hence, the feeling of bias in planning regulations by the other groups. Perceptions of cultural bias in planning could have detrimental impacts on the planning profession as a whole and seriously undermine the ability of planners to carry on with their work.

Cultural sensitivity in the application of planning standards with regards to the built environment is one more reason for the relevance of holistic planning. While the modernist bulldozer destroyed ethnic neighborhoods, there is now a resurgence to revitalize these neighborhoods and preserve, or even sometimes recreate, their historical character. Sen provides an in-depth discussion of this phenomenon in chapter 13. There is also a growing effort to incorporate cultural elements of ethnic vernacular to building restorations and new developments. Such ethnic vernacular is visible in many urban communities today, including the Mexican-themed

Guadalupe Plaza in Houston, and El Mercado and La Villita in San Antonio. In fact, these urban enclaves are now having an influence in the design of the built environment in many other cities and not just for historical purposes. As Lin has observed, the Chinatown redevelopment scheme in Houston "presents a mosaic of ethnic diversity in the emerging globalized metropolis. Rather than historicizing ethnicity to celebrate the past, it packages ethnicity as a culinary experience while presenting an image of the evolving urban future" (Lin 1995:639).

Despite these limited success stories, design review requirements in many cities continue to hinder the building of nonconformist architectural styles that have a peculiarly ethnic flavor (see, for example, Qadeer 1997). Hence, there is a need for flexibility in urban design standards to reflect the diverse architectural styles of ethnic and cultural groups. The urban future of holistic planning would be a mosaic of ethnic architecture and an urban form that is eclectic. Such an urban landscape will also have the effect of expanding areas of cultural consumerism in cities and help promote urban tourism.

Not only is flexibility needed in the urban design standards, but also in housing form and arrangement. Since the housing arrangements and planning needs of social groups vary, planners must address these different needs. In terms of land use, for example, some social groups, such as Chinese, are known to prefer higher densities and a mixture of housing types that allow elderly household members to live with the extended family or close by in the neighborhood so that visitation and supervision is easy. Ameyaw, in chapter 7, provides case study examples of such housing preferences in Canadian communities. Such an arrangement also reduces the necessity and cost of caring for the elderly in nursing homes. The segregation of housing into different land-use zones, through subdivision regulations, prevent this from happening.

Where planning has been sensitive to cultural differences, the results have often been satisfying to these groups. In Oakland, California, Michael Pyatok, an architect working with residents in a blighted Ohlone neighborhood designed an affordable housing complex that reflected the needs of the residents. The housing complex, called Hismen Hin Nu, "doorway to the sun," was built with stucco and cement-based siding rather than wood in order to help conserve trees. The housing complex also provided for a central courtyard that served as a meeting place for residents. This design would never have materialized had the conventional approach been used where the community was not involved in the planning process (Lyman 1997).

Female single parents may benefit more from the Swedish model of cohousing in which some aspects of living arrangements are shared. Residents in cohousing have separate bedrooms but share common kitchen and dining facilities. Such a housing type could foster closeness among the group and help facilitate baby-sitting arrangements that would allow mothers of infants to work outside of the home. Families that are forced to live in traditional apartment structures because of lack of options are deprived of this benefit because the traditional apartment structure is isolating for families and lacks a communitarian touch.

Finally, holistic planning is called for because of the need to broaden the epistemological conversation to include voices from the "borderlands." In order for planning to be more inclusive, other forms of discourse besides the bureaucratic and legalistic approaches, which usually characterize planning decision making, must be given legitimacy. This is because the formal and rationalistic approaches to planning are alien to some ethnic and social groups. For example, Tauxe (1995) observed in her ethnographic study of planning decision making in Mercer County, North Dakota, that there is a difference in the decision processes between rural and urban communities on the one hand and between planners and rural residents on the other. In her study she found that rural residents in Mercer County had a culture of agrarian populism that is characterized by neighborly morality, nonconfrontational norms of public demeanor, personal mediation, and moralistic ethics. However, this style of argument placed the local farmers at a disadvantage in the planning decision-making process because it was regarded by the planners as inferior to the more legalistic and bureaucratic decision-making processes with which planners were familiar. Therefore, planners must bring themselves to an understanding and appreciation of the different value systems and different discourse mechanisms of diverse cultural groups. This means that planners must legitimate other forms of conversation in order to be more inclusive of cultural and ethnic minorities.

CONCLUSION

The discussion in this chapter has highlighted the trajectory path of the planning profession as it has dealt with the changes in national ideology toward ethnic and cultural groups. From the profession's initial preoccupation with the improvement of the physical environment, planners later found it necessary to address the social and economic problems confronting cities; however, these concerns were pursued under the umbrella of a universalist doctrine. Today, with demographic changes looming, and an increase in demands for cultural identity, planners are again at the forefront of a revolutionary change. While we critique the inadequacies of planning responses in the past, however, it is worth remembering the admonition by Hancock, that the planners and the ideas that we now critique were

inseparably bound with the events to which they responded—while contemporaries must draw their own conclusions knowing today's planning needs are more complex and the procedures more sophisticated and potent, one judges historical significance according to how well a people approach the fundamental problems of their own time, not necessarily by how well they also anticipate ours. (Hancock 1967, 301)

Still, the discussion in this chapter raises a number of important questions that are critical to the planning profession and how we respond to current and future concerns: Could planners have practiced otherwise? Were planners vicious representatives of hostile interests? Were planners merely conforming adherents to dominant cultural assumptions?

In my view I can discern no malevolence on the part of planners toward ethnic and racial groups. I do, however, think that planners were responding to prevailing cultural assumptions of their time and to some extent planners were also the foot soldiers of the elite in society, carrying out the orders in the trenches for their masters. That is why planners must have greater sensitivity to the values and aspirations of the people with whom they plan. This sensitivity will be forthcoming if planners learn to plan *with* rather than *for* the people.

Holistic planning will sensitize planners to the diversity of cultures in the country, reduce conflicts between planners and ethno-cultural groups, and legitimize planning among these groups by presenting an unbiased approach to community development. These qualities are needed of the planning profession to make it relevant in the twenty-first century.

NOTE

1. Although there was discrimination against some European ethnic groups such as the Irish and Poles, these groups were able to assimilate more easily into mainstream American culture than racially different ethnic groups, such as the Chinese and African Americans.

REFERENCES

Alinsky, Saul. *Rules for Radicals: A Pragmatic Primer for Realistic Radicals*, New York: Vintage Books, 1971.

Adams, Frederick J. and Gerald Hodge. "City Planning Instruction in the United States: The Pioneering Days, 1900–1930." *Journal of the American Institute of Planners*, vol. 31, February 1965:43–51.

Banks, James A. "Multicultural Education: Development, Paradigms and Goals" in James Banks and Banks (eds.) Multicultural Education in Western Societies, 1986:2–28.

Banks, James A. "Multicultural Education: Development, Dimensions, and Challenges" *Phi Delta KAPPAN*, September 1993:22–35.

Baum, Howell S. "What is to be Learned? Alternative Views of Planning Theory-In-Use" Paper Presented at the Association of Collegiate Schools of Planning, 24th Annual Conference, Chicago, October 1982.

Beauregard, Robert. "Planning in an Advanced Capitalist State" in Robert W. Burchell and George Sternlieb (eds.) *Planning Theory in the 1980s: A Search for Future Directions*, New Brunswick, NJ: Center for Urban Policy Research. 1978.

Beauregard, Robert. "Without a Net: Modernist Planning and the Postmodern Abyss" *Journal of Planning Education and Research*, vol. 10, no. 3, 1991:189–94.

Constitution of the American Institute of Planners, Article II "Purposes" in *American Institute of Planners Handbook and Roster*, 1965.

Cubberley, E.P. *Changing Conceptions of Education*, Boston: Houghton Mifflin. 1909.

Davidoff, Paul. "Advocacy and Pluralism in Planning." *Journal of the American Institute of Planners*, vol. 31, no. 4, 1965:331–38.

Deacon, Thomas J. *Becoming American: An Ethnic History*, New York: The Free Press. 1983.

Fitch, Nancy E. "Multiculturalism and Diversity or Business as Usual in the Twentieth

Century." *Diversity*, vol. 1, no.1, 1992:43–64.

Friedmann, John. *Retracking America: A Theory of Transactive Planning*, Garden City: Doubleday/Anchor, 1973.

Friedmann, John and Carol Kuester. "Planning Education for the Late Twentieth Century: An Initial Inquiry." *Journal of Planning Education and Research* 14, 1994:55–64.

Gans, Herbert. The Urban Villagers. New York: The Free Press. 1982.

Grabow, Stephen and Allan Heskin. "Foundations for a Radical Concept of Planning." *Journal of the American Institute of Planning*, vol. 39, no. 2, 1973:106–14.

Hancock, John L. "Planners in the changing American City, 1900–1940." *Journal of the American Institute of Planners*, September 1967, vol. 33, no.5, 290–304.

Kraushaar, Robert. "Outside the Whale: Progressive Planning and the Dilemmas of Radical Reform." *Journal of the American Planning Association*, vol. , 1988:91–100.

Krumholz, Norman. "A Retrospective View of Equity Planning." *Journal of the American Planning Association*. Spring 1982:164–73.

Krumholz, Norman and Pierre Clavel. *Reinventing Cities: Equity Planners Tell Their Stories*. Philadelphia: Temple University Press. 1994.

Lin, Jan. "Ethnic Places, Postmodernism, and Urban Change in Houston." *The Sociological Quarterly*, vol 36, no. 4, 1995:629–47.

Lyman, Francesca. "Twelve Gates to the City: A Dozen Ways to Build Strong, Livable, and Sustainable Urban Areas." *Sierra*, May/June 1997:29–35.

Madsen, Richard. "Global Monoculture, Multiculture and Polyculture." *Social Research*, vol. 60, no.3, 1993:493–511.

Marcuse, Peter. "Integration and the Planner." *Journal of the American Institute of Planners*, vol. 35, no. 2, 1969:113–17.

Maruyama, Magoroh. "Human Futuristics and Urban Planning." *Journal of the American Institute of Planners*, vol. 39, no. 5, 1973:346–57.

Qadeer, Mohammad A. "Pluralistic Planning for Multicultural Cities: The Canadian Practice." *APA Journal*, Autumn 1997:481–94.

Sandercock, Leonie. "Voices from the Borderlands: A Meditation on a Metaphor." *Journal of Planning Education and Research* 14, 1995:77–88.

Sellers, Charles L. "Early Mormon Community Planning." *Journal of the American Institute of Planners*, vol. 28, no. 1, February 1962:24–30.

Stafford Walter and Joyce Ladner. "Comprehensive Planning and Racism." *Journal of the American Institute of Planners*, vol. 35, no. 2, 1969:68–74.

Tauxe, Caroline S. "Marginalizing Public Participation in Local Planning: An Ethnographic Account." *Journal of the American Planning Association*, vol. 61, no. 4, 1995:471–81.

Thomas, June Manning. "Coming Together: Unified Diversity for Social Action" in June M. Thomas and Marsha Ritzdorf (eds.), *Urban Planning and the African American Community: In the Shadows*. London. Sage Publications. 1997:258–74.

United States Commission on Civil Rights. *Civil Rights Issues of Euro-Ethnic Americans in the United States: Opportunities and Challenges*. Washington, D.C. 1979.

Warner, S.B. Jr. *The Urban Wilderness*. New York: Harper and Row. 1972.

Webber, Melvin M. "Comprehensive Planning and Social Responsibility." *Journal of the American Institute of Planners*, vol. 29, no. 4, November 1963:232–41.

Winch, P. "Understanding a Primitive Society" in B. Wilson. *Rationality*. Oxford: Blackwell. 1970.

CHAPTER 4

Neither Embedded Nor Embodied: Critical Pragmatism and Identity Politics

Robert B. Beauregard

In the United States talk about how we want to live, what our institutions are obliged to do, and how we expect others to behave is infused with the social and political weight of multiculturalism. We are urged to consider the cultural biases of literary canons, encouraged to take the point of view of Native Americans when considering the westward march of "civilization's" frontier, compelled to take race into account when accepting students into college, and asked to commemorate publicly the personal tragedies that constitute our history. Our public talk is organized on the premise that it is legitimate for groups (and the individuals who comprise them) to make claims based on their differences.

My interest is with how planners respond to these politicized differences. Public planning is meant to be democratic, thereby requiring the support of public institutions *and* citizens, and to serve "public" ends; that is, concerns that all or most groups have in common. Consequently, planners must consider both the differences and commonalities among groups. They can neither avoid multiculturalism (Qadeer 1997; Sandercock 1998) nor elude the identity politics that it has spawned.

More specifically, I am concerned with how one particular strand of planning theory, what is called critical pragmatism, handles the claims of a "strict" politics of identity. My argument is that critical pragmatism is silent about important tensions that emanate from multiculturalism. The democratic deliberations at the core of critical pragmatism rely excessively on the inherent enlightenment of reasonable individuals, the promise of an egalitarian proceduralism, and an assumption of shared values (either as precondition or consequence). These attributes rub against multicultural inclinations. The purpose of this chapter is thus to consider the issues that identity politics poses for critical pragmatism.

I begin with an overview of critical pragmatism as it has been developed by its planning proponents, turn to a brief discussion of multiculturalism and its related politics of identity and recognition, and then bring these two themes together in a critique of critical pragmatism.   My larger aim is to challenge the ascendent, communicative turn in planning, not because it is profoundly flawed but because it is neither sufficiently embedded in the historical moment nor sufficiently embodied in the actual participants without whom its deliberations are meaningless.

CRITICAL PRAGMATISM: AN OVERVIEW

The origins of critical pragmatism lie not only in a discomfort with how the practice of planning has been conceptualized but also with a shift in the way planning, at least in the United States and England, has been practiced. Drawing from outside the discipline—Jurgen Habermas' theory of communicative action and the recent resurgence of interest in American pragmatism (Bernstein 1992; Kloppenberg 1996)—a number of planning theorists have turned away from theories that focus on the functions of planning within the political economy, elaborate formal procedures for carrying out planning's values, or draw on postmodern arguments (Alexander 1984; Beauregard 1989; Friedmann 1987). Instead, they explore the connections between deliberation and action (Forester 1989).   Subsequently labeled critical pragmatism (Sager 1994:246–59), this approach to planning theory has become dominant (Innes 1995).[1]

Critical pragmatism's specific complaint is that prevailing theories of planning give insufficient consideration to the day-to-day behavior of practitioners, resulting in a paucity of professional guidance. It is dissatisfied practically with the ineffectiveness of planners and theoretically with threats to a liberal planning posed by both radical political economy and a full-blown postmodernism. Critical pragmatists argue that the emphasis on analysis and plan-making in the "rational model" of planning and the related de-emphasis of implementation make planners irrelevant to action. Planning procedures are too inner-directed. A political economy approach looks outward but then abandons the daily rhythms of practice, while postmodernism's epistemological assumptions and politics are too dismissive of liberal values of equality, tolerance, and justice.

At the same time, planning practice has evolved such that the connection between what planners propose and the social arrangements that make those proposals politically feasible is increasingly important. By comparison to the 1950s and 1960s, practice has become less centered on comprehensive, long-range plans and more involved with individual development projects and the day-to-day managing of land use and zoning. These tasks have shifted the core of planning from analysis and plan-making to negotiations and require practitioners to be more flexible. Instead of thinking about issues and formulate advice in isolation, planners must interact with residents, developers, and other stakeholders (Schon 1982).

This restructuring of planning has compelled theorists to address concerns that have haunted planning from its inception: its negotiation of diverse and incommensurate interests, the proper way for planners (experts) to interact with non-experts, and planning's contribution to democracy (Howe 1913). Planning theory thus began its communicative turn.

The important theoretical shift was from analysis as the fulcrum of the planning act to social interaction, particularly communication (Healey 1997:29–30). The key insight was that the ways that issues are defined, questions framed, attention directed, and agendas set are much more important than technical skills. It is not the scientific qualities of analysis that should rule but the sensibilities of those involved in the planning task and the usefulness of planning knowledge. This usefulness, though, cannot be manufactured by isolated professionals, but must be socially constructed. The objective is to forge an effective path that connects planning knowledge to social action.

Critical pragmatists thus opt for honest, open, and purposive communication as the basis for the crafting of collective actions. The central elements of good planning are the ability to communicate in an undistorted fashion (and to counter distortions) and to listen and learn from those with a stake in planning projects. Social learning empowers both planners and nonplanners and enables planners to educate and be educated by the public, thereby spreading planning's philosophy more widely throughout society.

Clearly, it is a short distance between planning as communicative action and a pragmatic philosophy that emphasizes democratic deliberations, personal experiences, and real-world consequences (Dewey 1954). Harbored within planning has always been an emphasis on practical results and a concern with educating the public. Consequently, communicative action theorists who had initially drawn on Habermas for their understanding of the "ideal speech" situation and the communicative act turned to John Dewey and William James (Blanco 1994; Hoch 1996, 1984a, 1984b; Verma 1996).[2] This enabled communicative action to be framed by pragmatism's more public understanding of the intersection of experience, inquiry, and participation. Planning was constituted as a deliberative and democratic process.

Using this framework, planners join with nonplanners to shape issues, set agendas, and work toward collective responses. Each participant has equal standing to speak and to be heard, and the legitimacy and efficacy of claims is negotiated publicly. Participants draw on their experiences, the imagined consequences of proposed actions, and their understanding of prevailing conditions. Planning is realized through public deliberation (Bowman 1996; Fishkin 1991).

Planners, of course, are making a trade-off. In return for relinquishing an aloof professionalism and allowing nonplanners access to planning's mysteries, planners become privy to alternative perspectives and subsequently are able to widen the commitment to planned actions. A "leveling" is being proposed, with planners less distant and less defensive of their professional authority. Planners' power and status are shared and planning is more deeply integrated in the deliberations that characterize everyday life. The hoped for result is a more democratic and effective planning.

On its surface critical pragmatism seems quite compatible with multiculturalism. Its openness, inclusivity, and sensitivity to different interests should easily incorporate different groups. As we probe more deeply, however, we discover that this is only partially true. A number of key "demands" of identity politics are not fully addressed. Before making my accusations specific, let me first indicate how I view the ideology of multiculturalism (particularly its "strict" version) and its politics of recognition.

MULTICULTURALISM AND THE POLITICS OF RECOGNITION

During the last twenty or so years, multiculturalism has become a familiar phrase in popular and academic discourse. It refers to the diversity of groups in society, a diversity driven (at least as regards the United States and many Western European countries) not only by recent immigration but also by "identity" movements that have articulated distinctions (among others) of race and ethnicity, sexual orientation, gender, physical handicap, and prior traumatic experiences (Calhoun 1995; Castells 1997; Habermas 1981; Young 1990).

Because such groups have distinct histories, they have "standing" in society. Multiculturalists, however, do not recognize all such groups but only those that occupy marginal social positions. To the extent that marginality violates the principles of inclusion and justice embraced by multiculturalists, it merges with group "standing" to make "differences" significant enough to warrant exceptional consideration in political deliberations.[3]

The thrust of the resultant identity politics is for acknowledgment of this distinctiveness; that is, for more than ameliorative responses to past or current injustices. A politics of identity is first a politics of recognition (Fraser 1995) and respect (Appiah 1997; Margalit 1996)) and only secondarily a politics of redistribution.

Identity politics is founded in two basic critiques, one directed at the dominance of a white, male European political perspective and the other at the notion of reason on which this perspective is based. The former critique is rooted in the realization that the dominant model of democratic politics precludes "difference" (Fraser 1990; Young 1990:96–121). The ideal citizen participating in the bourgeois public sphere embraces the common good (or public interest), searches for consensus, and subordinates passions to interests. This impartiality, critics argue, excludes different types of discursive engagement (for example, those grounded in emotions), assumes the desirability of existing structures of power (without which the public interest loses its force), and compels subsequent decisions to reinforce existing privileges. More pointedly, the dispassionate, other-regarding citizen is (historically) the white, European male. In order for others to participate in democratic politics, they have to adopt his persona and abandon the "difference" that establishes their identity. Consequently, the bourgeois public sphere is incompatible with a politics of recognition.[4]

More deeply embedded in multiculturalism is a rejection of a certain form of reason and the universalism that it implies (Beauregard 1989). The reasonableness posited for the ideal citizen embraces means-ends analysis, the existence of "best" solutions, and the possibility of shared values. This bourgeois rationality is associated with a belief in absolutes or at least universal political principles (that is, Enlightenment values) and a single, Archimedean point of view that places society in its proper perspective.

Universal values and the Archimedean perspective threaten multiculturalism. Universalism dissolves differences. It posits an underlying set of values and interests that knit society together and that have a higher priority than the values and interests of any particular group. In turn, the Archimedean viewpoint questions the legitimacy of diverse perspectives. If one "ideal" position—a totalizing discourse—exists from which to interpret society and frame its issues, then all other positions are inadequate.

Although society might be multicultural, diverse groups have no special standing within the bourgeois public sphere. For a common good to be attained, individuals must don the role of the ideal citizen and the views and interests of specific groups must be subordinated to universal considerations. These arrangements are incompatible with a politics of recognition and identity.

More germane to my argument, though, are the demands that a "strict" multiculturalism makes on the democratic deliberations in which critical pragmatism is anchored. Three are crucial: the initial and non-negotiable demand for recognition, the subsequent demand for the granting of a "special competence" in public deliberations, and the demand that the needs and desires of multicultural groups not be subject to a universalist resolution.[5]

The first two demands are that groups be publicly acknowledged and a special competence based on their cultural status be conceded. The symbolic act of recognition acknowledges the group as having special needs, desires, and interests as well as histories. Although these identities are socially constructed, they are formed prior to public engagement and, in the "strict" version, non-negotiable.

Recognition also includes acknowledgment of the important and irrefutable insights such groups have of themselves and thus of the distinct point of view they bring to public deliberations. This special competence, the most contentious of the demands, stems from the rejection of universal values and the resultant privileging of multiple perspectives and local knowledges. Only the group knows itself, only it can comment legitimately on its needs and desires. The "best" understanding comes from within the group. Consequently, one frequently hears in multicultural debates the accusation that "you cannot and should not speak for us; only we can speak for outselves." In the absence of this granting of special competence, recognition loses its political meaning.

Empowerment is at stake. Many identity groups think of themselves as being or having been oppressed and exploited. This oppression has involved "others" speaking for them; that is, interpreting their interests to those in power (Love 1991). In part, their marginal status is discursive and interpretive. Not allowed to speak for themselves, they are devalued. In the world of democratic politics where citizenship rests on the ability to give voice to interests, they are disempowered. Hence, these groups demand that only they speak to their interests and resist anyone else doing so. Recognition and the special competence associated with it are essential to their identity and to their future.

The third demand has to do with how claims made during democratic deliberations are adjudicated. The discussion of special competence signals the "strict" multicultural position: claims cannot be resolved by reference to universal values or to a purported common good. Rather, collective decisions about group claims must be resolved from the moral and social positions of the groups themselves. Their values must be paramount, undiluted in the solvent of universalism.

The dilemma this creates is obvious. If each group's claims must be taken on its own terms and if these claims can only be reconciled from the viewpoint of that group, then the group's claims cannot be challenged effectively from outside the group and claims that involve other groups cannot be resolved.[6] Under such conditions, redistributional issues pose insurmountable difficulties and even distributional concerns (since they leave material and status differences unchanged) are problematic. If all perspectives have to be respected equally and a common ground is absent, then claims that cross group boundaries will end in stalemate and democratic deliberations will preclude just resolutions (Hobsbawm 1996).

This is the paradox of multiculturalism. It began as a resistance to unequal treatment and marginality, yet a strict version casts aside the procedures that might insure equity and equality *across* groups. The paradox disappears only if one posits, much too simplistically, a democracy whose single function is to distribute resources and recognition from the oppressive haves to the marginalized have-nots, thereby conferring recognition and reducing inequalities but ignoring social interdependencies and thus producing only a crude justice.

The rejection of universal values thus presents a dilemma for identity politics. Because interdependencies exist, group claims are likely to be thwarted by the demand that they be resolved from a group perspective. Wrapped in solipsism, a "strict" multiculturalism founders on its own demands.

CRITICAL PRAGMATISM AND THE DEMANDS OF IDENTITY POLITICS

The three demands discussed above—for recognition, for the acknowledgment of special competence, and for a particularistic basis for resolving group claims—are problems that critical pragmatism has not yet adequately addressed. On these issues of identity politics, it is either silent or insufficiently attentive. This is a problem; planning's version of pragmatism is grounded in assumptions about the procedures and consequences of democratic deliberations. Such deliberations are meant to be inclusionary, open to all who wish to participate. They require that participants communicate honestly and reasonably, listen attentively, and respect others. General deliberative competence is assumed to be sufficient and participants are considered equals as regards the right to speak and the intrinsic value of their contributions (Beauregard 1998; Young 1996).

Agreement is assumed to stem from the reasonableness of individuals, shared moral understandings, and an underlying commitment to procedures, the latter ostensibly assuring agreement even when one's interests are excluded (Forester 1996b). The retention of liberal, democratic values serves as a basis for resolving group differences and finding common ground (Harper and Stein 1995). Regulatory structures that might "force" resolutions are absent as is any sense that individuals might organize in blocs designed to consolidate influence and shape outcomes.

Finally, critical pragmatism makes no mention of multiple public spheres across which citizens would be compelled to take different positions and thus to destabilize their claimed identities. Instead, it assumes a single forum in which all debates occur.[7] Within that forum, nevertheless, groups with different claims and perspectives can speak and be heard.[8]

Describing critical pragmatism in this way highlights the difficulties posed by a "strict" multiculturalism. Insufficiently embedded in specific social contexts and tending (ironically) to a disembodied practice, critical pragmatism flounders amid the deep conflicts of cultural pluralism. The friction begins with the first of these demands: the call for group recognition.

Within critical pragmatism, recognition vanishes in the face of inclusiveness and equality of standing. Critical pragmatism's openness supposes an "ideal citizen" much like the one that occupies the bourgeois public sphere; individuals are universally enfranchised; that is, they participate in democratic deliberations not because they are unique but because they are members of society. The differences that groups bring to planning deliberations are ones of interests rather than identities. Identity is important only to the extent that it produces incompatible interests that have to be reconciled through deliberation. Critical pragmatists believe that differences can be accommodated, and do so by redefining the differences of identity politics in terms of interests. This is less a solution than an evasion.

In turn, participants are disembodied. They are not included as gendered and ethnicized, holding allegiances to nations and religions, identified with specific places, and bearers of qualities that give them real presence. They are viewed simply as reasonable individuals who are open to the arguments of others and committed to the resolution of differing claims through democratic engagement (Beauregard 1998; Hopper 1992; Sandercock 1995). To embody participants would be to position critical pragmatism on a different ground, one where individual and group characteristics become salient, equality becomes problematic, and hierarchy emerges (Wolfe 1992; Young 1990:122–55). An embodied critical pragmatism would thus face identity differences in a way that it has heretofore avoided, and this would challenge its liberal inclinations.[9]

Theorists of critical pragmatism must specify in more detail how their liberal values are operationalized and include in this specification a recognition of the obstacles that make it easier for some individuals and groups to join the deliberations than others. Such obstacles exist and historically have been crucial to the attainment of democracy's ideals. Simply claiming to be inclusive leaves critical pragmatism out of touch with actual conditions. Problems of mobilization and incorporation cannot be disregarded.

A related issue is whether in certain situations certain individuals and groups might lack legitimacy; that is, might lack standing to participate. This is particularly important to an identity politics that fears powerful groups and institutions might usurp the voices of those on the margins. One cannot assume that groups that have no legitimate interest will opt not to be involved, nor does it seem reasonable to assume that all who participate have a legitimate right to do so.[10]

Critical pragmatists respond by retreating to proceduralism; those involved will debate who is a legitimate participant. Participating groups, however, are not disinterested parties and the power to deliberate and to arrive at a decision will be unevenly distributed among them. A just resolution might be forthcoming, but it might not. The question then becomes whether subsequent deliberations will be undemocratic and thus flawed.[11]

The second demand—that group membership confers special competence over group issues—is incompatible with the intellectual basis of planning and fits uncomfortably with the democratic deliberations posited by critical pragmatists. The dissonance is related both to the presumed scope of planning and to its rationale in a division of deliberative labor.

Planners are people who take the interests and needs of a variety of groups into account. Locating a light-rail transit stop, redeveloping a neighborhood commercial street, and regulating retail land uses require negotiating among diverse interests. The point of planning is to knit these interests together and mediate (potential) conflicts. Consequently, while critical pragmatism would seem to be safe in allowing for participation by nonplanners with general competence, special competence is problematic. Special competence erects a barrier to planners' engagement with the claims of the group. It places the claims of that group off-limits to planners and thereby hinders the search for a common or "public" resolution.

As experts in certain types of knowledge, one would expect theorists of critical pragmatism to be sensitive to the diverse and distinct contributions that individuals and groups can make to public deliberations and thus to have procedures for differentiating among types and degrees of competence. In fact, these theorists do just the opposite; they abandon a division of labor. Planning knowledge and deliberative competence are seemingly ubiquitous. How else does one explain the reduction of the planner to just another speaker in the deliberative process? The planner becomes merely one of numerous equally competent and knowledgeable individuals. For planners to be at all useful, however, they must make a unique contribution.

Planners have professional knowledge (Bender 1993) rather than amateur or common knowledge. They have elaborate insights into the city and how it functions. The competence they possess thereby stands apart from that of the groups with whom they plan. More importantly, it purportedly functions to synthesize group interests. Planning is not only inherently about the future, it is also about interdependencies that knit together issues, interests, places, and groups. Absent synthesis, planning makes no sense.

Under critical pragmatism planners place their knowledge and competence in contention. This is what it means to be an equal participant in democratic deliberations. The assumption is that what planners know about a given situation is insufficient to achieve a democratic resolution because it is partial (lacking common sense meanings), biased (all knowledge is socially constructed), and pre-democratic (that is, not yet democratically negotiated). Consequently, planners within critical pragmatism cast aside their special competence. This removes the hierarchy that is anathema to identity politics and breaks down the barriers between experts and nonexperts that stifle participation and democracy, but it also eliminates planners' status as professionals.

While these planners give up their unique competence, identity groups do not. A "strict" identity politics compartmentalizes issues in terms of stakeholders. Participants are divided by group identities and the overlap of knowledge and competence is minimized.

The issue is whether critical pragmatism can incorporate a division of deliberative labor. Because group interests overlap, democratically deliberated issues must be open to alternative points of view. Can critical pragmatists recognize that people come to these deliberations with different skills and knowledges, accept the need for "experts" (those who take private troubles as public issues), and still maintain inclusivity?

One solution is to allow each group to claim special competence, but not to allow it *a priori* that competence to be privileged. Rather, special competence must be articulated along with substantive claims and defended through mutual inquiry and argumentation. Once established in an earlier engagement, special competence must be re-established in subsequent ones. The problem with this solution, of course, is that it undermines the *prior* claim to special competence that is part of a "strict" multiculturalism.

Alternatively, one might posit procedural claims as subordinate to substantive claims, with the former disappearing if the latter are resolved. This is very much in the vein of disjointed incrementalism and its argument against the procedural bias of the rational model (Lindblom 1959). The focus is on consensus around outcomes rather than consensus on process, a reversal of the proceduralism of critical pragmatism. Making the resolution of substantive claims the primary goal, however, clashes with identity politics. Because a group's special competence is linked tightly to its identity and because this involves recognition and not redistribution, the substantive approach is unacceptable.

The third demand of a "strict" multiculturalism concerns the basis on which claims are to be adjudicated; doing so in terms of universal values or by reference to shared values is rejected. This severely hampers the deliberations imagined by critical pragmatists.

People are embedded in social positions that shape how they deliberate and to what they might agree. Those with the resources and power to insulate themselves from uncertainty, for example, are reluctant to act jointly or in ways that increase that uncertainty, making coalitions and agreements across social divides less rather than more likely (Marris 1996:87–104). More extreme are situations in which deliberations will never lead to a resolution, situations in which certain parties are so intransigent and single-minded that compromise is impossible.

Often, impasses need to be resolved and decisions sometimes need to be "forced." The *deus ex machina* of democratic deliberation—the inherent reasonableness of individuals who are committed to the avoidance of debilitating situations—seems to be the solution of choice for critical pragmatists.[12] This evades the issue. Moreover, it constitutes a surreptitious importing of universal values, another way in which critical pragmatism parts with identity politics.

In sum, by failing to embed its theory in a social context and by formulating a disembodied practice, critical pragmatism ignores and, when it does not, insufficiently addresses key issues raised by a "strict" politics of multiculturalism. It fails to provide a differentiated sense of its participants, ignores the division of labor that might contribute positively to collective action, and dismisses the difficult problems of adjudicating across groups. Consequently, critical pragmatists' claim to having formulated a planning theory that is more attuned to and more connected to practice becomes suspect.

CONCLUSION

The three demands of a strict identity politics—for recognition, special competence, and particularistic accommodations—are not easy to resolve. They rub against the tenets of deliberative democracy and the uniqueness of planning. Critical pragmatists, moreover, have not yet grappled seriously with these issues. Their commitment to proceduralism and constriction of planning encounters to communicative action disembeds and disembodies their argument, and this is not to its advantage.[13]

Certainly, critical pragmatism deserves praise for its emphasis on experience and consequences and its democratic inclinations. The close reading of what planners do is also important, particularly when it fuses theory and practice. Nevertheless, if we are to ground our theories historically and spatially, embedding them in the social diversity of existing societies, and speak to larger institutional forces and to political mobilizations without which social change is unlikely, then critical pragmatism must be further elaborated.

A "lax" identity politics, of course, would be more hospitable to the critical pragmatic project. Its demand for recognition accepts the inherent instability and multiplicity of identities, the limits of special competence, and the need for an interplay between a common ground and group interests as well as between recognition and redistribution. Its groups, moreover, are other-regarding, to a degree, and willing to cede (some) control. Still, theoretical problems do not disappear.

At the core of these challenges, of course, is toleration. People who are tolerant "make room for men and women whose beliefs they don't adopt, whose practices they decline to imitate; they coexist with an otherness that, however much they approve of its presence in the world, is still something different from what they know, something alien and strange" (Walzer 1997:11). Yet, tolerance is a social quality, one which, as Michael Walzer reminds us (1997), is aided and abetted by "regimes of toleration." Tolerance is only pervasive and possible when embedded in social structures that nurture it.

Tolerance, though, is insufficient. People must be willing to compromise in ways that convey mutual respect and balance group interests with interests that groups have in common; that is, which sustain cultural pluralism (Bowman 1996:95–104). Compromise also flows more generously from supportive social structures, and like tolerance, it is also embodied in socialized individuals with (often) politicized identities. These are the issues to which critical pragmatism must turn. Solutions are elusive, but better a messy and partial response than avoidance.

Such a response might begin with a number of questions, questions relevant not only to critical pragmatism but to all planning theories. First, what does it mean to plan in a political economy that exacerbates inequalities and is disinclined to a robust welfare state, in a society increasingly multicultural but suffused with discriminations, in a country more and more spatially organized along lines of class and race, with a civil society wedged between the pressures of commodification and the erosion of the governmental programs that support it? This question is an invitation to historical and spatial embeddedness.

Second, how should we plan in different institutional settings? What types of planning make sense in civil society? What are the costs of reducing planning to communicative action? These questions point to the need for institutional embeddedness.

Third, what does it mean that planning is carried out by real people with specific class backgrounds, gendered, racialized, and having strong ties to specific residential areas? Can any person, at any time, be a planner? Here, we embody planning.

Finally, how can planners engage democratically with those with whom they plan without abandoning a commitment to justice and without sacrificing their skills as planners?

NOTES

1. Harper and Stein (1995) call their version neo-pragmatism.
2. Michael Walzer, in a lecture titled "Deliberation and What Else?" labeled this turn to deliberative democracy as the American version of German ideal-speech theory, the former being less philosophical and more immediately and politically relevant. The lecture took place on December 2, 1997, at the New School for Social Research (New York City).
3. As will be obvious later, the "universal" principles of inclusion and justice pose internal dilemmas for a "strict" multiculturalism.
4. Feminists within planning have made similar arguments; see Hillier 1995, Hopper 1992, and Sandercock and Forsyth 1992. For a postmodern critique, see Beauregard 1991.
5. Essentially, I am focusing on the "deep conflicts" of cultural pluralism (Bowman 1996:75). Examples abound of "strict" multiculturalism, particularly in its political correctness mode. For illustration, see Orlando Patterson's (1997:83–123) discussion of

racial advocacy. The three demands of a "strict" multiculturalism bring to mind Walzer's (1992:3–19) three moments of the politics of difference: articulation, negotiation, and incorporation.

6. The inside-outside distinction corresponds to narrow and wide reflective equilibrium respectively as developed by Stanley Stein and Thomas Harper (this volume).

7. On the political theory behind this position, see Habermas 1996.

8. The need to deliberate across group boundaries was one of the impetuses for redirecting planning to greater emphasis on communication (Healey 1992b).

9. Tempering my criticism is that many critical pragmatists are quite attentive to the behavior of individual planners (Healey 1992a; Hoch 1994; Forester 1996a, 1992; Innes 1995). Nonetheless, the "identities" of the planners in their arguments are descriptive rather than functional.

10. Of course, a judgment of legitimacy is always problematic. Groups experiencing the lesser consequences and only symbolically affected would seem to have less legitimacy than those more substantively affected.

11. For discussions of how power mediates planning, see Forester 1989, Hoch 1992, 1984b, and especially Chambers 1994.

12. Along these lines, critical pragmatists and other theorists committed to deliberative democracy often conflate civil society with the spheres of political action, the former being less institutionalized and less implicated by power differences and strategic maneuvering (Young 1994).

13. Hoch 1984a and Forester 1989 do recognize that individuals are embedded in organizations and Verma 1996:10 notes the need to attend to the "communities" that influence sociological and psychological processes, but critical pragmatists stop short of institutional analysis. For a compelling exception, see Healey 1997.

REFERENCES

Alexander, Ernest. After Rationality, What? *Journal of the American Planning Association,* vol. 50, no. 1, Winter 1984:62–69.

Appiah, K. Anthony. The Multicultural Misunderstanding. *The New York Review of Books,* vol. 44, no. 15, October 9, 1997:30–36.

Beauregard, Robert A. Between Modernity and Postmodernity: The Ambiguous Position of U.S. Planning. *Environment and Planning D: Society and Space,* vol. 7, 1989:381–95.

Beauregard, Robert A. Without a Net: Modernist Planning and the Postmodern Abyss. *Journal of Planning Education and Research,* vol. 10, no. 3, Summer 1991:189–94.

Beauregard, Robert A. Writing the Planner. *Journal of Planning Education and Research,* vol. 18, no. 2. 1998:101–09.

Bender, Thomas. The Cultures of Intellectual Life: The City and the Professions in Thomas Bender (ed.), *Intellect and Public Life.* Baltimore, MD: The Johns Hopkins University Press, 1993:3–15.

Bernstein, Richard J. The Resurgence of Pragmatism. *Social Research,* vol. 59, no. 4, Winter 1992:813–40.

Blanco, Hilda. *How to Think About Social Problems.* Westport, CT: Greenwood Publishers. 1994.

Bowman, James. *Public Deliberation.* Cambridge, MA: The MIT Press. 1996.

Calhoun, Craig. *Critical Social Theory.* Oxford: Blackwell. 1995.

Castells, Manuel. *The Power of Identity.* Malden, MA: Blackwell Publishers. 1997.

Chambers, Robert. All Power Deceives. *ids bulletin.* vol. 25, no. 2, April 1994:14–26.

Dewey, John. *The Public and Its Problems*. Athens, OH: Swallow Press. 1954 (originally 1927).

Fishkin, James S. *Democracy and Deliberation*. New Haven, CT: Yale University Press. 1991.

Forester, John. *Planning in the Face of Power*. Berkeley: University of California Press. 1989.

Forester, John. Critical Ethnography: On Fieldwork in an Habermasian Way in M. Alvesson and H. Wilmott (eds.) *Critical Management Studies*. London: Sage, 1992:46–65.

Forester, John. *The Rationality of Listening, Emotional Sensitivity, and Moral Vision* in Mandelbaum, Mazza, and Burchell, 1996a:204–24.

Forester, John. *Argument, Power, and Passion in Planning Practice* in Mandelbaum, Mazza, and Burchell, 1996b:241–62.

Fraser, Nancy. From Redistribution to Recognition? *New Left Review* 212, July/August 1995:68–93.

Fraser, Nancy. Rethinking the Public Sphere. *Social Text*, vol. 8, 3-9, no. 1, 1990:56–80.

Friedmann, John. *Planning in the Public Domain*. Princeton, NJ: Princeton University Press. 1987.

Habermas, Jurgen. New Social Movements. *Telos*, vol. 49, Fall 1981:33–7.

Habermas, Jurgen. Three Models of Democracy in Seyla Benhabib (ed.) *Democracy and Difference*. Princeton, NJ: Princeton University Press, 1996:21–30.

Harper, Thomas L. and Stanley M. Stein. Out of the Postmodern Abyss: Preserving the Rationale for Liberal Planning. *Journal of Planning Education and Research*, vol. 14, no. 4, Summer 1995:233–44.

Healey, Patsy (a). A Planner's Day: Knowledge and Action in Communicative Practice. *Journal of the American Planning Association*, vol. 58, no. 1, Winter 1992:9–20.

Healey, Patsy (b). Planning Through Debate: The Communicative Turn in Planning Theory. *Town Planning Review*, vol. 63, no. 2, 1992:143–62.

Healey, Patsy. *Collaborative Planning*. Vancouver, Canada: UBC Press. 1997.

Hillier, Jean. The Unwritten Law of Planning Theory: Common Sense. *Journal of Planning Education and Research*, vol. 14, no. 4, Summer 1995:292–96.

Hobsbawm, Eric. Identity Politics and the Left. *New Left Review*, vol. 217, May/June 1996:38–47.

Hoch, Charles. Doing Good and Being Right: The Pragmatic Connection in Planning Theory. *Journal of the American Planning Association*, vol. 50, no. 3, Summer 1984a:335–45.

Hoch, Charles. Pragmatism, Planning, and Power. *Journal of Planning Education and Research*, vol. 4, no. 2, December 1984b:86–95.

Hoch, Charles. The Paradox of Power in Planning Practice. *Journal of Planning Education and Research*, vol. 11, no. 3, Spring 1992:206–15.

Hoch, Charles. *What Planners Do: Power, Politics, & Persuasion*. Chicago: Planners Press. 1994.

Hoch, Charles. A Pragmatic Inquiry About Planning and Power in Mandelbaum, Mazza, and Burchell, 1996:30–44.

Hopper, Barbara. 'Split at the Roots': A Critique of the Philosophical and Political Sources of Modern Planning Doctrine. *Frontiers*, vol. 13, no. 1, 1992:45–80.

Howe, Frederick C. The Remaking of the American City. *Harper's Monthly Magazine*, vol. 127, no. 758, 1913:186–96.

Innes, Judith E. Planning Theory's Emerging Paradigm. *Journal of Planning Education and Research*, vol. 14, no. 3, Spring 1995:183–89.

Kloppenberg. James T. Pragmatism: An Old Name for Some New Ways of Thinking? *The Journal of American History*, vol. 83, no. 1, June 1996:100–138.

Lindblom, Charles E. The Science of Muddling Through. *Public Administration Review*, vol. 19, 1959:79–88.

Love, Nancy. Politics and Voice(s): An Empowerment\Knowledge Regime. *Differences*, vol. 3, no. 1, 1991:85–103.

Mandelbaum, Seymour, Luigi Mazza, and Robert W. Burchell (eds.) *Explorations in Planning Theory*. New Brunswick, NJ: CUPR Press. 1996.

Margalit, Avishai. *The Decent Society*. Cambridge, MA: Harvard University Press. 1996.

Marris, Peter. *The Politics of Uncertainty*. London: Routledge. 1996.

Patterson, Orlando. *The Ordeal of Integration*. Washington, D.C.: Civitas. 1997.

Qadeer, Mohammad A. Pluralistic Planning for Multicultural Cities. *Journal of the American Planning Association*, vol. 63, no. 4, Autumn 1997:481–94.

Sager, Tore. *Communicative Planning Theory*. Aldershot: Avebury. 1994.

Sandercock, Leonie. Voices From the Borderlands. *Journal of Planning Education and Research*, vol. 14, no. 2, Winter 1995:77–88.

Sandercock, Leonie. *Towards Cosmopolis*. Chichester, UK: John Wiley & Sons. 1998.

Sandercock, Leonie and Ann Forsyth. Gender Agenda: New Directions for Planning Theory. *Journal of the American Planning Association*, vol. 58, no. 1, Winter 1992:49–59.

Schon, Donald. Some of What a Planner Knows. *Journal of the American Planning Association*, vol. 48, 1982:351–64.

Verma, Niraj. Pragmatic Rationality and Planning Theory. *Journal of Planning Education and Research*, vol. 16, no. 1, Fall 1996:5–14.

Walzer, Michael. *What It Means To Be An American*. New York: Marsilio. 1992.

Walzer, Michael. *On Toleration*. New Haven, CT: Yale University Press. 1997.

Wolfe, Alan. Democracy versus Sociology: Boundaries and Their Political Consequences in Michele Lamont and Marcel Fournier (eds.) *Cultivating Differences*. Chicago: University of Chicago Press, 1992:309–25.

Young, Iris Marion. *Justice and the Politics of Difference*. Princeton, NJ: Princeton University Press. 1990.

Young, Iris. Civil Society and Social Change. *Theoria*, October 1994:73–94.

Young, Iris. Communication and the Other: Beyond Deliberative Democracy in S. Benhabib (ed.) *Democracy and Difference*. Princeton, NJ: Princeton University Press. 1996:120–35.

CHAPTER 5

The Paradox of Planning in a Multicultural Liberal Society: A Pragmatic Reconciliation

Stanley Stein & Thomas Harper

This chapter points to certain tensions generated in the idea of a pluralistic liberal multi-cultural society. It shows how postmodernistic[1] critiques of modernistic approaches to planning can be reconstructed from a pragmatic point of view. Different ways of viewing multicultural planning (including a reconstructed Enlightenment position) have value in enhancing our understanding of a multicultural society and in seeking more just solutions to some of its problems. Thus, pragmatism (a) presents a different way of seeing the tensions (one that avoids the contradiction of the Postmodernistic approach), and (b) suggests a theoretical strategy for dealing with them.

North American society has always been composed of people with numerous different cultures of origin (including Aboriginal peoples), and has been enriched by a constant influx at varying rates of immigrants from many different cultures. In spite of this, North American society (at least until quite recently) has been characterized by a single dominant culture. This culture emphasizes a critical/analytical perspective, coming out of the Enlightenment, often referred to as "Modernism" (Harper and Stein 1995a).

As Burayidi has argued in chapter 3, the modernist worldview and its associated universalist planning approaches (Social Reform, pre–World War II and Rational Comprehensive Planning, post–World War II) (Friedmann 1987) tended to be assimilationist, pressuring all comers into conformity with the dominant culture. This approach has become more obviously problematic as immigrants increasingly come from cultures that are very different from the dominant culture; that is, they are "traditional" (nonmodern—they lack the critical/analytical perspective of Modernism). The more different from the dominant culture is the culture of origin, the more wrenching the process of assimilation.

POSTMODERN CRITIQUES

Postmodernists have critiqued the dominant culture and its vocabulary as hierarchical, reductionistic, scientistic, universalizing, anthropomorphic, and patriarchal. They have attacked the assimilationist tendency, and advocated a multicultural approach to public planning and policy, one that celebrates difference, one that encourages and facilitates maintenance of the identity of the originating cultures. Many of these critiques of planning in a multicultural society have a similar structure: (i) attack the dominant approach, (ii) provide a replacement, and (iii) plead for respect of other narratives.

Attack the Dominant Approach

The dominant planning approach (western, modernist, patriarchal) is attacked on grounds both theoretical (reliance on rejected notions like objective truth, rationality, theory, meta-narrative) and practical (oppressive consequences).

Postmodern feminism critiques what it calls logocentric (or phalocentric) thought; that is, they argue that the way of thinking that has come down to us through the Enlightenment is paternalistic, hierarchical, and leads to social structures that oppress women and minority groups. In presenting this view, postmodernists attack the vocabulary, ideas, and concepts which they feel are constitutive of logocentric thinking. These include: dualism, universals, reality, truth, rationality, absolute goodness, knowledge, scientific objectivity.[2]

Developmentalism as an approach to nondominant cultures (whether in our society or in the "third world") is critiqued as a distorting ideology, one that masks the dominant culture's attempt to assimilate non-dominant cultures. Marxist and other modernist views are seen as presupposing a notion of "development" that should be deconstructed. The "stages of development" model espoused by modernization theorists revolves around the dichotomies underdeveloped/developed and traditional/modern. Many Marxists also maintain the belief in evolutionary progress from precapitalism to capitalism and finally to socialism (Connelly et al. 1995). Postmodernists further critique the dominant culture's practice of imposing labels—like "backward" and "underdeveloped"—on nondominant cultures. Through the process of labelling and normalization, individuals, classes, genders, ethnic groups, and even nations become redefined according to one-dimensional labels that simplify and therefore belie their complex histories and motivations. They become portrayed as passive "clients," "victims," "target group members," "cases" in programs apparently intended for their benefit.

The labels of the dominant vocabulary are seen as insidious ideological distortions: "It is as if the label itself provides the diagnosis of the problem and proposes a particular solution" (Connelly et al. 1995:25). Planning agencies and experts are guilty of the imposition of the dominant culture's "categories and technical knowledge" (Connelly et al. 1995:26).

"Modernism's universalizing claims" are attacked by "unpacking or deconstructing the power relations, assumptions, and hidden agendas implicit in a body of language or discourse." Such deconstruction unmasks "political agendas embedded in key terms . . . environment, equality, helping, market, needs, participation, planning, population, poverty, progress, production, resources, science, standards of living, state and technology" (Connelly et al. 1995:27).

In sum, what these critics reject is the idea that there is (i) some universal account that predetermines the way things are to be, and (ii) some ahistorical standard that prescribes what should be. These ideas are viewed as myths or subterfuges, which act to suppress and control nondominant cultures in favor of the dominant culture.

Critical theorists[3] would say that the dominant culture's planning approach is an ideology and we should replace it with something more legitimate. So then, what do we replace it with?

Provide a Replacement

Postmodernists wish to replace the Modernistic vocabulary and ideas with their own notions. A radical paradigm shift, a new language game, a new vocabulary is advocated.[4] Within anthropology, a major paradigm shift has occurred since the 1970s. The challenge to evolutionary or stages models of historical change has led to a re-examination of the world system, and a critique of earlier studies that portrayed certain societies as "primitive."

The replacement usually appeals to thinkers like Foucault[5] or Derrida. Theory still enters, but as a critical account of power relations and "normalization" (Foucault 1980). Normalization is the process through which a citizenry becomes reorganized and labelled according to bureaucratically imposed categories that privilege or punish according to certain standards and rationales. The arbitrary nature of these standards is disguised, so that they come to appear as rational and self-evident (Connelly et al. 1995).

So the proposed (replacement) approach recognizes the significance of power relations, and celebrates difference and the significance of the "other." They talk of envisioning "alternative possibilities for human association generated by a range of new social movements (indigenous, peasant, feminist, environmentalist)" that are not "mere technical or managerial improvements on the existing developmental paradigm" (Connelly et al. 1995:26).

An alternative vocabulary is proposed. This creates an either/or situation. In providing a new vocabulary, they ask us to give up the old vocabulary of the dominant culture. No longer is there talk of progress or development. The "alternative" theories focus on people as the agents, or creators, of their own histories. Local histories are the focus of research: mini-narratives replace meta-narratives.

Plead for Respect for "Other" Narratives

The idea that there is only one legitimate perspective is seen as serving the patriarchal interests of the dominant culture. Postmodern feminists speak of different realities, different "voices and knowledge," different moralities, different ways of knowing (Gilligan 1977). They urge planners to respect the narratives of the "other" (Aboriginals, ethnic groups, women), to expand the worldview of the dominant culture to recognize and validate other cultural values and other ways of knowing.

Postmodernists seek the "recognition of the importance of identity," the "recovery and strengthening of difference," a "focus on identity, difference and culture," to "give rise to the complex diverse and multi-layered realities of the third world women's lives." They want to go beyond the (liberal pluralist) recognition of the need for public institutions to encourage respect and understanding of nondominant cultures; they advocate what Nussbaum (1997) calls the politics of identity, which is the view that public institutions should provide the individual with self-legitimation through identification with a particular minority culture. In this view, recognizing that different cultures, traditions, and genders have different views on these matters is not enough; they want us to accept the *legitimacy* of them all.

A corollary of this approach is that public institutions (both planning and educational ones) should de-emphasize the values of the dominant culture. This advocacy has had some influence in the United States and a great deal more in Canada, where we have a federal ministry of multiculturalism, which subsidizes a wide range of activities designed to encourage and legitimate nondominant cultures.

THE CORE TENSION

We believe that there is great merit in this perspective but it also presents difficulties. There is a tension between the second and the third steps. Whereas the third step (plead for respect for all narratives) presupposes that all accounts are equally good, the second step (provide a replacement meta-narrative) presupposes that some accounts are better or *truer* than others. What these critics really want to do is to distinguish between stories that are good, true, and liberating versus those that are not. They would like to reject the latter.

Herein lies the core tension. Rejection and replacement of the dominant approach presupposes criteria for evaluating some accounts as *better* than others. Then we no longer have a postmodernist proposal to eliminate meta-narratives, but a proposal for a *new* meta-narrative. What is being proposed by the postmodernists is just as much a universal, general, abstract description as the modernist account. But, by their own account, they aren't entitled to look upon their views as "better," or as closer to "the truth" or "reality" or "rationality" than any other. Another way to put it is that they want to claim their view is "right" at the same time that they argue there is no such thing as "right." While the Postmodernists want to reject the privileging of the dominant account, they have really not broken away from the (modernist) worldview of the dominant culture.

TWO USEFUL DISTINCTIONS

External and Internal Perspectives

In trying to resolve the tension just described, we find it useful to distinguish between external and internal perspectives. An internal perspective is the standpoint of the *participants* in a culture, an activity, or language game. It relies on concepts internal to the activity: "the use of the words in a language game cannot be described without using concepts which are related to the concepts employed *in* the game" (Putnam 1992:269). An external perspective is the standpoint of an external observer who is not involved in the culture, activity, or language game. External approaches usually involve the application of a general explanatory theory (and its concepts) of anthropological function or economic structure.

The relevance of external accounts to internal ones (and the closeness of the two) varies across cultures. The internal view is usually associated with accepted standards, beliefs, and practices. Thus, cultures that take a strictly internal perspective tend to be more static and conservative. These "traditional" cultures have little use for background theory, and resist external views. The critical, analytical, external view is not valued. An external observer attempting to gain an *interpretive* (internal) understanding usually does so by *participating* in the culture. In contrast, the external view tends to be associated with a critical attitude toward accepted standards, beliefs, and practices. Cultures that incorporate an external view are usually more dynamic.

However, the internal/external distinction should not be interpreted as necessarily coextensive with the distinction between members of a culture and nonmembers. Really it relates more to the distinction between cultures that are traditional, noncritical, and conservative versus those that are nontraditional, critical, and dynamic. So it is entirely possible for members of a culture (particularly a nontraditional one) to take an external view of that culture. Thus, Walzer can argue that the effective social critic must be "inside" the society. They must stand "a little to the side, but not outside: critical distance is measured in inches" (Walzer 1987:61).

This is possible in our dominant culture because the critical, analytical view is highly valued and the external view is almost part of internal practice. Here, internal and external are much closer. In Marxian terms our cultural superstructure includes a critical account of the relationship between superstructure and structure (economic relations). Such cultures are analytic, scientific, critical, in flux. A very clear example of this second type of culture is the culture of liberal academic planners.

Wide and Narrow Reflective Equilibria

For understanding the problems of accommodating nondominant cultures in a multicultural society, we have found that another related contrast is more useful—between wide and narrow reflective equilibrium. The notion of "Reflective Equilibrium"[6] is based on the work of Rawls (1971, 1993); Daniels (1985); and Nielsen (1991, 1996). They have attempted to describe how we might objectively devise the structure or rules for particular types of situations, independent of our own interests or position in society, within a particular set of value commitments. Reflective equilibrium is "a coherentist method of explanation and justification used in ethical theory, social and political philosophy, philosophy of science, philosophy of mind and epistemology" (Nielsen 1996:13). We have argued that it is an equally valuable method for planning (Harper and Stein 1995b). The idea is to get our "beliefs and practices" into the "most coherent pattern we can for the time manage" (Nielsen 1996:14).

An internal perspective might seek a Narrow Reflective Equilibrium (NRE), which focuses on the coherence of considered situational judgments and normative principles. This perspective gives expression to the mini-narrative—the local story of the culture. It does not give an explanatory or critical account of moral or other practices by bringing in (external) background theories and principles (normative or descriptive).

In contrast, a Wide Reflective Equilibrium (WRE) widens the NRE by invoking an external perspective that includes background theories and principles. These other elements add a *critical* capacity. Thus, in the moral realm, a WRE has been defined as a coherent set of beliefs that includes the following components: (i) a set of firmly-held, considered judgements (which may be intuitive); (ii) a set of normative substantive and/or procedural principles; and (iii) a set of background theories that show that the set of normative principles are more acceptable than alternative normative principles. These background theories may incorporate both other normative notions (different from those in the normative principles held) and empirical theories and observations.[7]

A WRE process[8] involves seeking *coherence* among the above elements, whether they are internal to a culture or external. It includes each participant reflecting on their own judgments and intuitions, ethical principles and theories, and background theories, critiquing and justifying intuitions by reference to principles; generating and critiquing principles that reflect intuitions; and using background theories to justify both judgments and principles. All of the interlocking elements should fit together as a coherent, consistent, organic whole. The starting point is to seek agreement among participants on an "overlapping consensus" (i.e., look for whatever is shared: moral principles, values, empirical facts, or specific judgments) and work from there to widen this circle of consensus.

When the WRE process is followed, progress and justification of judgments do not require an appeal to any absolute outside foundation that is independent of our social framework. In chapter 4 Beauregard considered the values of liberal democracy as "absolutes or at least universal political principles." It may be that these values can be deduced from particular philosophical conceptions, but for the Pragmatist, they need not be. These values arise out of a WRE process; they are practical and situationally contingent; not universal and not absolute. In no way do they presuppose or require an absolute, universal, or archimeadian point. They are merely accepted as necessary conditions for a pluralistic democratic society. A commitment to these values does not assume people are disembodied rationalists, nor does it require any denial of traditional culture as a source of their beliefs. Instead, justification depends on legitimate procedures. By legitimate, we mean open, uncoerced, fair, and fallible. These fair procedures provide for legitimation while avoiding the foundationalist pitfall of modernism (Harper and Stein 1995a).

As we have seen, many critics of modernist planning and development approaches want to eliminate the use of (external) dominant vocabularies (either Marxist or Capitalist) they describe as *a priori*, arbitrary, universalizing discourses. Instead, they want to use a postmodernist, Foucauldian (1980) analysis of power. But, aren't the proposed alternative vocabularies also based in the dominant culture? Does not the idea of recovering voices or traditions also reflect the dominant culture? They are simply substituting one external vocabulary for another; and they are still appealing to a wider equilibrium. Their analysis is just as *a priori*, arbitrary, and universalizing as any other external one. In Western enlightenment cultures, external perspectives—whether modern or postmodern—are usually from the dominant culture. The key distinction is not whether the views are from the dominant culture, but whether they look at a society from an internal view or an external view, whether they are satisfied with a narrow or a wide reflective equilibrium.

THE PARADOX OF MULTICULTURALISM

Nondominant cultures within a multicultural liberal society experience a tension between NRE and WRE, between tradition and critique. NRE tends to be static; to conserve both what is good and what is bad in the culture. WRE allows for dynamics and change; ideological distortions are more likely to be identified and corrected.

The Need for an Overlapping Consensus

The multicultural approach (which encourages an NRE in the nondominant cultures) creates its own problems, particularly if taken too far—the most extreme form being Beauregard's "strict" multiculturalism discussed in chapter 4. Rawls (1993) has argued that even a pluralistic liberal democratic society like ours requires an *overlapping consensus* regarding certain basic values, like tolerance. He traces our society's ability to accommodate diverse viewpoints to the western European experience with clashes between different substantive religious and moral conceptions of the "good" (which Rawls calls thick theories of the good). A conception of society was developed that tolerated different thick theories of the good within a framework of democratic political values, many of which are procedural. He refers to this conception of society as a thin theory of the good. It presupposes a recognition that other traditions one might not accept are still worthy of respect.

Each of the constituent cultures of a pluralistic society has to be able to accept the values of this thin theory of the good—impartiality, fairness, individual rights, democratic processes, and tolerance for multiple thick theories of the good. This is one reason why pluralistic liberalism emphasizes process and dialogue in the political realm. We try to leave as much as possible of the substantive ("thick theories") to the private realm. It is not that these beliefs are unacknowledged or denigrated or seen as unimportant. Rather, we have to learn to live with our differences over them. A procedural focus aims to accommodate significant substantive private differences. The aim in the political realm is not to discover truth, but to devise institutions and practices that have political legitimacy.

People from originating cultures that do not accept these values will have to adapt, changing some values in order to be part of a pluralistic society. For example, if a culture believes in a theocratic state that enforces their particular thick theory of the good and imposes it on everyone, then people from that culture have to give up that aspect to become part of a pluralistic culture. To this degree, they have to accept the values of the dominant culture. This doesn't mean that they have to give up the rest of their internal thick theory of the good. It doesn't mean that they have to give up their identity to participate in the political realm. Nor does it require, as Beauregard claims in chapter 4, that they give up claims to "special competence" in interpreting their own "local knowledge." However, a "strict" multicultural approach to planning that seeks to preserve *all* aspects of the originating cultures will be in a paradoxical position if they refuse to accept the very values that cause the pluralist society to be willing to try to accommodate them.

Arguments for a Widest Equilibrium

Many theorists (Nielsen, Rawls, and Daniels) believe that moral theory should be seeking the *widest* possible reflective equilibrium. Rawls remarks that "it is clearly WRE that we should be concerned with in moral philosophy," because in WRE, "we are presented with all the possible sets of moral principles, together with the relevant philosophical arguments for them" (Nielsen 1985:27–28). Whereas an NRE (because it is not critical) is likely to "leave our sense of justice pretty much intact," a wide process entails the "realistic possibility that our sense of justice may 'undergo a radical shift'—there are no judgments on any level of generality that are in principle immune to revision" (Nielsen 1985:27–28).

In other words, the argument for seeking the widest possible equilibrium is that it allows for critique and change, which are highly valued in our enlightenment-based culture. The difficulty with the claim that we should always seek the widest possible equilibrium is that it underestimates the negative effects of the critique involved—a problem to which planners need to be sensitive.

Arguments Against a Widest Equilibrium

On the other hand, there are arguments that wide reflection and critique are not always salutary. Williams (1985) argues that scientistic cultures (in which science and analysis are important values) tend to undermine the very possibility of moral knowledge. As Putnam puts it: "If we become reflective to too great a degree, if we absorb too much of the absolute (i.e., scientistic)[9] conception of the world, we will no longer be able to employ our ethical concepts...we cannot stop being reflective, but we can be *too* reflective. We are in an unstable equilibrium" (Putnam 1992:90).

Thus, he believes that too much reflection and external criticism undermines cultural practices, leading to the destruction of valuable social practices, including moral values. In a "true common culture," Scruton argues that change will not be valued; it may be seen as a threat to the continuity of tradition:

There is only limited scope...for change and innovation. Indeed, innovation is never a value in itself, but at best a necessary accommodation to changes arising from outside. Too much innovation—especially in those customs and ceremonies which provide the core experience of membership—is inherently threatening to the culture. Tradition, on the other hand, is of the essence...through membership, I see the world as it was seen by those who went before me, and as it will be seen by those who are yet to be. (Scruton 1990:119–20)

Accepting an external account can be destructive of these valued social practices. As Scruton warns:

To the observing anthropologist steeped in functionalist and utilitarian thought, the dance is a means to raise the spirits, to increase the cohesion of the tribe, in time of danger. Thus, description explains and justifies. But it does not tell us what the dance means to the dancer. If the tribesman thinks of the dance in that way he is alienated from it. He loses his motive to dance, once he borrows the language of the anthropologist. (Scruton 1990:109)

So the external account of the functionalist anthropologist can rob the social activity of its meaning and lead to its demise. Thus, a problem for highly reflective cultures is that those who take a critical external perspective and are sympathetic to change seem to be prone to alienation; and this alienation can damage the social fabric. This is one of the key criticisms of Rawls' political liberalism levelled by Communitarians. They believe that a Rawlsian overlapping consensus, regarding a thin good theory of the good, does not provide the necessary social and institutional bonding necessary to cement members of a culture into a unified whole. They advocate the revival of civic virtue, character formation, and substantive moral discourse (Sandel 1982; Etzioni 1993). Too much critique will tend to dissolve the social glue.

The Dilemma

When we contrast these two views, we understand why some traditions (e.g., circumcision) are criticized by some observers external to the culture and defended not only by its participants, but also by other observers who are external. How would postmodern critics respond to the following? When all is said and done, fully informed, sophisticated, and educated Muslim women may decide to maintain a traditional (internal) position regarding certain social relationships, which from an external perspective are patriarchal and subservient. Are they wrong? Yes, wrong if they accept an external functional, structural account. But why *should* they? There is no *a priori* answer; there is no compelling reason why they should. There are very obvious tensions regarding whether, and to what extent, feminist analysis should be accepted by other cultures, and at what cost.

A postmodernist observer of a traditional custom (e.g., wife-burning or circumcision) may disapprove (i.e., find it morally wrong), yet refuse to intervene on the grounds that we should respect the other culture and its (internal) standard, holding that we have no right to judge them. This is a completely inadequate response—we must attempt to engage a culture when its practice is so clearly oppressive. Here we have a choice. Either we remain silent (say nothing normative/evaluative at all), or we speak from a particular perspective—not a universal, historical one, but our own.

The tension for Postmodernists is: are they willing to take an external perspective, to adopt a form of meta-narrative? The Postmodernists should recognize that saying we should never intervene is a meta-narrative that requires an external perspective just as much as does saying the practice is wrong. Even to claim that each culture is right internally, they must take at least a minimally external perspective.

The dilemma faced by observers of other cultural practices is that the participant's internal understanding gets them (at best) to an NRE. The external critic points out how these conceptions work from an outside view. Someone like Habermas (1984) might say that the internal NRE is ideologically distorted. How do we decide?

A PRAGMATIC INTERPRETATION OF CULTURAL DIFFERENCES

What is required is a replacement for the modernist approach, one that acknowledges the postmodernistic critique of dominant cultural practices, yet gives us some grounds, something to hang on to that can still be a means of human betterment. The problem is that the postmodernist's step #2 (the replacement meta-narrative) and step #3 (respect for other narratives) don't do the job. Why? They leave us nothing to hold on to. The fact that there are different realities, different voices, different ways of knowing, different truths, different meta-narratives (all claiming legitimacy) gives us no way to evaluate any of them (to decide whether they are a better replacement). This is the dilemma of relativism.

Our response to this situation comes from a Neo-pragmatic perspective. This is an alternative response to modernism—one we believe is much more productive than postmodernism. Unlike postmodernism, Neo-pragmatism (i) is not relativistic—it allows for objective justification within context; (ii) retains useful contrasts as end points of continua; (iii) retains a legitimate role for science; (iv) doesn't view differences between communities as incommensurable; (v) can integrate different frames; and (vi) retains our enlightenment tradition regarding rationality, truth, and objective (liberal) values.[10]

In other respects, Neo-pragmatism is similar to postmodernism and very different from modernism in that it: (i) is naturalistic, nonfoundational, anti-essentialist and fallibilistic; (ii) rejects the idea of absolute dualism; (iii) rejects the idea of metaphysical realism; (iv) is nonreductive and nonscientistic; and (v) de-emphasizes the importance of meta-narrative and theory (Harper and Stein 1995a). Our Neo-pragmatic interpretation of different accounts of planning is that each narrative is a language game. Differing views are seen as different vocabularies—no one nearer to the truth than the others.[11] This allows us to recognize alternative accounts. Then we try to bring them into a noncoercive dialogic planning process.

From a pragmatic perspective, a strong moral critique, appealing to both normative and empirical theories, using science as the servant of your moral position will be part of this dialogue. Yet a moral critique is internal; it does not provide an absolute position. Its success depends on whether or not it convinces in a noncoercive way.[12]

Both internal and external perspectives are relevant, important, and legitimate; however, neither perspective is superior to the other. A Neo-pragmatic view sees this distinction as a continuum; a balance is possible. For most purposes we need both kinds of understanding. Ignoring either the internal or external perspective is dangerous.

When dealing with practices (moral or otherwise), which are not part of the dominant culture in a multicultural society, planners may be more inclined to take an external perspective—this is most likely if they are from the dominant culture, as they often are. What they are in danger of missing, then, is the significance or meaning of the institutions or traditions to those who participate in them. To the external observer, the legitimacy of the internal view can be hidden; she may be too quick to condemn without understanding the meaning to the participant. She may assume that there is oppression and ideological distortion, which gets the participant to accept practices that are not in her own true interest. Here, it may be more important to be reminded of the internal meaning rather than the external view of structure.

The participant may disagree. From her own internal perspective, the practice is believed to be justified. The danger here is that she may not see the belief as ideologically distorted, to understand the way her own culture works. This may be due to the fact that she is not part of a highly reflective culture (i.e., issues of how cultures work are foreign to her). This is more likely in a nondominant, "traditional" culture. Thus, a purely internal account is likely to lack a critique of the status quo. When dealing with their own culture, the external, structural relations are more often hidden, and many people are likely to settle for an internal view. Here, pointing out these relationships may lead us to liberation.

Is the situational choice regarding how wide the equilibrium (i.e., how much reflection is appropriate) objective? Say what you like, but for the Pragmatist, this question is not a concern. The notion of objectivity drops out because it serves no purpose.

A danger arises from the functionalist anthropologist's positivistic idea that an external understanding of the mechanism underlying a social practice/institution *replaces* the internal understanding. This is a reductionistic myth. The external understanding may be relevant; it may even replace the internal, but it does not necessarily do so. Certainly a critical WRE does not *require* giving up the internal account. For example, suppose that morality can be explained genetically or functionally. This doesn't undermine or replace the moral practice. Understanding the mechanism doesn't replace moral motivation—why should it? If Postmodernists argue that the external view should supersede the internal one, then they are being reductionistic; that is, retaining the modernistic assumptions that they claim to reject.

The key question is: lacking a God's eye perspective, how do we determine the extent to which the internal NRE is ideologically distorted? Is there really ideological distortion? The problem is that there is no objective "fact of the matter" outside of the process. What are legitimate true interests can be ascertained only *within* a context. There is no absolute answer. This is where the Neo-pragmatist differs from Habermas (1984), who believes that ideological distortion can be objectively identified.

A PRAGMATIC RECONCILIATION

The Neo-pragmatic reconciliation is to engage in a noncoercive open dialogue, where the external critic seeks to understand the internal participant's view, and seeks to convince them that their understanding is distorted and their practice is oppressive and wrong. The Neo-pragmatic hope is to engage participants in a consensus-seeking dialogue, using all available means, involving reason, passion, intuition, and experience. This needs to be done in a sensitive noncoercive way. As Nielsen says:

I am not trying to set reason and passion in opposition to each other. And I am not trying to collapse the distinction either or to give one precedence or authority over the other. Wide reflective equilibrium appeals to both. Within the holistic, largely coherentist method that is reflective equilibrium, both what it is reasonable to believe and to do and our sympathies . . . play an important role. (Neilsen 1996:448)

We try to help participants see the structural, power, class, gender relations which we believe are oppressive. What many planning theorists have argued—that planning needs to stress the dialogical, communicative, deliberative, consensus-building aspects, and to design new institutions for fostering dialogue—is particularly true for a multicultural society.

From this perspective, evaluation is pragmatic, guided by this interactive, noncoercive dialogue. Does each approach to planning help us to understand and solve social problems? What is the pragmatic value of these different perspectives? Different purposes will be better served by different vocabularies. The choice of perspective then is made on pragmatic grounds. The distinctions we have made here (internal and external, wide and narrow) should be seen as pragmatic ones that are endpoints of continua. The ultimate goal of a dialogic process is to reach a consensus, ideally where the distinctions disappear.

The degree to which a reflective equilibrium is "wide" (i.e., invokes a critical external perspective) is a continuum. We should not assume as an absolute *a priori* meta-narrative principle that WRE has a privileged position[13] (i.e., that wider is always better). Both modernism and postmodernism tend to assume that their external accounts are privileged. They may be underestimating the impact of a WRE's external critique. As we have seen, too much reflection and criticism can destabilize social values and institutions—particularly moral ones (Williams 1985). We should recognize that a WRE undermines cultural practices and beliefs that are inconsistent with the pluralistic liberal democratic state. Of course, as critical liberal theorists, in general we do believe WRE to be the best approach. Here the communitarians have a point; our social institutions (particularly planning and educational ones) need to uphold and promote essential liberal democratic social values, if we want to have a functioning pluralistic liberal state. And this may not be consistent with the politics of identity.

This is the dilemma of a multicultural society. How much of the nondominant cultures is to be protected and how much is to be changed? Going too far in either direction can lead to disasters. A pragmatic perspective looks for a situational balance. The trick is to restrict the extent of reflection in order to preserve as much as possible of those parts of a tradition critical to personal identities. This is particularly true for marginalized groups, who may require such identity to rectify past injustices and to gain self-respect. This delicate balance acknowledges differences, while retaining a basis for cooperative action in a pluralistic society. It recognizes both the need to preserve identity and the requirements of a decent pluralistic society.

The Pragmatist claims no absolute answer, only the hope that a dialogical planning and political process (with participants sharing at least some liberal democratic values, seeking to understand each other and to build a wider consensus) will lead to a workable resolution of these tensions. But it may not. There are no guarantees. Some traditions may have values that are simply unacceptable and cannot be accommodated in a pluralistic liberal society.

The pragmatist sees the dominant culture as having both good and bad sides. The bad side may be more obvious—domination, exploitation, and oppression. But there are some things for which the dominant culture need not apologize—insisting on tolerance is one of them. Some aspects of the dominant vocabulary can be liberating. We want to retain and promote these aspects.

The only sense of "better than" that is consistent with post-positivistic critiques is this pragmatic one. It is not absolute! What will count as improvement will emerge from the dialogue. The only meta-narrative we need for this purpose is one that connects human practices (linguistic and other) to the possibility of human flourishing, as it is defined by this process. All of the different accounts (including a reconstructed enlightenment position[14] without metaphysical aspects) can be looked at pragmatically, in terms of their contribution to improving the situation of nondominant cultural groups in our society.

CONCLUSION

From a Neo-pragmatic perspective, we should acknowledge and respect the stories of all cultural groups, but they should be heard critically and evaluated carefully. A Neo-pragmatic approach does not seek a meta-narrative; it does not provide any universal solutions. Judgments must be made about particular situations in context.

For observers from the dominant culture, the difficult question is determining when there is oppression and distortion in a more traditional culture. The pragmatic reconciliation is an open and noncoercive dialogue, which will give us a more internal understanding of the other culture, and give them a wider, more reflective and critical view of their own practices. Ultimately, the liberal goal is for each person to have autonomous choice.

But there are limits to what can be accommodated. A WRE process is necessary at some level if we want to have a pluralist society. Beauregard's "strict" multiculturalism is a nonstarter; it guarantees that a pluralist society will not work. The idea that we should accept everything in every tradition is in itself a universal principle, one that would destroy pluralism. It leaves us few options—at best, separation; at worst, violence. There is no reason why we should accept it. We argue that not only are political liberal ideals consistent with accommodation of other cultures; consensual acceptance of these (largely procedural) ideals is required for a pluralistic society.

Too long, we've seen the powerful elites of the dominant culture impose their views on nondominant cultures, often as a tool of economic and social exploitation. We believe Neo-pragmatism (even though it comes out of modernism) can bring some of the advantages of the dominant culture without its exploitive features. Avoiding the relativism of postmodernism and the universalism of modernism, Neo-pragmatism can acknowledge the legitimacy of nondominant cultures, while reflectively critiquing their oppressive aspects. This is the promise of pragmatism in a pluralistic liberal multicultural society.

NOTES

1. By "Postmodernism," we mean "a way of understanding and conceptualizing that forms a radical break with modernism," one "not commensurable with the Enlightenment values" (Milroy 1991:183).

2. See Harper and Stein (1995b) for a discussion of weaknesses in this critique.

3. Critical Theorists following Habermas (1984) are not postmodernists in the sense we are using the term.

4. See Stein and Harper (1996) for a discussion of the problems arising from radical paradigm shifts.

5. Foucault need not be taken as providing a universalist account. His genealogies can be regarded as completely contextual. Then they're very similar to our view.

6. The term "reflective equilibrium" seems to have originated with Goodman (1965). Rawls (1971) brought it into ethical discourse; Rawls (1974) first distinguished "wide" and "narrow" equilibria; Daniels (1985) popularized the term "wide reflective equilibrium" to distinguish it from the narrow reflective equilibrium of ethical intuitionists (Nielsen 1991).

7. This definition is adapted from Daniels (1985).

8. A "WRE" is a state where all the elements outlined are in coherence; a "WRE process" is a process of seeking to move toward such a state.

9. We have added "scientistic" for clarification.

10. However, these notions are no longer viewed as foundational absolutes.

11. Neo-pragmatists reject the scheme/content distinction: the notion that one conceptual scheme (account) is better or truer or "closer to reality" than another.

12. It is very problematic whether a government authority (particularly one providing financial support) can ever be seen as noncoercive by nondominant cultures.

13. If advocates of WRE make this claim (which they seem to come very close to), then they have slipped into a new form of foundationalism.

14. As we have argued elsewhere (1995b), we should retain the liberal, and discard the scientistic, aspects of the enlightenment.

REFERENCES

Connelly, M.P., T.M. Li, M. MacDonald, and J.L. Paspart. Restructured Worlds/ Restructured Debates: Globalization, Development and Gender. *Canadian Journal of Development Studies*. 1995:17–38.

Daniels, N. Two Approaches to Theory Acceptance in Ethics in D. Comp and D. Zimmerman (eds) *Morality, Reason and Truth*. Totowa, NJ: Rowman and Allanhold. 1985.

Etzioni, A. *The Spirit of Community: Rights, Responsibilities and the Communitarian Agenda*. NY: Crown Publishers. 1993.

Foucault, M. *Power/Knowledge*. C. Gordon (ed.). C. Gordon, L. Marshall, J. Mepham, and K. Koper (trans.) NY: Pantheon Books. 1980.

Friedmann, J. *Planning in the Public Domain: From Knowledge to Action*. Princeton, NJ: Princeton University Press. 1987.

Gilligan, Carol. In a Different Voice: Women's Conceptions of Self and of Morality in M. Pearsall (ed.) *Women and Values: Readings in Recent Feminist Philosophy*. Belmount, CA: Wadsworth. 1977:309–39.

Goodman, N. *Fact, Fiction and Forecast*, 2nd ed. New York: Bobbs-Merrill. 1965.

Habermas, J. *The Theory of Communicative Action*. Boston: Beacon Press. 1984.

Harper, T.L. and S.M. Stein (a). Out of the Postmodern Abyss: Preserving the Rationale for Liberal Planning. *Journal of Planning Education and Research*, vol. 14, no. 4, 1995:233–44.

Harper, T.L. and S.M. Stein (b). Contemporary Procedural Ethical Theory and Planning Theory in S. Hendler (ed.) *Planning Ethics: A Reader in Planning Theory, Practice and Education.* New Brunswick, NJ: Center for Urban Policy Research, Rutgers University. 1995.

Milroy, B. Into Postmodern Weightlessness. *Journal of Planning Education and Research*, vol. 10, 1991:181–87.

Nielsen, Kai. *Equality and Liberty: A Defense of Radical Egalitarianism.* Totowa, NJ: Rowman and Allanhold. 1985.

Nielsen, Kai. *After the Demise of the Tradition: Rorty, Critical Theory, and the Fate of Philosophy.* Boulder, CO: Westview Press. 1991.

Nielsen, Kai. *Naturalism Without Foundations.* Amhurst, NY: Prometheus Books. 1996.

Nussbaum, M. *Cultivating Humanity: A Classical Defense of Reform in Liberal Education.* Cambridge, MA: Harvard University Press. 1997.

Putnam, H. *Renewing Philosophy.* Cambridge, MA: Harvard University Press. 1992.

Rawls, J. *A Theory of Justice.* Cambridge, MA: Harvard University Press. 1971.

Rawls, J. Independence of Moral Theory. *Proceedings of the American Philosophical Association*, vol. 49. 1974.

Rawls, J. *Political Liberalism.* New York: Columbia University Press. 1993.

Sandel, M.J. *Liberalism and the Limits of Justice.* Cambridge, MA: Cambridge University Press. 1982.

Scruton, R. *The Philosopher on Dover Beach.* Manchester: Carncanet Press. 1990.

Stein, S.M. and T.L. Harper. Planning Theory for Sustainable Development. *Geography Research Forum,* vol. 16, December 1996.

Walzer, M. *Interpretation and Social Criticism.* Cambridge, MA: Harvard University Press. 1987.

Williams, B. *Ethics and the Limits of Philosophy.* Cambridge, MA: Harvard University Press. 1985.

CHAPTER 6

Objectives and Values: Planning for Multicultural Groups Rather than Multiple Constituencies

Peter B. Meyer & Christopher R. Reaves

Public policy in general, and planning in particular, have always had to address the diverse interests and concerns of different groups. Neither policy analysts nor planners historically have been particularly sensitive to the needs and priorities of interest groups other than the dominant, or politically most powerful, parties in their environments. This myopic understanding of the factors relevant to decision-making has gradually been broadened in recent decades, but planning still has a long way to go to incorporating all the issues that are germane to selection of plans and strategies for action. In particular, the advances that have been made in addressing the diversity of interest group perspectives by and large have been limited to recognition that class differences and minority group concerns exist. Progress has been far more limited in planners' understanding of and response to the even greater diversity associated with a multiplicity of cultures and cultural values present in almost any society.

There is substantial literature that addresses the problems of multiple constituencies for any given social policy or planning decision. The entire discussion of distributional effects that appear as an overlay on the core welfare economics analyses of most cost-benefit analysis writing constitutes one massive subset of the writing on the subject (Gramlich 1981; Mishan 1976; Sugden and Williams 1978; Thompson 1980). Another strand is the growing body of material on conflict resolution and negotiations that has emerged as more room is made for citizens' groups and neighborhood associations at the table at which policies and plans are drawn up (Meyer 1994). Taken in combination, these two components of the literature suggest that decision-making processes may be moving toward better representation of diverse interests than existed in the past.

However, there is ample evidence, both in the underlying theory and conceptualization, and in planning practice on the ground, that this progress in addressing *multiple constituencies* does not necessarily constitute advance in responding to *multicultural groups*. The fundamental problem in addressing diverse cultures, rather than interests, lies in the prevailing assumption that decision-making criteria are held in common by all parties and that there is some basic agreement on the relevant constraints on the range of possible solutions (see, for example, Godschalk et al. 1994). Neither premise is valid and, as we shall see, the institutions to which the prevailing culture accords the decision-making powers may, themselves, not be accepted by some divergent cultural groups.

In this chapter we take current argument about planning for multiple constituencies with different objectives and extend the logics and principles derived to apply them to the divergent groups that comprise a multicultural society. The central questions of this essay are essentially twofold: "How do multicultural groups differ from multiple constituencies?" and "How can planners and planning practice best respond to those differences?" In effect, we begin with the assumption that planning is doing a relatively decent job of addressing multiple constituencies but may not be handling multiculturalism well.

Some clarification of our language and usage in this discussion is critical to the argument here. When we refer to multiculturalism we do *not* mean simply different ethnic groups or classes in a society. Some minority groups may appear different and exhibit lifestyles that vary from those of others but may share most of the values of the dominant ethnic groups in a society. These populations do not necessarily pose a planning problem beyond that associated with interest group diversity. On the other hand, subpopulations may be indistinguishable from the majority in terms of race, ethnicity, or even observable lifestyle but may adhere to completely different value premises. This form of cultural diversity may result from differences in acceptance of a capitalist, or even monetized, economy, from variation in the practice of a common religion, or, under some conditions, even something as fundamental as a geospatial or temporal frame of reference. Our definition thus forces examination of the conditions under which what has been characterized as a multiple constituency problem really reflects multiple and divergent cultural norms, and simultaneously avoids the false presumption that multiculturalism is simply a reflection of the number and types of minority groups in a society.

The distinction between different constituencies operating within the same cultural frame and a frame encompassing different cultures can be drawn very neatly within the conceptual logic of the traditional economic problem of constrained optimization; we begin with a section elaborating the points of correspondence and divergence, dwelling on how the divergences account for the variation in the capacity to plan for diversity using any form of pursuit of a single optimum solution. Next, we will turn to examples of planning problems that permit us to highlight the special issues raised by cultural conflicts, drawing on both U.S. and overseas experience. Finally, we will speculate about possible approaches to the problems posed by efforts to plan for multicultural societies, drawing in large part on the approaches to environmental mediation that have developed in the past decade.

Constrained Optimization

Perhaps the best way to consider the progress made on addressing some differences in impacts of plans and policies is to describe the decision problem that is addressed. Whatever the characteristics of the decision—on a comprehensive plan, on specific land uses, on preservation standards or policies, and programs for home-ownership or blight removal, and so on—the choice is generally conceived of as a matter of *constrained optimization.*

This sort of choice can be seen as an effort to *maximize* the value of some "objective function," subject to limits on resources and possible courses of action. Recasting this verbal statement as an equation can actually assist in illustrating key ways in which diverse cultures differ from multiple constituencies within a single culture in the problems they pose for decision-making. Let us assume, for simplicity, that an objective function, Q, is expressible as a *weighted sum* of a number of results or outputs of a plan, program or policy. The actual decision criterion is probably a more complex mix of the elements, but this simple formulation serves well to illustrate the problem. We can then write:

$$\text{Max } Q = \text{Max } (w_1 A_1 + w_2 A_2 + ... + w_i A_i + ... + w_I A_I)$$

Subject to Constraints $= F_j(w_1, ..., w_I, A_1, ..., A_I, L_1, ... L_K)$, where the "$w_i$" are the weights or values (prices) assigned to each unit of an outcome or "activity," A_i, the constraints, F_j, are a series of functions placing limits on possible values of all the weights and the levels of the activities, with the limits L_k defining the ranges of what is "acceptable"to a cultural group.

A society with many different constituencies, then, can be envisioned as one in which groups disagree on the weights to be assigned to different outcomes—assigning a zero weight, for example, to benefits that accrue to groups other than themselves if they are very parochial. The groups are, however, willing to negotiate within a commonly defined range on all the major weights and have few disagreements over the constraints they consider relevant, generally accepting the same set of limits L_k.

By contrast, a multicultural society may be characterized as incorporating far more diversity, since it includes:

(1)   Groups that differ in the *components* they recognize as present in the objective function, Q, not just in the weight assigned to elements, such that each may consider a different set of outcomes or activities, A_i^*, to be appropriate outcomes to address and weigh;
(2)   Groups with different valuations (w_i) of commonly accepted outcomes (A_i) that may be unwilling to negotiate or compromise on the weights they assign to activities (a condition that may be understood in terms of strict constraints such that w_i must be less than or equal to some particular limit L_k); and/or,
(3)   Groups that perceive or accept different constraints (F_j) on the range of acceptable decision choices or actions, especially groups that place very particular limits on impacts or activities (L_k).

Conflict resolution is needed for broad acceptance of a decision, even in the simplest cases of multiple constituencies, such as situations with a fixed possible gain in the value of a commonly accepted objective function and allocation of shares in a zero sum game. Additional conflict may emerge from different values assigned by different groups to the outcome elements in the objective function. That is, the weights assigned to "increased income," "safe neighborhoods," and "a clean environment" may differ between groups in a city or metropolitan area. In general, the constraints that are recognized as acceptable factors shaping possible outcomes are held in common by the different constituent groups and a relatively uniform culture. None of these sorts of planning conflicts come close to those posed by culturally diverse populations.

For example, any of these types of diversity, but especially the third, could account for the Native-American sacred land conflicts, in which mainstream society seeks "compromise" over preservation of sacred sites, which may be seen as an absolute constraint by the tribal groups. In many of these cases, old grave sites have been uncovered by new urban excavations; while the dominant society may see these sites as already compromised by prior construction, native peoples have pursued preservation of the sites, once identified, or at least special treatment for the remains uncovered. The conflict resolution mechanisms and procedures themselves, from consensus-building efforts to the inherently adversarial judicial process, may not be viewed as legitimate by many cultural groups in a society. Judicial efforts to strike a "balance" between urban economic development needs and the necessity of honoring grave sites have a built-in cultural bias—the criteria for "balance" that are related to the weights w_i in Equation 1 above—that may not be acceptable to one of the affected parties.

The ability to plan so that all affected members within the citizenry agree on the appropriate distribution of costs and benefits is an arduous task. It may be impossible. But it may not be necessary to pursue full *agreement* if the resulting objective function value, Q, can be *accepted* by constituent groups. There may, for example, be differences of opinion about the desirability of inequality in a society—or in the impacts of spatial decisions on different groups. However, those pursuing no inequality at all may be willing to accept *some* unevenness in impacts. In other words, the extent of inequality may be a constraint that cannot be violated, with equality not appearing as an element of the objective function.

In a one-culture setting, acceptance may be relatively easy to attain. This relative ease makes unacceptable the all-too-common instances of planners and elite decision-makers failing to involve affected constituents in decisions that affect them. Planners know of these failures and have a long history of efforts on the part of some subset of the profession to address the issues, generally under the labels of advocacy, equity, or participatory planning (Clavel 1983; Davidoff 1965; Krumholz 1982; Marris 1987; Peattie 1968). The general failures of most planning regimes adequately to address even the distribution of commonly accepted gains and losses stands as a challenge to the far greater problems posed by multicultural settings. The intensity of some conflicts the "cultural diversity" planners need to address does not necessarily emanate from differences in race, religion, or national origin, but may still exceed that of the allocative disputes that are by now recognized as serious by the profession.

In *any* complex society, some cultural norms, and thus values and decision principles, differ across population groups. Absent systematic efforts to involve all parties in a democratic decision process, the values and interests held by the dominant cultural groups will tend to preempt those held by minority cultures. As has been evident in case after case in urban economic development efforts, buildings, communities, and lifestyles deemed valuable by one or more minority groups (or even neighborhood organizations) are not included in the decision outcome variables, A_i, or the constraints, F_j, and limits, L_k, incorporated into the decision problem statement. If entire factors or considerations, such as neighborhood integrity or patterns of interpersonal interaction, are sacrificed on the altar of urban economic development, the problem may be dismissed as simply disagreement about relative weights for outcomes, that is, the w_i in Equation 1; they may, however, as we have suggested here, be better understood as reflecting decisions in the face of cultural diversity. Efforts to improve planners' sensitivity to the issues posed by cultural diversity should, therefore, simultaneously protect minority interests in the decision-system as a whole, whether or not these divergent concerns constitute actual differences in cultural norms from those of the mainstream decision-makers. We return to this issue in examining some of our cases below.

Conflict of Cultures

We offer here a number of case examples to illustrate how pursuit of human development, as it is perceived by different cultures, can lead to irreducible conflicts. In the process we will note, in passing, features of the decision-making processes that may act to heighten or reduce these policy dilemmas. We begin with examination of two different dam-building efforts, one in the United States and one in India, since human actions to reshape landscapes have the potential to generate both religious and economic questions. Next, we turn to two urban planning conflicts that illustrate the problems caused by economic reductionism, even within a single culture: both cases involve inter-governmental conflicts, and are types of decisions that have generally been treated as allocation problems within a common culture although they appear to actually embody one or more of the three cultural conflicts we have identified. The limits of the economic perspective are further illustrated by two additional cases, both reflecting the problems economic "development" can raise for planners in a single jurisdiction, one of which raises some question about who should be decision-makers. Finally, we examine a case that directly challenges the legitimacy of the decision-making system itself.

Damming the Mattaponi River, Virginia, U.S.

The Mattaponi, a Virginia Indian tribe, has had recent conflict with the State of Virginia in confrontation over the proposed development of a 1500-acre King William County Reservoir. Due to development pressures and a large population increase, Virginia is in need of additional fresh water supplies and damming the Mattaponi river could provide this needed facility. The Mattaponi tribe, however, relies on shad fishing in the river and on the sale of those fish and their eggs for their livelihood, and they claim that their fishing would be threatened by a dam.

At a March 31, 1997 hearing, local politicians urged the Virginia Department of Environmental Quality to approve the project as vital to the region's economy, which is attempting to diversify and reduce its dependence on the region's Naval bases. The Mattaponi argued that their own economic vitality was threatened by the reduced water flow the dam would create, which would harm their fishing and spawning (Lavelle 1997:A12).

Each of the divergent parties in this case is predominantly interested in maintaining or bolstering its own economic objectives. They can be seen as accepting a shared set of outcomes, A_i, but disagreeing on the weights, w_i, in the optimization formula. If the State can devise a plan for a dam that would both sustain the vitality of the river and provide the increasing local population with the water supplies it demands, both parties could agree on a solution. Engineering the dam with fish ladders or other features that would preserve fisheries, while potentially very expensive, could satisfy the relevant parties.

A more economical decision, perhaps, might be simply to reimburse the Mattaponi Indians for their lost incomes and just disregard the decline of the river ecosystem. However, reliance on this compensation approach would open up the issue of cultural conflict in a way the engineering approach would not: (i) the engineering solution implicitly accepted maintenance of the lifestyle of the Mattaponi as an outcome to be pursued, while the compensation solution narrowed this to maintenance of income; and (ii) the engineering approach would not severely challenge any environmental quality constraints, but the compensation approach ignores the environment. Putting it differently, in this instance the engineering solution does not directly challenge inclusion of objectives, A_i, and constraints, F_j, that extend beyond profit or income maximization and equitable allocation, but the compensation decision explicitly narrows the focus of the optimization decision to income maintenance or enhancement.

An excessively narrow, largely economistic perspective does, however, dominate much decision-making and planning for economic development. The myopia inherent in such plans appears to derive in part from a failure to recognize that cultural change and economic change do not always move in tandem. Cultural and economic values can thus clash in ways that transcend simple disagreement over the weights, w_i, in the decision formula, especially if some of the people in a society adapt to the economic change while others resist it.

Damming the Narmada River, India

The narrow economic focus characterizes the decision in India to build dams on a river sacred to Hindus despite the fact that the religion is the dominant faith in the country. In 1987 construction began on the Sadar Sarovar dam on the Narmada River. The project was intended to spur economic development by generating an estimated 500 million megawatts of electricity, irrigating more than two million hectares of farmland, and bringing higher quality drinking water to thousands of villages (Elliott 1994). While the intended economic benefits of the Narmada Valley project are substantial, the cost, even in economic terms, may be excessive: "The dams will displace 200,000 people, submerge 2,000 sq. km of fertile land and 1,500 sq. km of prime teak and sal forest, and eliminate historic sites and rare wildlife. The expansion of irrigated agriculture is likely to leave impoverished farmers upstream with even less water than before" (Elliott 1994:48). Beyond the economic calculations, however, lie cultural conflicts, exemplified by the vow on the part of the non-Hindu tribal people of the Madhya Pradesh region that they would drown in their homes rather than resettle (Miller and Kumar 1993).

In fact, the headlong pursuit of economic development in the Narmada Valley plan has actually created a cultural conflict between the government and its own dominant ethnic group: all Hindu inhabitants of the valley are supposed to walk the entire length of the river at least once in their lifetime (Elliott 1994). This obligation creates a special constraint, F_{j*}, with a very rigid limit, L_k. Specifying that the river has to be a series of dams will make this observance impossible, and the project continues to be resisted by those who are fighting for their strongly held religious principles. Compromise is not an option in this conflict if the river will no longer be walkable after the completion of the dams. This example may be dismissed as not germane, since it is a case of a conflict between modernism and traditionalism, but it does represent cultural conflict and is an exemplar of many similar projects around the world (see for example Burayidi 1993).

The sacrifice of cultural or societal values or goods to economic development objectives is also evident in industrialized urban settings. The history of economic development practice has illustrated many times that excessive economic and social burdens have fallen on the shoulders of the poor and minorities (Mier 1993). By filling the role of advocate for these disadvantaged groups, urban planners have helped to ensure that the costs, as well as the benefits, were disseminated more equally among all affected constituencies (Clavel 1986; Davidoff, Davidoff, and Gold 1970; Krumholz and Forester 1990; Marris 1994; Peattie 1994). In many instances it was not the planning objective that was questioned, but rather the distribution of the cost and benefits, with professional advocates fighting for "fair shares" for their constituents. The picture changes drastically when the adherents to the different views do not come from the same professional ranks and share the same socialization as the government planners and decision-makers.

Developing the Docklands, London, U.K.

The decades-old conflict over the redevelopment of the London Docklands provides a case in point. By the early 1970s the decline of shipping to the docks in the center of London and the loss of 150,000 jobs in the adjacent neighborhoods was well recognized (Docklands Joint Commission 1976). The recommended responses were never undertaken, in large part because of a shift in political control of the national state in Britain in 1977. The Conservative Party–controlled Parliament created the London Docklands Development Corporation (LDDC) in 1981 with the rationale that the area "represents a major opportunity for the development that London needs over the last 20 years of the 20ᵗʰ Century: new housing, new environments, new industrial development, new facilities for recreation, new commercial development, new architecture; all calculated to bring these barren areas back to more valuable use" (LDDC 1984:7).

As stated, these objectives seem unobjectionable, but their implementation caused problems. The actions and transformations of local economic activity designed by the LDDC "to bring these . . . areas back to more valuable use" served the interests of the London metropolitan area economy, but not the needs of the impoverished population living in the Docklands. The new housing constructed, office facilities erected, and jobs created were, by and large, inaccessible to the local residents, either due to cost or due to the skill requirements for the employment generated (Meyer 1988). What arose in this case was a fundamental conflict over the objectives of the regeneration effort, especially the stated political intent of transforming the local economy to fit better with that of the adjacent financial district at the center of London. The Labour Party–controlled local London Boroughs wanted jobs and better housing for their residents, while the Parliament wanted to maximize property values and attain the so-called highest and best use for the land. In addition, the LDDC, the first of Britain's Urban Development Corporations, was the archetype of the Conservatives' effort to "emasculate local authorities and usurp the local democratic process" (Parkinson 1988:111).

Despite a shared "common culture," the Docklands residents and the national legislature disagreed on a level so fundamental that it fits our description of a cultural conflict: beyond clear differences in the w_i they assigned to different outcomes, there was disagreement about the set of outcomes, A_i, to be considered, and there was additional conflict over the decision-making process, including local demands for maintenance of a sense of community identity (a limit L_k) and for the democratic control that the national state was trying to weaken, constituting very different sets of F_j—the constraints to which the process and strategy was to conform.

Rezoning the Danada Farm, Wheaton, Illinois, U.S.

Conflict among parties in a common culture that parallels that which may arise in multicultural contexts may also arise within a more local decision context, as a case described by Rubin (1988) illustrates. In 1978 the estate of Dan and Ada Rice petitioned the city of Wheaton, Illinois, to annex the 1355-acre Danada Farm and rezone it for commercial and residential development. To Wheaton, the Danada Farm represented an opportunity to encourage tax-producing commercial growth and to expand its residential base. Wheaton's plans for the Danada Farm conflicted with those of the DuPage County Forest Preserve District, which considered the land a major segment of a greenbelt intended to slow urbanization. Clearly, this is a case of vastly divergent sets of objectives, A_i. Maintenance of the greenbelt might even be seen as a rigid constraint, paralleling the argument Native Americans may articulate about their lands. The difference between this case and the Docklands example is that the conflicting objectives are amenable to a compensation solution (payment in lieu of taxes to Wheaton from DuPage County—and possible compensation to the Danada estate itself), a resolution that was not possible given the political objectives inherent in the British case.

The preceding cases are just two of many evident in the literature on urban development that illustrate the need for a more comprehensive multicultural approach to planning. There is a need to develop an approach that considers not only how to equally allocate costs and benefits among all parties, but how to satisfy those groups that hold objectives contrary to those pursued by the majority, or politically dominant, culture.

The Use of Roads in Mexico City, Mexico

Some planning conflicts emerge from shifts in orientation of use of different municipal assets such as infrastructure. Therefore, they involve the need to respond to a change that has caused a problem; however, the problem may be invisible unless the fact of cultural diversity and conflict can be recognized. Consider, for example, Ivan Illich's 1983 description of the changes visible in Mexico City: streets used to comprise a common area in which people came to engage in social activities and in economic enterprises as well as travel; they functioned as a widespread and readily acceptable urban "commons." The spread of motorized transportation and the need to make existing roads carry ever more traffic as the metropolitan area grew drove the nontransportation uses off the streets (cited in *The Ecologist* 1993:61).

In Mexico City in the 1980s, different subsets of the local population utilized roads for a variety of purposes, some of which conflicted with others; there was no consensus on the A_i. Those involved in the emerging automobile culture sought to increase the efficiency of streets as channels for travel. Others not dependent on the automobile or in need of a common space for other purposes suffered economically and culturally as increased economic development forced them out. For the latter, their loss of a gathering place could be replaced, albeit at some cost, and only if the authority recognized the loss in its decision function, that is, modified the outcomes and activities set, A_i.

The Mexican case, like that of the Narmada dam, illustrates that a planning body intent on "modernization" and adapting to and promoting economic and population growth may fail to be sufficiently sensitive to the cultural and economic damage it causes by its failure to recognize the value of more traditional uses of limited resources. This failure to recognize the multiple purposes that limited resources serve is an inherent characteristic of another set of conflictual urban planning decisions, those involving environmental assets.

Land "Reclamation" in Hong Kong

Hong Kong is the densest urban settlement on the face of the earth. Land "reclamation"—dredging to create usable land in what have been ocean shallows—has been the focus of major municipal effort. Through 1994 existing and committed reclamation plans amounted to 543 hectares, but post-1994 plans proposed reclamation adding a total of about 2300 hectares to the land area of Hong Kong, about a third of which was to be taken from Victoria Harbor, the waters between the Asian mainland and the island of Hong Kong (Ng and Cook 1997:9). The government has argued that the reclamation of the land is needed both to increase the quality of life by reducing the density in which the current and projected future population of the city will have to live and to provide central dock facilities to serve the expanding hub functions of Hong Kong in Pacific Asia.

Opposition to the plans from a variety of private sector parties and public interest groups has focused on the negative effects of the reclamation that would reduce the width and depth of Victoria Harbor:

(i)   Decreased volume of water flow in Victoria Harbor will result in lowered capacity for cleansing pollution caused by port operations;

(ii)   Dredging and dumping operations may adversely affect fishing areas and ecologically important habitats;

(iii)   Dredging may also release heavy metals deposited deep in the seabed, thus polluting the harbor area;

(iv)   Part of the reclamation will be a public waste dumping site for construction industry, providing an inequitable subsidy;

(v)   Creation of new available land close to the urban core creates more competition for the decaying center and diverts investment that might otherwise regenerate older areas;

(vi)   Inadequate infrastructure, especially roads, will be subjected to even heavier burdens as the result of reclamation, and there are no plans to upgrade those facilities;

(vii)   Reducing the width of the harbor may weaken its capacity to function as a vital city lung to improve ventilation and reduce air pollution for the population of Hong Kong; and,

(viii) Funnel effects in a narrower water channel in Victoria Harbor may result in stronger tidal currents and more choppy water, thus adversely affecting the shipping industry that is supposed to be served by some of the new land. (Ng and Cook 1997:15–16)

These arguments reflect a mix of economic and environmental concerns, and disagreements with the municipal authorities on aspects of virtually all the features of the decision equation, the A_i, the w_i, and the F_j, and some acceptance of limits, L_k, not recognized by decision-makers.

While it is possible to sort these objections to the plans of the government of Hong Kong, and other issues raised that we have not enumerated, into those that reflect concerns over the distribution of costs and benefits, the totality reflects what can only be considered a different *worldview* of what should be considered in making decisions on economic expansion and the use of scarce resources. This difference clearly represents divergent cultural perspectives and may best be addressed by planners in the same manner.

The Hong Kong case, in which there was no public participation in the planning process, other than notification about plans after decisions were made, raises another question that we have not yet addressed: the issue of the legitimacy of the institutional decision-making and adjustment mechanisms in the eyes of the parties to a possible conflict. Advocacy planning efforts and calls for greater participation have attempted to address the need for participation, but the question of legitimacy in a multicultural context extends beyond provisions for public involvement, as the next case illustrates.

Native-American "Religious Use" of Land

The problems of the legitimacy of the decision-making body itself are neatly illustrated by a U.S. example. The American Indian Religious Freedom Act (AIRFA; Pub. L. No. 95-341, 92 Stat. 469 1978 codified at 42 U.S.C par. 1996 1993) articulated a specific congressional intent and policy of protecting and preserving the inherent right of Native Americans to "believe, express, and exercise" their traditional religions, including, but not limited to, assuring access to religious sites. Notwithstanding this intent, U.S. policy seems, at times, to have conflicted significantly with Native-American religious belief and practice.

A dispute between the Navajo tribe and the U.S. Forest Service over proposed road construction and logging led to claims by the Indians that such development would violate their AIRFA Free Exercise rights. The case, *Lyng v. Northwest Indian Cemetery Protective Association*, rapidly rose through the judicial system to the U.S. Supreme Court, with a result that raises questions of decision legitimacy. Justice Sandra Day O'Connor, rendering the court decision in 1988, raised a fundamental issue in her ruling on behalf of the Forest Service, the definition of what constitutes "religious use" of the lands in question. Her argument, that the land in question was not used actively for ritual purposes and did not contain a specific religious site, raised, but did not resolve an issue inherent in different perceptions of the value of land. The ruling raises the broader question of how the secular U.S. society can develop laws that will protect Native Americans' "sacred" land when it has been extensively documented that land *in general* is sacred to Native Americans (Neal-Post 1994:445). Obviously, any decision that accepts the

Native-American standard supports what has been labeled the "Indian veto" for religious use over other uses for federal land; protection for Indian religious uses could result in the *de facto* ownership by Native Americans of large tracts of public land. Justice O'Connor and the Court ruled that, so long as federal land management decisions did not prohibit Indians from exercising their religions, they had no veto power over other legitimate federal programs.

This finding, however, begs the central question in planning for a multicultural society: it imposed a form of Judeo-Christian standard of "exercising one's religion" on Native-American cultures. That is, the Court decision explicitly presumed that if land was not used directly in religious ceremonies, then denial of access to that land or its transformation to another use did not infringe on the exercise of religion. Not all religious practice is bound in time and space as are the church-based belief systems of the dominant U.S. cultures, so the Court decision is based on criteria and understandings that are limited by a cultural perspective. Put differently, the *decision system* failed to be sensitive to the problems posed by the diversity of religious practice and failed to structure the constraints on optimization, F_j, to incorporate appropriate constraints on optimization.

LEGITIMACY OF DECISION-MAKING INSTITUTIONS

The failures to address nonaccounting costs and benefits in the London Docklands, Illinois, and Hong Kong cases and the cultural conflicts of the Narmada dam, Mexico City road use, and the Navajo land claims share a common problem: the legitimacy of the decision-making institutions taking action. Multicultural groups are likely to pose greater problems for planners than multiple constituencies in that they are more inclined to challenge the legitimacy of decision criteria. But the decision-making institutions themselves must first be modified to permit the representation of more diverse interests, a point that is elaborated by Allor and Spence in chapter 12 with regards to local planning commissions. A first step has been taken by advocacy and community planners in the United States who have forced planning bodies to consider the perspectives of their clients and their different values, w_i^*. A second step has been forced by the environmental movement that has lobbied for the incorporation of new decision criteria, A_i, and acceptance of some new constraints, F_j, and limits, L_k, albeit with inconsistent results. These forces remain in place, continuing their efforts to broaden the perspectives of the planning profession and political decision-makers while accepting their decision logic, the process of compromise.

The step that has yet to be taken is one that will serve both of these constituencies while furthering the interests of an increasingly diverse population. It involves the recognition that some principles and constraints may not be divisible, allocable, or subject to compromise. Planners' and decision-makers' pursuit of the chimera of the "win-win" solution has yet to confront that, in a polity of sufficient diversity and an ecology of limited resources and resilience, such an outcome is unlikely, and that sacrifice of some objectives to others, or to permit adherence to some constraints, may be necessary.

The planning process itself needs to be reshaped to address the reality of multiple cultures and diverse—potentially divergent or conflicting—values. This will require that we modify the planning problem as posed—that we recognize that "the planning question" becomes multiple questions in a context of multiple objective functions with different outcome elements and constraints. It further necessitates the recognition on the part of planners and decision-makers that some conflicts may be irreconcilable or irreducible in a multicultural society, and that plan implementation cannot be pursued strictly within the decision frameworks of the dominant cultures or politically powerful groups.

This chapter cannot provide a blueprint for a series of changes in planning practice and in the training of planners that will have to evolve through the interaction of the diverse cultures that participate in the process. Recent developments in the literatures addressing conflict resolution, however, suggest that some foundations for approaches that may serve to better incorporate diverse values and attitudes are being laid in theory, if not yet in practice.

The first key is to realize the limitations of past decision-making practices. Susskind and Cruikshank (1987) enumerate a number of well-known systemic and structural problems in existing decision-making mechanisms that inhibit response to the challenges of multiculturalism: reliance on transitory majorities in majority-rule decisions, the absence of long-term commitments to decisions, excessive reliance on the limited choices provided by voting procedures, over-dependence on legal and procedural approaches, and failure to acknowledge the technical dilemmas, scientific uncertainty, and legal complexity that undermine planners' capacity to identify clearly the elements of the optimization equation and constraints.

The emergent communicative turn in planning theory and practice (Healey 1992, 1996; Innes 1995) clearly responds to the observation that "by directly confronting their differences in values, . . . contesting parties are able to achieve insights that contribute to reduced conflicts and better relationships" (Druckman, Broome, and Korper 1988:489). The ability to see the situation as the other side sees it, as difficult as it may be, is one of the most important skills a negotiator—or, we should add, a planner providing input to decision-making—can possess (Fisher and Ury 1991). Once each party is able to identify the reasons behind the stated interest of the other parties, communication of interests is easier; better yet, a relationship and real communication may be established. Thus, the very recognition by planners that they have to respond to the inherently multicultural settings in which they operate represents a major step toward improved practice.

Central to communicative efforts is acceptance of the rationality and legitimacy of the different cultural perspectives that exist. That is, adherents of any one perspective—a set of particular outcomes or attributes A_i, weights w_i, constraints F_j, and rigid limits L_k—have to understand that equally rational people may arrive at totally different formulations. It is not sufficient to simply recognize that other groups may assign different weights, or even some additional outcomes, to the optimization formula itself. Unfortunately, much of the contemporary planning literature and guidance still fails to recognize so much as the possibility of rational and politically acceptable different constraints and, most significantly perhaps, of any rigid limits on acceptable choices.

The Urban Land Institute's widely used manual on *Pulling Together* for conflict management and resolution in potentially contentious development decisions (Godschalk et al 1994) still focuses almost totally on differences in objectives and largely ignores the issues posed by constraints and limits. Kunreuther and Easterling (1992) acknowledged the legitimacy of rigid constraints in suggesting that decision-makers citing noxious facilities should only consider communities willing to accept the facilities. Their argument, however, is characteristic of the risk management literature in that they effectively ignored the role of economic coercion in site acceptance and thus skirted the issue of "fairness." Even while emphasizing "fair citing procedures" and the inadequacy of financial compensation alone in decision-making for citing of nuclear facilities in Switzerland, Frey and Oberholzer-Gee (1996) still failed totally to address the problems posed by locally perceived limits and constraints. These works, and myriad others, especially those in the social psychology and economics literatures, concentrate on addressing—and reshaping or "correcting"—perceptions, which they distinguish from "realities." They, thus, never address the legitimacy and rationality of the range of different optimization objectives, weights, constraints and limits that may be held by groups in a society. In other words, much of the literature continues to ignore the reality of multiculturalism.

Resolving Conflict Between Multicultural Groups

The challenge facing urban planners and planning educators in a multicultural society can be addressed with the insights from our discussion of how disagreement on constraints and limits differs from the more widely recognized differences on the weights assigned to activities or outcomes. We close by enumerating some of the more obvious approaches available, mixing education and practice considerations.

First, planners need to make explicit all the points of agreement and disagreement between the diverse cultural groups affected by, and interested in, each planning problem. This pursuit of openness and disclosure can be described by way of an illustrative twelve-step process toward maximization of the objective function, Q, assuming that public notice about proposed plans provides all interested parties with access to the decision-makers and their advisors.

(i)   Catalog points of agreement on objectives and outcomes, shared A_i, and any disagreements on importance assigned to these decision elements, that is, variation in w_i;

(ii)   Enumerate additional objectives, A_i^*, that are particular to one cultural group or another and ascertain any nonzero weights that other groups would assign to those outcomes if they were to be included in the optimization function;

(iii)   Identify all the limits, L_k, and rigid or tight constraints, F_j, that any of the different cultural groups bring into the decision;

(iv)   Consult with all the cultural groups as to their willingness to accept the L_k and F_j articulated in step 3 (and, in the process, elicit other constraints and limits that may not have been made explicit by other groups);

(v)   Identify and publicize the irreconcilable subset of L_k^* and F_j^* that define the differences between the interest of cultural groups that cannot be resolved by simple compromise and that thus constitute the greater sources of potential conflict;

(vi)   Provide an arena for negotiations between those cultural groups with irreconcilable limits or constraints, L_k^* and F_j^*, with the condition that discussions be limited to the specifics of those requirements and that they exclude any consideration of the implications of the limits or constraints for attainable values of the objective function Q;

(vii)   Initiate plans and other efforts to pursue those consensus objective elements A_i that can be attained without compromising any of the constraints or limits while not precluding progress on the nonconsensual objectives A_i^*, arranging for compensation between cultural groups where such payments appear due on the basis of divergent w_i valuations (in order to show all parties that the planning process and its implementation will not be immobilized by the irreconcilable differences);

(viii)   Compute, for each cultural group that defined limits L_k or tight constraints F_j, the reduction in the attainable value of its objective function Q (using its own A_i and w_i) caused by the various constraints and limits it specified, in order to make explicit to each the cost it bears for the conditions it imposes on the range of acceptable planning outcomes;

(ix)   If any participant cultural group redefines its L_k and F_j, recycle through steps 5, 6, and 7;

(x)   Establish if the value of Q attainable in light of the remaining constraints and limits is acceptable to the population at large (i.e., to all of the individual cultural groups);

(xi)   If the attainable Q is acceptable, then the planning process should be considered completed, regardless of the extent to which the accepted value of the objective falls short of the theoretically attainable level for one or more of the cultural groups; and, finally,

(xii)   If the attainable Q is not acceptable to one or more of the cultural groups with a stake in the planning process, then further negotiation over the irreconcilable differences in L_k^* and F_j^* may need to be pursued, enfranchising all the participating groups and broadening the focus of discussion to include the impacts of the limits and constraints on the attainable Q values.

This process may not cure the planning system or society of conflicts associated with its multicultural character, but it will help to control any tendencies toward conflict between the diverse populations.

Second, once the issues for negotiations are well specified through a formal process that explicitly acknowledges the legitimacy of the interests and value perspectives of all cultural groups affected by the proposed plans, the mediation and communicative planning strategies that have been articulated in many literatures can be employed in situations such as those defined in steps 4, 6, and 12. The precedents suggesting only limited successes in past efforts at inter-group negotiation may be ignored in large part, given their tendency to operate from an ethnocentric or unicultural perspective, or to focus overwhelmingly on balance sheet accounting and monetized economic factors.

Finally, with respect to the training of new planners and further theoretical development in the planning field, scholars need to explicitly identify the limits of the acceptance of multiculturalism exhibited in the literatures on which they rely for different insights and understandings of causes and consequences of planning outcomes.

REFERENCES

Burayidi, M.A. *Managing Urbanization through Rural Development: Lessons from the Tono Irrigation Project in Ghana*. Doctoral dissertation in Urban and Public Affairs, University of Louisville. Available from University Microfilms, Ann Arbor, MI. 1993.

Clavel, P. *Opposition Planning in Wales and Appalachia*. Philadelphia: Temple University Press. 1983.

Clavel, P. *The Progressive City: Planning and Participation 1969-1984*. New Brunswick, NJ: Rutgers University Press. 1986.

Davidoff, P. Advocacy and Pluralism in Planning. *American Institute of Planners Journal*, vol. 31, no. 4, 1965:331–38.

Davidoff, P., L. Davidoff, and N.N. Gold. Suburban Action: Advocate Planning for an Open Society. *American Institute of Planners Journal*, vol. 36, no. 1, 1970:12–21.

Docklands Joint Commission. *London Docklands Strategic Plan*. London, UK: Greater London Council. 1976.

Druckman, D., B.J. Broome, and S.H. Korper. Value Differences and Conflict Resolution: Facilitation or Delinking? *Journal of Conflict Resolution*, vol. 32, no. 3, 1988:489–510.

Elliott, J. *An Introduction to Sustainable Development*. New York: Routledge. 1994.

Fisher, R. and W. Ury. *Getting to Yes*. New York: Penguin. 1991.

Frey, B.S. and F. Oberholzer-Gee. Fair Siting Procedures: An Empirical Analysis of Their Importance and Characteristics. *Journal of Policy Analysis and Management*, vol. 15, no. 3, 1996:353–76.

Godschalk, D.R., D.W. Parham, D.R. Porter, W.R. Potapchuk, and S.W. Schukraft. *Pulling Together: A Planning and Development Consensus-Building Manual*. Washington DC: Urban Land Institute. 1994.

Gramlich, E.M. *Benefit-Cost Analysis of Government Programs*. Englewood Cliffs, NJ: Prentice-Hall. 1981.

Healey, P. A Planner's Day: Knowledge and Action in Communicative Practice. *Journal of the American Planning Association*, vol. 58, no. 1, 1992:9–20.

Healey, P. The Communicative Turn in Planning Theory and Its Implications for Spatial Strategy Formation. *Environment and Planning B*, vol. 23, no. 2, 1996:217–34.

Innes, J. Planning Theory's Emerging Paradigm: Communicative Action and Interactive Practice. *Journal of Planning Education and Research*, vol. 14, no. 2, 1995:128–35.

Krumholz, N. A Retrospective View of Equity Planning. *Journal of the American Planning Association*, vol. 48, no. 2, 1982:163–83.

Krumholz, N. and J. Forester. *Making Equity Planning Work*. Philadelphia: Temple University Press. 1990.

Kunreuther, H. and D. Easterling. Gaining Acceptance for Noxious Facilities with Economic Incentives in D. W. Bromley and K. Segerson (eds) *The Social Response to Environmental Risk: Policy Formation in an Age of Uncertainty*. Boston: Kluwer. 1992.

Lavelle, M. 320-Year-Old Treaty May Dam Water Project. *The National Law Journal.* Monday, April 12,1997:A12.

London Docklands Development Corporation (LDDC). *Corporate Plan 9/84: Objectives, Policies, Strategies.* London, UK: Author. 1984.

Marris, P. *Meaning and Action: Community Planning and Conceptions of Change.* Revised edition. Andover, Hants, UK: Routledge and Kegan Paul. 1987.

Marris, P. Advocacy Planning as a Bridge Between the Professional and the Politician. *Journal of the American Planning Association,* vol. 60, no. 2, 1994:143–46.

Meyer, P.B. *Who Should Control the Urban Economic Development Agenda? The Policy Conflict Over London's Docklands.* Paper presented at the Urban Affairs Association Annual Meeting, St. Louis, MO. 1988.

Meyer, P.B. Economic "Development" and Environmental Threats: Institutional Factors Shaping Socio-Economic Impacts. *Working Paper 94-7.* Louisville, KY: Center for Environmental Management. University of Louisville. 1994.

Mier, R. *Social Justice and Local Development Policy.* Newbury Park, CA: Sage. 1993.

Miller, S. and S. Kumar. Narmada Dam Fails World Bank's Final Test. New Socialist, vol. 138, no. 1868, 1993:5.

Mishan, E J. *Cost-Benefit Analysis.* New York: Praeger. 1976.

Neal-Post, J. Sacred Sites and Federal Land Management: An Analysis of the Proposed Native American Free Exercise of Religion Act of 1993. *National Resources Journal,* vol. 34, no. 2, 1994:443–65.

Ng, M.K. and A. Cook. Reclamation: An Urban Development Strategy Under Fire. *Land Use Policy,* vol. 14, no. 1, 1997:5–23.

Parkinson, M. Urban Regeneration and Development Corporations: Liverpool Style. *Local Economy,* vol. 3, no. 2, 1988:109–18.

Peattie, L.R. Reflections on Advocacy Planning. *Journal of the American Institute of Planners,* vol. 34, no. 2, 1968:80–88.

Peattie, L.R. Communities and Interests in Advocacy Planning. *American Planning Association Journal,* vol. 60, no. 2, 1994:151–53.

Rubin, H. The Danada Farm: Land Acquisition, Planning and Politics in Suburbia. *Journal of the American Planning Association,* vol. 54, no. 1, 1988:79– 90.

Sugden, R. and A. Williams. *The Principles of Practical Cost-Benefit Analysis.* New York: Oxford University Press. 1978.

Susskind, L. and J. Cruikshank. *Breaking the Impasse: Consensual Approaches to Resolving Public Disputes.* New York: Basic Books. 1987.

The Ecologist. Whose Common Future? Philadelphia: New Society Publishers. 1993.

Thompson, M.S. *Benefit-Cost Analysis for Programme Evaluation.* Beverly Hills: Sage Publications. 1980.

PART II

Planning with Ethnic and Cultural Communities

Appreciative Planning: An Approach to Planning with Diverse Ethnic and Cultural Groups

Stephen Ameyaw

This chapter starts with an outline of its theme: "Appreciative planning" as an approach to urban planning in a multicultural context. Appreciative planning is a model based on mutual respect, trust, and care-based action. It is a two-way learning and problem-solving approach to planning. Appreciative planning is a multi-faceted process that unites rational and nonrational processes of social interaction and social learning to enable citizens and professionals to share the work of problem solving and decision-making for the benefit of their communities. By so doing, it enables planners to celebrate the valuable assets multicultural groups bring to city life and planning deliberations.

The "appreciative" concept is important in today's pluralistic society because it confronts the real conflicts, issues, dissent, and trade-offs in city planning. Appreciative planning is a proposal to create contexts in which planners and multicultural groups can continuously learn and experiment, think systematically, engage in meaningful dialogue, and create visions that energize action and inclusion in city planning.

I have borrowed the word "appreciative" from Bushe and Pitman (1991), and Barrett (1995), who use it as an intervention model in organizations such as NGOs and corporations. Given the strong push to involve multicultural groups in the urban planning process, appreciative planning will help provide valuable insights into the many problems and issues facing planners and multicultural groups in urban environments.

The appreciative planning approach I am proposing here can bring citizens and professionals together in fruitful cooperation despite their cultural differences because appreciative planning is a process model based on flexibility rather than on a rigid, rational planning approach and its universal notions, and it allows planners to reach out to minority groups and address their social and human living conditions. Appreciative planners learn to escape from the scientistic, one-way problem-solving process by engaging in networking, communication, and dialogue with community groups.

An example of an appreciative approach to planning is the proposal in Vancouver to utilize large, unsafe, abandoned playgrounds for allotment gardening: not to eliminate the grassy areas, but to surround smaller playgrounds with ever-present, watchful elders. Strathcona, a community of older homes with much street crime, is putting front porches back on the houses so it becomes natural again for residents to "live on the street." From the comfort of park benches and porch rockers, citizens keep an eye on what is going on.

HISTORICAL PLANNING PRACTICE

In the rational comprehensive tradition, city planning has historically concerned itself with the physical environment. There have been several planning projects such as housing developments, schools, and recreational facilities that have failed to take into account socio-economic, racial, and cultural factors of the intended beneficiaries. City planners often fail to understand racial and ethnic problems because the mechanistic approach to physical planning hinges on the belief that land-use problems can be isolated from socio-economic, racial, and ethnic concerns. Although the rational comprehensive planning approach has led to some improvements in city life, this approach to meeting the needs of multicultural groups has several limitations.

The analytic, reductionist, problem-solving techniques and tools employed by city planners often further a fragmented view of the city. Rational comprehensive approaches to problem solving require isolating complex problems into small parts. As such, city planners become experts in narrowly focused areas such as land-use planning and housing and often ignore the systemic, interactive nature of city problems.

Furthermore, because the analytic problem-solving approach fragments their view, it prevents them from seeing the city as a holistic entity. This holds true even though the problems and issues confronting planners—for example, developing zoning and administrative policies, provision of housing, recreation services, transportation, public participation in city plan making—are all interactive. Planning departments often segment and address these problems separately. Their distinct separation from each other—and the mixed messages that result—makes it difficult for racial and minority groups, in particular, to relate to the city planning process. Thus, rational comprehensive planning loses its guiding force when it deals with less than the whole of its public. In fact, it becomes markedly irrational.

Friedmann (1987), who reviewed the intellectual traditions and ideologies from the perspective of "four corners" of planning and development (i.e., policy analysis, social reform, social learning, and social mobilization), characterized the rational comprehensive position, which many city planners adhere to, as representing professional disciplines that accepts the existing power relations as a given. In advancing the public interest, these planners place their faith in technical reason, social engineering, and centralized directed planning. Such a planning approach nonetheless resists the participation of some ethno-cultural groups because of its universal regulations.

Cities such as Richmond, Surrey, and Vancouver in the Lower Mainland of British Columbia have now been translating planning information documents into Chinese and other minority languages and taking steps to involve ethno-cultural groups in the planning process. This is an acknowledgment of the kind of disadvantages minorities encounter with the planning profession. However, it is important to note that some of the approaches used to address these problems, such as translating English into ethnic languages, using cultural organizations as mediating contact with ethnic groups, and other communication techniques, may be inadequate. Rationalistic ideas simply do not translate well into cultures with radically different value systems.

For instance, "community policing" and "block watch" programs have "warm and fuzzy" nostalgic connotations for those who remember the British bobby and Norman Rockwell's blue-coated neighborhood Irish cop. The City of Vancouver developed these programs in response to the growing crimes against citizens in their homes. Yet, they were met with resistance from Chinese residents, who were most affected by home invasion gangs. This is not just because "triad brotherhoods are a feature of Chinese culture," as cultural relativists would have it, but because "community policing" in imperial, nationalist, and communist China has been a euphemism for secret police spies. Thus, these programs are viewed with suspicion by Chinese neighborhood groups.

MULTICULTURAL POLICY RESPONSE IN CANADA

Ethnic inequality and racial discrimination have political and economic roots in the history of Canadian social institutions. Our national myth is of "Two Founding Nations," both European (ignoring the Aboriginal First Nations). But today, Canadian society is more diverse than ever. The past two decades, in particular, have seen a dramatic increase in the number of immigrants from Asia, Latin America, and Africa.

The federal and provincial governments have given serious attention to the task of defining and developing policies for coping with diversity. The Canada Multiculturalism Act (1985) and the Charter of Rights and Freedoms (1982) have promoted and addressed barriers toward diversity and individual rights. Most of these policy initiatives totally or partially affirm the right for cultural, ethnic, and racial groups to live free from all forms of discrimination and to have the opportunity to participate fully in Canadian society.

Thus, in Canada "multiculturalism" has three meanings. First, it recognizes the many cultures in the country. Second, it affirms that cultures and heritage of ethno-racial communities must be respected and, when necessary, incorporated into the programs and services of organizations and institutions. Third, it requires that the work environment, methods of service delivery, communications, and agencies' aspirations reflect the diverse cultural background of the clients, staff members, and managers. To what extent do we find reflections of these policies and laws in shaping the development of cities? Canadian cities now have multicultural groups of significant social weight that multiculturalism is no longer an abstract ideal. It has become a concrete social skill, routinely demanded in society. In the section that follows, two brief cases and an extended case study of multicultural and planning related issues are examined to give a context for the appreciative planning approach.

Two Brief Cases: Multiculturalism in Planning

Surrey's Mega-Homes and Neighborhoods

Every culture, ethnic group, and race attaches symbolic meaning to a particular service or set of services and policies. Among some groups, for example, the East Indians in Surrey, housing is thought to symbolize the sense of community where the extended family and communal life is of great importance. As a result, these groups often seek housing that meets the needs of the extended family. In recent times a new social mosaic is becoming evident in Surrey. The real estate market has built several mega-homes in Surrey to accommodate the larger family sizes of the East Indian community. These neighborhoods are gradually becoming ethnic residential concentrations. Also, sidewalks and streets have become active public places in these neighborhoods. This trend has raised tensions between the East Indians and other residents whose individualistic and nuclear family lifestyles conflict with the extended family lifestyles practiced by the East Indians. Thus, there has been a greater need for planners to reconcile the needs of racial and ethnic communities with those of other residents of the neighborhood and with the city's land-use plans. Planners in this community are faced with the task of mediating between the competing interests of stability and change in a community that is undergoing rapid social transformation.

The Battle for Single Room Occupancy in Vancouver—1997–98

In Vancouver a debate is currently raging on with respect to the provision of single-room occupancy (SRO) in some neighborhoods. Planners and developers wanted to demolish several blocks of low-cost, single hotel rooms in Chinatown, Downtown Eastside, Gastown, and Strathcona. They planned to increase the capital return for the land by intensifying its use with high-rise apartments, commercial space, and social housing. The planners and developers intended to seek approval from the City of Vancouver for public assistance in several forms, including massive upgrading of water and other services in the area. The issue has, however, raised tensions between business groups and socio-cultural groups in these neighborhoods. Each of these groups has formed citizen organizations to protest the city's plans. For example, the ethnic Chinese merchants have joined forces with other merchants to seek the removal of the poor and drug addicts from the area because they undermine the tourist trade, while the poor have asked for fair treatment and accommodation of their needs for low-income housing.

The planners' response to this debate has been to take a more technical or functional approach to the problem and to separate the planning issues from the concerns of the merchants, the poor, and the developers. This has created a battleground for competing interests. The planning system has become an arena not only for contending ethnic or class interest, but for more personal conflicts between groups.

The two case histories cited in this chapter point to the fact that planning cannot be divulged from its social context, especially so in a multicultural community. The planners' use of public hearings, town hall meetings, zoning changes, and official plan design in responding to the demands of divergent groups often creates further tensions and conflicts between competing groups because these methods are too abstract and do not address the "real" concerns of ethno-cultural groups. What is needed is a balancing act that appreciates the values and assets of different groups and includes them in the planning process.

The preceding analysis has also identified several areas of concern within city planning that need to be addressed, especially when dealing with issues related to racial and ethnic groups. The areas of concern are: (i) planners' inability to critically examine and analyze issues from a multicultural perspective; (ii) planners' inability to adapt the universal rational planning process to address the concerns of multicultural groups; and (iii) planners' inability to design participatory processes that bring racial and ethnic groups into the planning process.

Despite concerted efforts by city planners to include ethnic communities in city plan making (for example, the Vancouver's citizen circles process, the SRO town hall meetings and hearings), these efforts have often been seen by ethno-cultural groups as cooptation. What is needed is a broad-based planning process that includes minorities, multicultural groups, and women in the decision-making bodies, an approach that was used by the City of Surrey in the extended case discussed below.

Extended Case Study: Task Force Report on Intercultural Inclusivity in the City of Surrey

Background

Surrey is one of the fastest growing cities in Canada. The 1996 Census figures show that immigration was a major part of Surrey's population growth between 1991 and 1996. During that five-year period, 24,230 new residents came to Surrey from another country, accounting for 41 percent of Surrey's total population growth.   Asian Pacific countries were the most common origins of recent immigrants.   The majority, 37 percent came from India, with 20 percent from Taiwan, 7 percent from the Philippines, 7 percent from Fiji, and 4 percent each from South Korea and China.   The profile of immigrants coming to Surrey was quite different from other cities within the Greater Vancouver Regional District (GVRD).

Over the past five years, 24 percent of immigrants coming into GVRD were from Hong Kong, 14 percent from China, 12 percent from Taiwan, 9 percent from India, and 7 percent from the Philippines. Interestingly enough, many of the Hong Kong immigrants (44%) chose to settle in Richmond, while 24 percent chose to settle in Vancouver. The majority of immigrants from India (56%) settled in Surrey, while 19 percent settled in Vancouver. The changes in population over the past five years have greatly increased the ethnic diversity of Surrey and other GVRD cities (City of Surrey Planning & Development Department 1998). The demographic picture of the Lower Mainland has changed from an Anglo Saxon majority to an emerging multicultural society.   Yet, the rational technocratic planning methods and tools were still being applied to developing policies and providing alternative solutions to the city's problems.   The city, thus, saw a need for broader planning approaches that are more inclusive of ethno-cultural groups in the community.

City of Surrey's Taskforce Report—Case Illustration

Based on an earlier report conducted by Surrey's Parks and Recreation Department (1994), the following areas of concern were outlined: (i) there were gaps in the services and programs provided to ethnic groups; and (ii) there were concerns about the increasing population of ethnic groups and the need to provide culturally sensitive programs and services to meet these needs.

In March 1995 a ten-member task force was formed with people who have expertise in multiculturalism. They included people from different ethnic and racial backgrounds, race/ethnic relations committees, municipal government, nonprofit organizations, and social service agencies. It is interesting to note that included in the task force membership were three planners from the City of Surrey's planning department. The mandate of the task force was to develop a multicultural mandate which embraces all the department's operations, and identify and develop strategies which advance the objectives of the multicultural mandate.

These inclusive community participation project activities took place in Surrey between March 1995 and September 1996. The research methods and activities were divided into two phases as outlined below.

Phase One: Finding Out. A series of staff and community surveys were conducted in addition to focus group sessions.   Nearly thirty-two representatives ranging from ethno-specific and multicultural organizations, the school board, and the department of parks and recreation in Surrey participated in the project.   About seventy-nine community meetings were held and attended by 122 Surrey residents. Three focus group sessions were conducted with fifty parks and recreation staff and

103 responses were received from the staff survey. About seventy-three ethno-cultural volunteers translated and interpreted the project information, survey, and processes, totalling 820 volunteer hours. The outreach initiatives led to contact with forty Surrey ethno-cultural groups and organizations and a range of ethnic and mainstream media helped to inform the public about the project and its outreach activities. A total of about 1,400 people participated directly in the project and contributed much of their time and resources. As well, it is estimated that indirectly, more than 15,700 people received information about Surrey's parks and recreation program and gained greater insights into the cultural barriers experienced by multicultural groups.

Community focus groups were held with the objective of answering two questions: What principles would make the Surrey Parks and Recreation Department multiculturally sensitive? and, What are the community's expectations for the work of the Task Force on Intercultural Inclusivity? With respect to the first question, the focus group session suggested an acceptance of diversity at both the organizational and community level. Also suggested was that a plan of action be adopted with a timeline for implementation. The Parks and Recreation Department should also recruit volunteers from ethno-cultural groups and examine partnership opportunities with these groups. In addition, the department should provide diversity training for all levels of staff, including management, staff, and volunteers.

Regarding the second question, it was suggested that the department establish a multicultural council or advisory board and appoint or designate a staff person to work with the community. The Parks and Recreation Department should also seek to become more knowledgable by identifying how recreation/leisure is defined by different ethno-cultural groups. The activities of the department should also be advertised in various mediums such as ethnic papers, radio, and through schools.

Phase Two: Taking Steps. The primary goal of "Taking Steps" in phase two was to consult with the general ethnic communities in Surrey to identify barriers which limit their access to parks and recreation department's programs and services. This phase of the project was contracted out to consultants. The main objectives were to gather quantitative and qualitative data and information that would allow for assessment of the program and service delivery needs of Surrey's ethno-cultural communities, validation of the multiculturalism mandate, and development of strategies to advance each of the mandate's objectives. The rationale was that if the Parks and Recreation Department and community ethnic groups began to research together to identify barriers toward diversity, both groups would gain more knowledge about each other and the problems that need to be addressed.

In many of the community meetings, participants shared openly their contacts and experiences with the Parks and Recreation Department. One Aboriginal woman described how her two teenage children were harassed and pushed around while visiting the local youth center. She complained that the people in the housing complex in which she lived do not permit their children to play on the grounds anymore because other kids would pick on them and call them names. She also stated that the children in the housing complex do not have the chance to play on their own because they are not safe in the community. Another Indo-Canadian gentleman talked about his terrifying experience at Bear Creek Park. He was walking the track mid-afternoon when three boys approached him and started swearing and yelling racial slurs. He tried not to get involved but the boys continued and threw punches at his turban, trying to knock it off. This was a frightening and humiliating experience for him. The community meetings allowed for open and frank discussions of residents' concerns and helped the Parks and Recreation Department to identify residents' needs.

A community survey also helped to identify the population of new ethnic residents in Surrey. Twenty-three percent were of South Asian origin, 24 percent Asian, and 43 percent of Spanish origin. These figures indicated a recent and substantial influx of new immigrants to Surrey. However, these new residents have had limited participation in parks and recreation programs and services.

Overall the use of facilities by language groups was 84 percent South Asian, 72 percent Asian, and 77 percent Spanish. These groups used at least one indoor facility in 1995. The two most frequently used indoor facilities were the community hall and the indoor swimming pool. In terms of outdoor facilities, the three groups identified large city parks and neighborhood parks as the ones most frequently used.

Language was sometimes a barrier to use of facilities. The study reported that there was a strong correlation between English as a household language and the number of facilities used. About 22 percent of English-speaking household respondents have used three or more facilities. Comparably, 93 percent of the nonusers do not speak English as the primary household language. This correlation also indicated that language was a strong barrier to participation in the Parks and Recreation Department's activities and the use of its services. It also pointed out that there is lack of a cultural sensitivity in the provision of these services in the department.

The major concern from the majority of the participants was that most of the multicultural groups had little understanding of the services provided by the Parks and Recreation Department. They complained about the lack of translated information on policies, procedures, signage, brochures, and leisure guide and the fact that their organizations were not included in the departments mailing lists.

Some of the ethno-cultural groups indicated that the Parks and Recreation Department does not offer culturally appropriate programs and services and in some cases, when they were offered, many of the programs and services were seen as incompatible with their religious beliefs. Another point raised by some of the groups was that the department's staff often treated them poorly and were rude to them at times.

The primary objectives of the multicultural community surveys were to identify ethnic community group usage of Parks and Recreation Department services and to find out if barriers existed when using these services. Based on the findings and analysis, five key areas were identified: (i) cultural barriers; (ii) communication barriers; (iii) limited program choices; (iv) security and safety issues; and (v) institutional enhancement, change, and accountability.

In November 1995 the task force completed its research and analysis of information generated from the survey. A draft multicultural mandate was prepared. This was then reviewed and discussed with the Parks and Recreation Commission and adopted in December 1995. Following this, the mandate was then discussed with community and staff, resulting in the following statement from the department:

The City of Surrey's Parks and Recreation Department acknowledges cultural diversity and multicultural community groups as sources of enrichment and strength, with significant contributions to the life of the entire community. The department, therefore, supports the rights of all persons to freedom from cultural or racial discrimination and to be included with equal opportunity and participation in department and community affairs.

The department itself set up the following principles to implement this Mandate:

1.   Inclusion of ethno-cultural groups in the design, implementation and evaluation of the department's service delivery model with a primary goal of ensuring that all services are accessible;
2.   The development and support of cross-cultural understanding and respect among employees and the community to produce suitable and effective programs and service delivery;
3.   To ensure that staff, volunteers, and public advisory committees and the commission is reflective of the diversity of the community currently and in Surrey's future; and
4.   Elimination and prevention of discrimination based on race, national or ethnic origin, language, culture, and religious beliefs.

In March 1998 a draft implementation plan was presented to the social planning committee and the consensus was to appoint a multicultural project coordinator to start working beginning May 1998. The coordinator's role will be to develop strategies to facilitate effective outreach services and provide support for members of diverse ethno-cultural communities. The other roles are to work with the Parks and Recreation Department to effectively implement all four principles in the multicultural mandate.

In short, the Surrey Task Force policy formulation experience cautions planners to endeavor more to understand the nature of problems and issues confronting ethnic and cultural groups with whom they work. The appreciative model provides the most suitable approach for formulating policy with diverse ethnic and cultural groups. This is because the appreciative planning process helps to develop networks, create innovative ways of gathering information from various groups, and above all, promotes effective community building initiatives and effective implementation strategies.

Table 7.1 examines some of the key elements of the community building research design framework—jump start, plugging in, emerging sense of diversity, and collaboration. This multicultural community building approach played a major role in bringing ethnic and cultural groups together into focus group sessions not only to talk about race and cultural issues, access to parks and recreation services, but to also find ways to build an effective multicultural community through learning and inclusion.

THE APPRECIATIVE PLANNING PROCESS

Table 7.1 presents the four phases of multicultural community building and their respective elements. These elements are examined below.

Jump-Start

Many planners are deeply committed to multiculturalism and community building as abstract principles, but often feel quite helpless by not knowing where to start. Communities faced with the very negative factors listed in the first column of Table 7.1 are deeply troubled. It seems that there is no other way than to jump-start community building initiatives. But how do we do it?

Table 7.1
Phases of Multicultural Community Building

JUMP START	PLUGGING IN	EMERGING SENSE OF DIVERSITY	COLLABORATION
No sense of multicultural identity	Small core multi- racial group	Effective multicultural community leaders	Realization that multicultural agenda is furthered by joining with other groups who have separate agenda
No multicultural community leaders	Mixed and loose organization and limited community resources	Strong institutional organization On-going multiracial community-based projects	But "add value" by participating in community projects
Few volunteers with interest in multicultural issues	Emerging sense of multicultural identity	Desire to create diversity	Many well established and effective multicultural organizations
Very limited institutional support	Limited awareness of multicultural community needs	People linked to issues outside the boundary of culture, race, and ethnicity Strong volunteer base	Large number of volunteers Clear sense of multicultural identity Focus on inter-connections of issues
Old buddy power base Hostile racial tensions	Limited interest in multicultural community-based projects	Significant multiracial identity and recognition Welcome new ideas Some political power Many assets to draw upon	Integrated community projects Widespread public support and involvement Training and educational opportunities for emerging leaders and volunteers Strong political power

Plugging In

Searching out the less visible positive factors in column two and identifying the groups and individuals associated with them is the first action step, which I call "plugging in." It is important to find out whether there are core multi-racial groups, or if the community has an organizational capacity to raise ethnic and racial awareness. It means starting where the community is, in a positive sense, in the now. Most of all, it means starting with small, highly visible projects that invite community curiosity and are "do-able" on a scale that does not overburden existing groups, individuals, and resources. Communities that can initiate visible projects with these various cultural groups can start to plug into community building with ease.

Emerging Sense of Diversity

Once these projects start to demonstrate success, their effectiveness can be publicized and the model promoted across cultures. Once they begin to be adopted across those boundaries, a sense of diversity emerges that begins to take on the sense of a "mutual admiration society." People feel they clearly understand ethnic and racial differences, but "difference" loses its confrontational sense and has a chance to become cause for celebration. Crucial to this stage are strong leadership and a desire to form alliances among the cultural groups. Without these, the models will not be carried across the cultural boundaries.

Collaboration

The purpose of collaboration in the appreciative planning process is to link community groups for the objective of addressing shared interests. Collaborative efforts can lead to effective participation and inclusion. It also adds value to the "rainbow" agenda and taps into unused resources. A community that engages its citizens to address racial and ethnic issues can grow in self-esteem.

The goal of multicultural community building is to improve race and ethnic relations and promote diversity. Communities are at different phases of multicultural community-building, and, therefore, each must examine the best strategies that work for it. Those in the early phases of community building need to focus on the jump-start process or plug-in by expanding their core base of interest and support. Those that are more mature can expand their identities and ties to gain diversity and influence. The well-organized communities will draw from both inside and outside support to gain value for themselves through collaboration.

Most of the elements shown in Table 7.1 were incorporated into Parks and Recreation research methodology design. The focus group sessions, ethnic specific interviews, volunteers, staff, and organization survey were attempts by Parks and Recreation Department to reach out to the multicultural community during the research process. Implicit in the methodology was a sense of multicultural community building that brought many ethnic and cultural groups together to identify their needs and contribute to the development of a multicultural mandate.

APPRECIATIVE PLANNING LESSONS

One of the appreciative planning lessons drawn from the study was that the Parks and Recreation Department and community ethnic groups began to research together to identify barriers toward diversity. This represented a two-way research or problem-solving approach that helped both sides to gain knowledge about their own strengths and problem areas. The second aspect of the appreciation element was based on reaching out to individuals and specific ethnic groups and to provide them the opportunity to tell their own stories and experiences of life in the community. By providing opportunities and focus group forums for residents to communicate and share ideas, this instills learning, builds trust, and develops networking among members and staff. Networking is important because elitist planning processes are often associated with lack of recognition of the multiple actors with legitimate interest in planning issues who need to be consulted.

The development of the multicultural mandate not only confirmed the successful outcome of the project but also helped build confidence and trust that has improved the social and human conditions' of Surrey's multicultural communities. It also demonstrated that the City of Surrey, in dealing with its conflict, dissent, and tradeoffs, has recognized the unique assets of multicultural groups and integrated them in the planning process.

With respect to the mega-homes in Surrey and SROs in Vancouver, the appreciative planning model would create dynamism between the various ethno-cultural groups and enable planners to go beyond their familiar ways of thinking and reach out to these groups. Some of the other examples cited in this paper (e.g., Chinese experience in neighborhood block watch and community policing, Vancouver's initiatives to utilize large, unsafe, abandoned playgrounds for allotment gardening areas, Strathcona's plan to redesign old buildings to fight street crime) require an appreciative planning approach, one that goes beyond adapting to challenges and solving problems. If planners' major tasks are to promote efficient physical and human organization of space, then more care and attention must be given to the increasing multicultural nature of today's urban communities.

What is needed is an overall review of planning policies and standards to reflect multicultural views and power sharing through inclusion of ethnic minorities in decision-making bodies. The lessons from the Surrey Task Force Report, and others cited in the paper, demonstrate how planners can articulate planning decisions affecting multicultural communities in meaningful ways that will achieve intercultural inclusivity and appreciation.

CONCLUSION

Planning in a multicultural environment has come to mean expanding the depth and scope of city planning. This means not just changing the planning process, but also rethinking how planning issues are identified, conceptualized, and prioritized.

Involving ethno-racial communities in planning is a critical component of the multicultural/anti-racist planning process. Despite more enlightened attitudes toward ethno-racial groups, planners often fail to acknowledge the gifts these groups bring to the city planning environment. The most successful communities are those that can identify the gifts of all residents, including multicultural groups, and draw them into the planning process.

Appreciative planning shifts the role of the planner from one of directing programs and delivering services to supporting partnerships, enabling multicultural community directed assets and needs to be addressed, and facilitating local initiatives. Appreciative planning promotes empowerment, builds confidence and competence in the community to do things for themselves. It is about a cooperative approach to planning or a two-way approach to problem solving. When planners focus on fixing multi-racial problems based on rational principles, multicultural groups often develop defensive postures and seek to escape from blame. What is needed is an approach that gives credit to groups and communities as having the ability to become their own problem-solvers and generating new ways of looking at planning issues.

In the past decade or so, planners have become more sensitive to issues of race, diversity, and culture. Talking incessantly only about problems, issues, and failures, however, serves to deepen the sense of despondency that is all too common in the multiculturalism and public policy debate. On the other hand, talking about successes (such as the Surrey Parks and Recreation Inclusivity Initiative) can convey the message that there is hope and that sustainable multicultural community is possible. The challenge today is for planners and policy-makers to learn the characteristics of the appreciative model as it can be manifested in multicultural and city planning contexts and situations. We need to focus more on what works, not what has gone wrong; on successes rather than failures. There are several examples of successful efforts of planning with diverse ethnic and cultural groups. We need to document, describe, share, and most importantly, replicate them in all our individual efforts.

REFERENCES

Barrett, F. "Creating Appreciative Learning Cultures." *Organizational Dynamics*, vol. 2, no. 2, Autumn 1995.

Bushe, G., and T. Pitman (eds). Appreciative Method for Transformational Change. *Organizational Practitioner*, vol. 23, no. 3, 1991:1–4.

City of Surrey. Parks and Recreation Task Force Report on Intercultural Inclusivity. Surrey, Canada. 1994.

City of Surrey. Planning and Development Department. Immigration Profile. Surrey, British Columbia. 1998.
Friedmann, J. Planning in the Public Domain from *Knowledge to Action*. Princeton, NJ: Princeton University Press. 1987.

CHAPTER 8

Culture Matters—But It Shouldn't Matter Too Much

Howell S. Baum

Planning is an effort to help groups reflect on their conditions, identify what dissatisfies them, imagine alternatives, and develop strategies for realizing better possibilities. Planners must help groups see themselves realistically, get critical distance that allows reflection on their past and present and recognition of different possible futures. How should planners approach this challenge, and how does the nature of communities affect the possibility of planning?

Communities have cultures, which prescribe members' relations with the community, orient their actions, and, among other things, suggest how they might use formal planning processes. Each community's culture, while partly resembling others, is distinctive. In addition, cultures vary in coherence and many are pluralistic. Multiculturalists alert us to these facts and some implications. Here we examine, first, the meanings of multiculturalism. The second section articulates a multicultural sensibility for planning. The third section presents a case study of community planning that illustrates predicaments of planning with groups that have strong, inclusive cultures. The final section draws conclusions for planning practice and education.

MEANINGS OF MULTICULTURALISM

Multiculturalism is a pluralistic movement (see, for example, Goldberg 1994). For many it is a political, rather than a social scientific, project. It is useful to distinguish political multiculturalism from anthropological multiculturalism. To begin, multiculturalism has two components, represented by "multi" and "culture."

"Multi" represents two arguments—one empirical, one normative. First, multiculturalists observe that the United States, as many nations, is an increasingly complex society, more complex than many inhabitants imagine, more complex than governance institutions recognize or can accommodate. Groups have diverse ways of living, perspectives, interests, identities, and loyalties. Moreover, some groups are more powerful and privileged than others. Some benefit from the rules of the game more than others, and some gain at others' expense. As a result, some groups are neglected in public discourse and public policy.

These observations have normative implications. Ordinary citizens and policymakers should consider that ways of living different from their own—indeed, many ways of living—make sense to others and, therefore, have validity and value. Succinctly, people must accept not just the complexity of the world, but also the reasonableness and legitimacy of alternatives to dominant arrangements. Different groups may require, and hence deserve, different policies and programs. Moreover, to create conditions whereby the gamut of groups, including the historically powerless, can effectively make their needs known and influence public decisions, extraordinary steps is necessary. Rules of the game must be changed to allow broader participation, ensure each group has the resources to know its interests and make them known, and, perhaps initially, compensate for past inequalities and disadvantages.

This is familiar territory for planners: pluralism, equity for minorities, the disadvantaged, and the powerless, and participation in public decisions (Arnstein 1969; Checkoway 1995; Davidoff 1965; Forester 1989; Krumholz and Forester 1990; and Thomas and Ritzdorf 1997). Still, as planners discover, fair and reasonable principles turn up prickly predicaments in practice (Baum 1997a and 1998; Marris and Rein 1982; and Medoff and Sklar 1994).

"Culture" is a second, more challenging theme. Multiculturalists hold that something "cultural" is essential to community identity and produces a multiplicity of distinct groups. For anthropologists, "culture" refers to a relatively coherent system of meanings, more or less integrated with social relations, practices, and material objects (Geertz 1973; Parsons 1951; and Stein 1994).

Many political multiculturalists, concerned with promoting minority group interests, have taken a narrower view of culture (Turner 1994). For them, "culture" refers to social groups assumed to have common political interests and, associated with these, common ways of thinking. "Culture" is often identified with race, ethnicity, sexual orientation, gender, or class. The language of "culture" is used to label groups because it is assumed members hold the same beliefs and aspirations. But this usage is only weakly empirical. More often than not, the existence of a unifying culture is just assumed, perhaps inferred from actual or potential political interests, not derived from careful observation of or dialogue with group members.

A political wish to argue that all group members have common strategic interests encourages distorting and reifying group characteristics. Advocates exaggerate the homogeneity of groups, playing down differences. Many multiculturalists exaggerate the role of ideas in defining groups and holding members together. Sometimes this stance is a way of minimizing the significance of social differences within a group or category of persons: despite situational differences, everyone can be said to think the same about essential matters.

Different multiculturalists talk about group beliefs differently. Some argue that tacit, unconscious, quasi-archetypal ideas unify group members even when they look different. Core ethnic assumptions, for example, persist and hold everyone together. Other multiculturalists treat whatever people say as an expression of underlying culture. While that view may seem to emphasize the superficial and transient in contrast with the deeply unconscious, both positions encourage finding group unity and optimism about improvement. Whereas the first tends to assume unity without analysis of differences, the latter is likely to take common statements in surveys or at public meetings as evidence of agreement about not only particulars, but basic ways of living. The first view tends to assume cultural unity; the second makes it easy to find unity, if only there are circumstances where people can say similar things.

This emphasis on ideas misses the range and depth of thoughts and feelings that lead or enable persons to identify with groups and hold groups together. Many of the important thoughts are, as the first view suggests, unconscious, but they are not necessarily realistic or rational. For someone who is part of a racial, ethnic, or religious group, for example, the specific ideas espoused by group leaders or even a political agenda may be less important than how belonging to the group brings self-esteem, identity, and feelings of being powerful, virtuous, safe, and loved. Moreover, people do not acquire, hold, or test these premises in formal indoctrination so much as in social and emotional relationships. Culture takes and makes meanings in personal relations with their pleasures and pains. These meanings are normally tacit, often elusive, and resiliently resistant to change. Attachments to groups may be rationalized as loyalty to ideas, but the personal and emotional weigh heavier than the intellectual.

Many multiculturalists exaggerate the exclusivity of groups. In stressing homogeneity, they emphasize differences among groups. They suggest that everyone belongs to a single cultural group, or at least that one group identity matters much more than others. In reality, people have complex, multiple identities. Many belong to several communities and they are normally untroubled by seeming contradictions among formal tenets associated with different communities (Mandelbaum 1996).

The political multicultural agenda tends to produce fictive labels. For example, the five conventional "racial" categories—Whites or Euro-Americans, African Americans, Asian Americans, Hispanics or Latinos, and Native Americans—lump together people of different races and/or cultures, often groups with little or no common past and sometimes groups with long-standing animosities. There may be good strategic reasons for creating coalitions, but thinking of these categories as culture is bad anthropology (Hollinger 1995). The labels don't capture the ways people think of their problems or aspirations (Wallace 1994).

Still, both political and anthropological multiculturalism emphasize two points planners should heed: to see the social world as pluralistic and to take seriously the role of culture in shaping how groups see things and try to influence them.

A MULTICULTURAL SENSIBILITY FOR PLANNING

If planners took culture seriously, they would assume every group they encounter has a culture. The culture may be total or partial, affecting all or some of members' actions. It may be thick or thin, thoroughly or only partially defining and directing actions. Some people may identify more deeply or thoroughly with the group and may be more centrally or intricately part of it than others, who may move among and identify variously with several groups. Still, at some times and in some ways, the culture will shape members' ways of seeing things and norms for their interactions with one another and outsiders. It will affect how members view their interests and prescribe rules for making decisions. To some degree, members will be attached to these ways of thinking and acting, as well as to other people who share them. Individuals will identify with the collectivity, equating their personal welfare with group well-being. Members will be loyal to the group, and they will feel special as a result of this connection. Crucially, these ties may move members to act in ways that are not realistic or rational in terms of apparent interests.

Anthropologists remind us that every observer—here, the planner—also has a culture. There is no detached "objective," "scientific" analysis of a group, only encounters between persons who see the world through lenses that differ in some ways and are similar in others. The latter point bears emphasis: others are always both different from us and similar to us. Those who stress the "multi" in multiculturalism call attention to the differences. Those who stress the "culture" direct us to commonalities: we all desire, participate in, and are guided by culture.

In approaching any group, particularly when people resemble us physically and use the same words, we are tempted to assume they see things as we do and are just like us. And it is easy to believe that when they say or do something we would not, they are simply being illogical, drawing faulty conclusions from shared premises. On the other hand, once we recognize that others think differently in some ways, we can be tempted to assume they differ in all ways, that even what seems understandable must be elusively exotic. The answer is empirical. Anthropologists observe what people do and ask them to explain how they think and act. It may take months or years to uncover the meanings that matter.

Planners do not need to understand groups in the depth that anthropologists seek, nor are some of the groups planners encounter as different from them as many societies anthropologists enter. Anthropologists' methods give guidance, however: ask people how they see things, what they want, and why they look at things as they do or want what they prefer. For planners, this research requires more than a few formal meetings or a need assessment survey. Understanding depends on spending time in a community. It calls for in-depth talk with not just formal leaders, but informal leaders and others who do not lead. Unlike anthropologists, planners do not have years to study a group's culture, but they may have months to work on particular projects, and they may have ongoing relationships over years.

Recognition and appreciation of simultaneous differences and similarities requires a special mental attitude.[1] It depends on being able to see differences without necessarily considering them wrong or bad and being able to see similarities without necessarily considering them right or good. It depends on being able to recognize that others act with their own integrity. It depends on being able to identify with others with regard to both how they are similar and how they are different. In particular, it requires being able to see how what one may dislike in the group may also be present in some way, not necessarily identical, in oneself.

This attitude is crucial because of the peculiar culture planners bring to these encounters. Some planners insist on seeing themselves as disinterested, objective, scientific observers who are outside culture, who bear no biases, who not only see things perfectly, but hold up what they see to universal norms for logical action. In fact, these premises delineate a singular culture, and they encourage intellectual and emotional certitude that ensures misunderstandings, mutual animosity, and difficulties working collaboratively or effectively.

Yet even a less self-assured, more sophisticated, view presents problems for planners *qua* planners. Even when planners recognize differences between other cultures and their own, they hold to assumptions that challenge those cultures. Planners are committed to viewing conditions realistically and acting in ways likely to be instrumentally effective. This stance does not presume there is one correct way to see things or that interventions are governed by immutable natural laws. It does mean that people should see things in ways that have coherence and a reasonable chance of contributing to effective action. Planning, after all, is concerned with analysis for the sake of action. Thus, planners insist that communities reflect on their assumptions, that at least momentarily they make premises explicit, cease taking them for granted, examine their purposes and consequences, and consider alternatives.

Groups often experience this stance as hostile.[2] It requires them to open themselves to judgment; considering, for example, whether they are acting in ways that contribute to problems, whether they have acted in ways that did not make sense or were morally objectionable, or whether they may have been foolish. The group may no longer seem special, its traditions wonderful, or its members exalted.

Thus planning is a cross-cultural encounter where principles of the planning culture must prevail. To make this work possible, planners must attempt what anthropologists try. They must create political and psychological conditions for members of a culture to be in their culture but also sufficiently outside it to reflect on it. This should be a moment when members can step aside from their culture, when they can take parts of it, mentally rework them, and imagine different configurations. This is what Stein and Harper refer to as the Wide Reflective Equilibrium in chapter 5. People must be able to do these things without feeling anxiously unmoored or guilty about betraying the past. They should be able momentarily to give up responsibility for their community without feeling irresponsible, to imagine a different community for which they might take responsibility. And then they can return to the present, back to the community now transformed and the culture subtly also altered. This is the work of planning.[3]

In short, taking culture seriously requires planners to take a dual stance. They must respect the ways in which a group's culture matters. They must be able to recognize how members think and develop a process that respects group assumptions. At the same time, planners must not go along with the culture uncritically, but must help adherents step aside from it and reflect on it. For planners who are outsiders, the first position may be more difficult; for planners who are part of a culture, the second is harder.

A CASE EXAMPLE: THE ASSOCIATED

The following case presents episodes from planning by an organization of a cultural community. The planners take their community's culture seriously in defining the ends and designing the process of planning. If anything, they exaggerate the community's homogeneity. In fact, they respect the culture in a distorted way: they cannot question it and they do not push members to reflect on it, even when cultural assumptions contribute to problems and hinder addressing them. The case illustrates what it means to take a community culture seriously. At the same time, by negative example, it shows the costs of not looking critically at the culture.

The case study shows a strategic planning process by The Associated: Jewish Community Federation of Baltimore.[4] The Associated (also called the federation) is one of about 200 federations in local Jewish communities in the United States and Canada (Elazar 1976). It grew from late nineteenth- and early twentieth-century agencies created by philanthropists to provide and regulate charity for needy Jews (Cahn 1970; Fein 1971; Kellman 1970). The Associated raises funds in the Baltimore Jewish community and allocates them to local, national, and international programs. It funds seventeen local service agencies in areas such as health, education, social work, housing, vocational counseling, and drug abuse.

The Associated's primary role is fund raising, and it manages a budget of about $30 million. Its main constituency is Jews who have the means to contribute. Approximately one-third of the households in the Jewish community of 95,000 donate to The Associated, and a few hundred families give most of what it gets. The federation involves significant donors on boards and committees of The Associated or its agencies.

In 1987 The Associated initiated strategic planning to set spending priorities and revive philanthropists' interests in the federation. Seventy people participated in committees that produced a plan in 1989 (Levin and Bernstein 1991; and Strategic Planning Committee 1989). Task forces and other committees involved many more people in implementation.

The episodes described here involve one part of implementation. The strategic plan recommended The Associated work with synagogues to develop a shared "vision," and the federation created a Joint Commission on Associated-Synagogue Relations. The federation assigned a staff member to the Commission, and other staff, including the Associated community planning director, sometimes attended meetings. With the Commission trying to plan for institutional collaboration, these staff members may be considered planners.

Culture

The Baltimore Jewish community includes several cultures. This simplifying summary emphasizes themes that arose in planning for synagogue-federation collaboration.

Ethnic and Religious Identity

The Associated has raised funds with the slogan "We are one." Although most Baltimore Jews might agree, many disagree about the community's core identity. One group, who are likely to be affiliated with a synagogue, especially a more traditional congregation, believe that Judaism, the Jewish religion, defines the community. They assert that only the religiously observant are good community members. Others less likely to belong to a synagogue and, if they do, probably a liberal congregation, consider the Jews an ethnic group. They have a common history in which people have developed and modified a culture and they choose to participate in Jewish life in ways consistent with this culture. For them, religion is only one part of the culture.

Whereas those in the religious group observe rituals for their link to the transcendent, those in the ethnic group more likely engage in religious practices because they are part of tradition. At the same time, Jews may participate in the community in ways with no religious connection; for example, by socializing or doing business with other Jews, participating in secular Jewish organizations such as the federation or its agencies, eating certain foods or attending cultural events, or simply thinking of themselves as Jews.

The religious position considers Jewish culture a body of normative prescriptions. The ethnic position is more liberally empirical: Jewish culture is what Jews do.

Religious Differences

Still, some who are not religious give religion special standing. They feel that others who have the time or faith to be religious are most legitimately Jewish. Even so, strong disagreements divide those who consider religion central to the culture. Definitions of appropriate practice range from the liberal Reform and Reconstructionists through the more conservative Conservatives to traditional, including fundamentalist, Orthodox. Rabbis articulate normative beliefs and practices more clearly than do the laity, who vary in general ways. Liberals define essential religious practices in terms of what makes sense in the modern world. Traditionalists, particularly the Orthodox, interpret the Torah (the Pentateuch) literally and insist on following prescribed practices even in conflict with modern life.

These religious differences shape divergent attitudes toward public life. Liberal modernists draw a line between religious activities and a larger secular, or civil, domain. In the latter, where they work and participate in community organizations, for example, they draw on contemporary social and political ideas. In contrast, traditionalists recognize no distinction between religious and civil spheres. Religious tenets, they hold, should govern all actions (see Liebman 1973 and 1988).

The Associated as a Civil Institution and Community Organization

The Associated has an organizational culture. As other federations, it was the creation of liberal, secular Jews, many of them successful in business and the professions. Leaders acknowledge religion but run the federation in ways more consistent with their business and professional lives. The federation is a secular institution because its leaders consider philanthropy a community, rather than religious, activity and because they want to avoid conflicts over religious differences.[5]

In fact, avoiding conflict is central to federation culture (Elazar 1976). Because The Associated claims to represent all Jews and because leaders want to present a united front to the outside, the federation makes decisions by consensus. Unanimity symbolizes and reaffirms the community's unity. Even acrimonious discussion unnerves participants, and Associated norms discourage aggressive advocacy and public disagreement. Routinely, top staff and federation leaders conduct backstage negotiations to resolve conflicts with positions where everyone can publicly agree. When consensus is elusive, leaders may decide to avoid action. Although a majority vote could produce a decision, it would also divide winners and losers.

At the same time, this way of proceeding, which federation leaders consider inclusive, conflicts with the norms of religious traditionalists, whom The Associated want to include. Many federation leaders want to increase the organization's fund-raising appeal by making it seem more deeply Jewish, and for them this means developing religious ties. The Associated closes for all religious holidays observed by the Orthodox, serves kosher food at meetings, and closes the Jewish Community Center Friday night and Saturday for the Sabbath. In addition, The Associated has invited some Orthodox and some rabbis to participate in its work. This diversity broadens the federation's fund-raising appeal but also introduces disagreements.

On balance, religious traditionalists bring more socially conservative and explicitly religious positions into deliberations. Liberal federation leaders see decision making as a matter of creating agreements from plural legitimate interests and are prepared to negotiate consensus. Traditional Orthodox, in contrast, believe rabbinical interpretation of the Torah reveals single appropriate policies. For them, disagreements are matters of understanding and error, and differences may be resolved by textual exegesis, not bargaining. Thus, two groups often take conflicting positions and lack common ground rules for making decisions or resolving differences.

Associated leaders and staff try to resolve these conflicts by translating positions into interests that can be served by programs with budgets. The Orthodox stubbornly exploit consensus norms, which allow a minority to prevent decision, while they push for agreement on their principles. Yet, practically, they can be satisfied with Associated funding for their institutions. The non-Orthodox majority, more or less, readily goes along with Orthodox wishes in a tacit, partly unconscious bargain. While federation leaders have great wealth, many admire Orthodox observance and faith. They may feel guilty about what they consider their own laxity, and they desire amity and unity. Even in the face of Orthodox criticism, many want approval from the Orthodox and peace with them, hence they give the Orthodox funds.[6]

Synagogues and The Associated

Synagogues are entangled in the differences between religious and ethnic, religious and civil, and Orthodox and non-Orthodox. In addition, they have institutional interests. They need to pay staff and maintain buildings. They depend on volunteers for much of their work. Small congregations, including many that are Orthodox, have part-time staff and barely adequate equipment and facilities. For all of them, the best targets for fund-raising, leadership, and volunteering are the same people to whom The Associated appeals. Many synagogue leaders feel they come out second best to the federation, which seems to get the biggest contributions and the lion's share of people's time by using full-time staff to recruit them more vigorously and rewarding them more generously.

Synagogue resentment toward the federation expresses more than conflicting interests. Rabbis vocally take the view that The Associated distorts community values by subordinating religion to secularism and materialism. Although synagogue leaders appreciate the social services provided by federation agencies, many wish the federation would give more to religious education and congregational expenses. They see themselves fighting for the community culture.

Culture and Planning

Baltimore Jewish culture is pluralistic. To speak of "the Jewish culture," as of such counterparts as "the African-American culture" or "the Asian culture," is to put a fiction in place of realistic understanding. There is no easy, unambiguous response to multiculturalists' adjuration to respect each group's culture. Thus, a planner who would work with this community, as any community, must anticipate not just that it has a culture, but that it contains several cultures, that they may conflict, and that working with the community depends on learning to recognize the ways people express various cultures in what they say and do. Culture matters deeply, but not necessarily in consistent ways.

The Case Example

During strategic planning, a Relationships Subcommittee was charged with strengthening the community's internal and external relations. One concern was improving the relationship between The Associated and synagogues.

Federation activists had two interests in bringing The Associated and synagogues closer. First, synagogues' autonomy and recurrent criticism of the federation challenged The Associated's claim to be the community's "central address." Federation leaders wanted to bring synagogues at least partly under The Associated umbrella. Second, when synagogue members mistrusted the federation or saw it as irrelevant to their Jewish lives, they did not donate. If the federation could help synagogues with their needs and work with them on projects, congregants and other community members might see it as a warmer, more deeply Jewish institution, and they would be more likely to contribute.

Still, there is no monolithic "synagogue community." Orthodox, Conservative, Reform, and Reconstructionist congregations have different views and interests. Large institutions, with congregations of more than a thousand families, have greater human, financial, and political resources than small congregations of a few dozen families. Within any congregation, members form a board, which hires a rabbi or rabbis and other staff. Rabbis have interests in promoting religious observance. Their congregants may agree or disagree with them about their religious positions, their style, or other matters. One interest shared by all denominations, congregations, clergy, and congregants is increasing resources.

The Associated and synagogues each wanted something from the other. Still, developing closer institutional relations would be complicated, particularly in the context of synagogue grievances.

The Relationships Subcommittee held hearings on synagogues in April 1988, when several rabbis spoke. They voiced old complaints: The Associated recruited leaders and contributors away from synagogues and led people to believe that religion was a secondary part of community membership; the federation rarely consulted synagogue leaders on issues about which they knew and cared; the federation offered services that synagogues might more appropriately provide; instead, The Associated ought to help synagogues raise funds, develop programs, and nurture leadership.

Yet, the Subcommittee could come to no more agreement on these issues than a general recommendation in the plan: "Seek a shared vision of mutual responsibilities, and improve communication" (Strategic Planning Committee 1989:14). The text called for a working group of federation and synagogue representatives to agree on roles, responsibilities, and joint projects.

The Joint Commission on Associated-Synagogue Relations: First Meeting

In February 1992 The Associated convened the Joint Commission on Associated-Synagogue Relations. Yet the eighteen-member "Joint Commission" resembled an

Associated committee. The federation designated members. An Associated activist was chair. Challenged on these things by synagogue members, federation leaders said they were following normal procedures. Even introductions were complicated. After everyone identified him- or herself, a rabbi asked people to reintroduce themselves by synagogue affiliation.

Then, as if none of this had happened, the chairman proceeded to read a script prepared by staff. He defined the group as an outgrowth of strategic planning and read a list of twenty proposals the Commission would consider, grouped under "community organization," "resource development," and "Jewish continuity." As soon as he finished, a synagogue member spoke up: "Some of these are interesting ideas, but who prepared this?" "A small steering group, including staff," responded the chairman. "Who from the synagogue community?" the questioner persisted. The chairman took a stand: "Me. I'm synagogue affiliated. Doris. Dan." Doris spoke up: "Staff did it. And don't be divisive, talking "we" "they" all the time. We are all synagogue people."

A rabbi put the issue explicitly: "Whether the perceptions are accurate or not, we have to start with the synagogue community's perceptions of The Associated. We don't feel involved with The Associated process in an empowering way. The ideas are interesting but ahead of things. We need to look at process questions."

"You mean turf?" Doris, one of his congregants, pushed. "No. Process." "What is a process question?" she asked, puzzled. He explained, "The synagogue community participated early in the process of talking about how we might work on our relationships, but then The Associated finished things up by setting up this committee. Who chose the synagogue community representatives?" "Don't talk about these things today," she warned him, and the chairman and a staff member joined her in attacking the rabbi for creating division.

The rabbi persisted: "The Associated is hierarchical, centralized. The synagogues are decentralized. There are four different [synagogue] units here, none with staff, unlike The Associated." The chairman struck back: "And the synagogues are so different among themselves. They cannot have a single structure. The synagogues introduce turf battles. They interfere with real work. The synagogues are part of community problems." Ignoring the attack, the rabbi suggested a mission for the Commission: "This is the challenge: how does a centralized, hierarchical Associated deal with a decentralized synagogue community?"

A second rabbi addressed the chair angrily: "I feel rejected by you as a rabbi. I would have preferred a generation of ideas at this meeting or from a group with synagogue representation. There are congregational groups." "What," the rabbi pushed, "was the chairman's vision for this group?" "The continuity of the Jewish people," the chairman declared.

As if on cue, the Commission's staff person stood up and wrote the words on a flip chart. Simultaneously, another staff member insisted the recommendations on the chairman's list weren't invented by staff, but were gleaned from earlier statements, before the Relations Subcommittee and elsewhere. The second rabbi took a stand. His rabbinical group "was shocked that this Commission was being created as a result of the testimony earlier." In response, the chairman suggested they "go around the room, and everyone can describe a vision for the group."

A synagogue member started, "If this is to be a cooperative effort, we should have someone from the synagogue community as co-chair." The first rabbi followed by describing at length how hard rabbis work, how much people ask from them. He noted that federations describe synagogues as central to sustaining the Jewish people and he asked for support.

An Orthodox rabbi then staked out distinct ground:

I dissent from the other two, non-Orthodox rabbis. I am speaking for a portion of the Orthodox community. We don't feel competitive with The Associated. We feel separate. We want lines of communication between synagogues and The Associated, to see the needs and resources. We need to get the center to the right (the most traditional parts) of the Orthodox community more involved in The Associated.

Soon after, a Reform rabbi laid out his position:

We need financial resources. Synagogues are always identified with their non-givers or small contributors. They are never identified with their major contributors. They are always claimed as The Associated's major contributors in Associated publicity. I want some credit for that. Also, when The Associated sends members of my congregation to Israel on trips, where travelers are expected to contribute to the federation, I want to know about it, so that I can say a special prayer for them on Shabbat (the Sabbath) before they go and ask them about their trip after they get back. I would also want to tell them about things of interest to them as Reform Jews in Israel. . . . There is the slogan of The Associated "We are one," but I have another version: "We are one—and we are many." The Reform, Conservative, Orthodox, and Reconstructionist—there is tension among them and we need to discuss it. Also, agencies and synagogues have tensions. Is the synagogue or The Associated 'the address' in terms of the outside religious community?

He ticked off religious issues that concerned the community. In short, he said the federation was mainly concerned about raising funds from the wealthy, rather than improving everyone's spiritual well-being and religious education, and the latter should be primary.

An Orthodox rabbi picked up on the acknowledgment of religious differences within the community.

The religious community is diverse, not unified . . . and Orthodox synagogues are small and poor. Many rabbis have another job. People tell me to fax them something from my office. I say, what fax machine, what office? . . . 'Jewish continuity' means different things to different people. For example, for The Associated and for synagogues. For us, it means *halakhically* committed, according to religious law. . . . We (Orthodox) are 15% of the community and we are highly decentralized. There is no real address for the Orthodox community. We have built a parallel community. My congregation doesn't understand what goes on in Reform synagogues and I am sure that the Reform don't understand what goes on in ours.

A congregant of the first Orthodox rabbi endorsed his rabbi's statement, noting divisions within "the synagogue community" and hoping that "The Associated helps bring the synagogue community together." Yet moments later a member of a Conservative synagogue added, "It should also be made clear that there is a difference between the synagogue community and the rabbinical community. It is important to involve the rabbinical community in The Associated. The synagogue community is the laity and they are already involved in The Associated."

A woman began to describe her worries over her children, who didn't seem likely to identify with the Jewish community: "They see the Jewish community as ghettoized and insular. They don't feel ritual as something special the way I do. They think it's something you first turn your brain off before doing." Her children were like many others, she feared, and the community's future was in jeopardy. Another woman agreed. "My children," she said, "need to have pride in being Jewish. I remember when television first came out, and my parents would look at Milton Berle or Groucho Marx and say with pride, 'He is Jewish.'" Although the first woman mentioned religious ritual, the second emphasized ethnic identity.

Seeking to gloss over the many differences proclaimed by speakers, an Associated official focused on the earlier challenge from a Reform rabbi: "We are different and we are the same." Yet, then, one of the Orthodox rabbis attacked a basic premise of federation activity: "The federation adopted the separation of civil and religious. The separation of church and state is a Christian concept. We Jews don't separate these things." The Commission, he concluded, should reassert the religious. After some general conciliatory comments, the Commission staff member politely asked whether people wanted to meet again.

Here, for all to see, are many cultural differences within the community. Significantly, many are associated with distinct, even if not monolithic, institutions. The problem of Associated-synagogue relations involves institutions with different cultures and interests, not personal beliefs or even distribution of funds. The Commission faced the challenge of creating space for members of these institutions to speak respectfully, reflect thoughtfully, and imagine ways of being together while also being separate.

Joint Commission on Associated-Synagogue Relations: Second Meeting

Associated staff circulated minutes that included a list of issues mentioned at the meeting and a request to prioritize them in a mail ballot. Staff convened some of the Commission's Associated activists and some of its synagogue dissidents. They reviewed the polling on issues and agreed on a tripartite agenda. "Community organization" involved institutional relations between synagogues and the federation, "resource development" concerned raising and allocating funds, and "Jewish continuity" involved promoting identification with the community.

When the Commission met again in April, the chairman summarized the pre-meeting, invited discussion of the voting, and then divided people into three groups to set priorities within the categories. After the groups reported back, the chairman asked people to volunteer for one of three subcommittees. He suggested the subcommittees aim to produce a report by December. A rabbi suggested an alternative: "The work of the subcommittees is more significant than the report itself because the process will allow people to establish new relationships. Therefore, we should allow more time. The subcommittee process is the work. And then the report would describe the success or failure of this work."

In federation culture the normal way to address issues is convening a committee, preparing a report that summarizes discussion and recommends a program, and implementing the program. The rabbi was saying that developing relationships among institutions with different cultures required more than a program. After little further discussion, the meeting broke up without agreement on deadlines or procedures beyond constituting three subcommittees.

Apparent ambiguity about the subcommittees' work might be seen as opening space for working on institutional relationships. At the same time, the quick creation of subcommittees could be interpreted as allowing federation activists and synagogue members to flee from the conflict that arose in the arena where, in fact, they had begun to confront differences. In the latter perspective establishment of subcommittees, while a culturally normal way to work at The Associated, might be a retreat from work that aroused anxiety.

The subcommittees began to meet during the summer. Although their histories, all brief, differed, they followed similar courses.

The Subcommittees

The Community Organization Subcommittee met only once—in August. Discussion acrimoniously echoed the disagreements of the first Commission meeting. Associated staff pushed the group to adopt a project, but synagogue members insisted on dealing with institutional relationships first. Perhaps out of anxiety over the conflict, some people left before formal adjournment and the group never met again.

The Resources Development Subcommittee had a longer life, but its course mirrored Community Organization. After frank exchange of biases and grievances at the first meeting, in August members moved in the next meeting to deeper talk about how synagogues and the federation could work together to preserve community life. However, Associated staff came to a third meeting to tell the group to suspend operations while the Jewish Continuity Subcommittee developed a project proposal, after which Resources Development should look for funds. Committee members bargained for their existence by agreeing to survey synagogues about their financial needs and how the federation might help them. The group lost steam, however, after getting back a few questionnaire responses and then hearing from federation staff that Jewish Continuity would survey synagogues. Again, community members began to examine institutional relations, and The Associated displaced that work with project development.

The Jewish Continuity Subcommittee also began in August.[7] It met four times and concluded in April 1993. Meetings were easy going and good humored. Six of the seventeen members were rabbis. Six members were Orthodox, though most from a liberal Orthodox congregation. With staff support, the group moved quickly toward developing a federation-synagogue project for the continuation of meaningful Jewish community life.

The project was a weekend family camp. Synagogues from different denominations would send families. They might worship differently and separately, but shared social and educational activities, would encourage them to discuss their differences, and recognize their commonalities. Assumptions and prejudices, for example, about the Orthodox and non-Orthodox, would break down when people saw one another as similar, for instance, in having common family concerns.

The committee concluded with self-congratulation at having designed a program that represented the success of the Joint Commission. Details remained, such as what The Associated and synagogues would contribute to the camp and how to make it affordable to anyone. More significantly, programming would entail deciding on which Jewish practices to encourage—making judgments about cultural norms. In addition, it was unclear how much a two- or three-day camp could affect everyday lives. Finally, it was uncertain how to attract the Orthodox to observe the Sabbath with non-Orthodox; if that weren't possible, was the community unified?

The camp proposal was more an expression of a fantasy about unity than a realistic plan for it. Quickly developing a project was a way to avoid facing cultural differences. The fact that every denomination has families cannot alone overcome major religious differences. In the end the program was not implemented.

Interpretation of the Case

One could interpret these episodes as normal fund-raising activities designed to interest wealthy contributors. A central feature of the meetings, the suppression of conflict, can be seen strategically. Staff avoid unpleasant experiences that could push donors away. In this way, the story reveals the culture of philanthropy (see Seeley 1989).

This is a story about a particular fund-raising organization, however. Its culture values avoiding conflict, including everyone, and creating consensus. At the same time the federation faces specific, volatile community conflicts, centrally, between Orthodox and non-Orthodox. These tensions threaten Associated claims to represent a single, unified community.

Moreover, The Associated is part of the larger community. On the one hand, the community is pluralistic. On the other hand, many Jews are joined by anxiety about the outside world. Particularly for the older generations, the Holocaust epitomizes the dangers of anti-Semitism. In this context "Jewish continuity" has two meanings. One is positive: a reason to feel Jewish and act Jewishly. The other is negative, or defensive: a need to stay strong against threats. With the latter concern, The

Associated represents Jews across many divisions in a desire to keep relationships amicable and create at least the appearance of unity, so as to discourage attack.

These views can be justified in religious terms. Many Orthodox, for example, believe all Jews were present with Moses at Mount Sinai. Kaplan (1981) gave voice to the view that Jews have a common "peoplehood." Yet for many, the norm of unity has less explicit origins and impulses for harmony come from their everyday experiences living as Jews. From these various roots, these ideas come to the core of Jewish culture.

Strategically, Associated staff and leaders encourage agreement and unity in several ways. First, they try to avoid or suppress conflict. Then they treat differences as matters of self-interest, amenable to negotiation. Staff move away from big issues to immediate stakes. They translate issues into programs, which, in turn, can be translated into funds. Although religious or other cultural differences are not divisible, budgets are.

In practice, these approaches often succeed in bridging conflicts and raising funds. The Orthodox accept whatever they can get from The Associated. Still, they most vociferously criticize federation culture for suppressing the discussion of basic cultural (they would say religious) issues. The case study shows this pattern. At the same time, it offers no evidence to support Associated confidence that harmonious planning is necessarily realistic or effective.

Moreover, cultural differences were not abstract. Synagogues, themselves diverse, and the federation are institutions with different cultures and interests. The case demonstrates the failure of a culture of programs and budgets to deal with institutional relationships. The work of the Joint Commission suggests that when cultural and institutional issues are forced quickly into a program planning framework, the result may look like planning, but it is more likely fantasy.

One might still argue that the case describes planning success. The Associated valued keeping peace more than addressing the problem on the formal agenda and no serious harm ensued from the proceedings. The federation raises a slightly increasing total in each new annual campaign and leaders have since made occasional overtures to synagogues. The Associated, however, also had self-interested reasons for building relations with synagogues, it failed to make progress, and federation activists and synagogue members left confirmed in their beliefs about the incompatibility of the two institutions.

In this frame these episodes show the limits of the Associated culture. They also demonstrate what can happen when a planner uncritically accepts elements of a community's culture. Empathy may lead to a respect narrowly focused on polite acceptance and an identification too close to permit question and challenge. Here, language of "continuity" encouraged planners to believe that understanding and supporting the community required maintaining whatever was part of traditional norms or practice. As a result, planners felt forced to define issues in terms that were familiar but, if the issues were to be taken seriously, unrealistic. They avoided leading community members into reflecting on themselves and perhaps finding new ways of being members of their community.

IMPLICATIONS FOR PLANNING PRACTICE AND PLANNING EDUCATION

Culture matters. The Associated culture led members and staff to define issues in ways that defied resolution. They could not understand that synagogue members' disagreements with them and among themselves expressed different cultural assumptions. They could not see that institutional relations involved culture as much as political or financial interests. Consistently, they did not try to design a planning process that opened cultural assumptions to discussion.

One might explain these lapses politically: Associated planners served what they took to be organizational interests. But they also thought they were serving the community, whose members cherished the past, regarded the outside world warily, and feared losing what was familiar. Thus, the planners kept faith with their community's culture. Crucially, they did not do so just out of abstract belief, but because they cared about the activists with whom they worked, and they cared about what these activists thought of them. Associated leaders did not have to say at any moment that they wished to avoid critical discussion or disagreement because they had tacitly made their preferences known many times. When remarks at a meeting threatened to lead to conflict, palpable anxiety enveloped the room, impelling speakers to cease and auditors to suppress. It was hard for planners to do otherwise.

In these respects, The Associated and the Baltimore Jewish community do not differ much from other communities. They most resemble those that emphasize an ethnic, national, or racial culture, where tradition matters, and where loyalty is important. They are like other minority groups who warily watch the larger world. Planners in this case show the special vulnerabilities of planners who belong to a community: their identity, attachments, and innocent understanding hinder their work. Planners from outside start out differently, but they face some of the same risks in trying to understand local culture.

Practicing Planning

A planner should anticipate that a community's culture will influence who participates in planning, what issues they put on the agenda, how they want to address or avoid issues, how they want to make decisions, and who they believe should benefit. Further, most communities contain several cultures, whose members share some premises but also diverge. A planner should work with community members to design a process that encourages and enables people to discuss their culture with the planner and among themselves. To understand the culture, planners need to get close enough to community practices to identify the assumptions they express. At the same time, planners need to keep enough distance to let them reflect on inconsistencies among assumptions, their overt and latent purposes, and problems to which they contribute. Because this task is difficult and a planner is subject to political and psychological pressures such as those in this case, planners should work in teams. Team members can test their perceptions with one another, consult when they feel confused, and help each other in complicated work.

To say planners should study culture does not mean economic or political interests do not matter. Rather, they have force because community members share assumptions about how things should be. Some beliefs, such as the rules of the game, may resist examination, much less change. Moreover, those advantaged by them may be well organized to protect their interests. In conjunction with understanding local politics, planners should study local culture.

In addition, to say planners should study culture does not mean they should search for esoteric rituals. Culture shows itself everywhere. For example, how community members respond to a planner when he or she enters the community or initiates planning expresses their beliefs about what distinguishes community members from outsiders, what is valued in the community and should be protected, and what is needed to secure community boundaries (Baum 1994). Meetings reveal a great deal about communities: Where they are, who attends, who sits where with whom, who addresses whom, who participates actively and who holds back, how people speak. Besides what people say about their community, all these things present the culture.

Public and private documents tell stories. Some offer explicit accounts of community conditions. Meeting agendas and minutes present someone's version of what matters. At The Associated, as in some other organizations, staff prepare scripts for chairmen; both the text and the fact that leaders use scripts reveal the culture. In addition, planners can ask people about the meanings of events, reasons for doing things, and the like. Finally, mundane events can open the door to understanding. For example, early on at The Associated, I overheard two women on the planning staff talking about one's new hairdo. This talk about personal appearance, later echoed by others in other settings, led me to pay attention to organizational and community concerns about having things look neatly in place—themes highlighted in the case study. This is multicultural sensibility in planning practice.

Preparing Planners

To practice this way planning students must acquire specific substantive knowledge. They need to learn about culture—what it is, what shapes and maintains it, what it influences, how it is related to social structure, how and why it varies, how and why it changes, and how one's own culture affects one's ability to understand others. They need to learn about group and community dynamics—how and why people form groups, how groups interact with one another, why relationships change, and how one's own group attachments affect one's ability to interact with others. They need to learn about individual, group, and community psychology—what people desire from one another, what makes them anxious, how these desires and anxieties affect cultural beliefs, how culture shapes the expression of desires and anxieties, how these feelings influence individual affiliations with groups, how they influence group and community dynamics, how group attachments influence the expression of feelings, and how one's own desires and anxieties affect one's ability to interact with others and understand their culture.

In addition, planning students need particular skills. They must be able to conduct research in and about communities in ways described above. They must be able to organize and work with groups ranging from small teams to community task forces or assemblies. They must be able to act deliberately and self-consciously with others, reflecting on their conscious intentions and unconscious motives, observing the consequences of their actions, and learning from the results to design new actions.

Finally, planning students need to conduct their work with a special attitude. They must question the meanings of what they encounter. They should assume that communities have cultures that give members' activities and interactions meaning, but they should not assume they know these meanings until they encounter community members. In addition, they should anticipate diversity—not simply that one group may differ from others, but also that any group may contain internal differences.

Universities offer courses in areas such as cultural anthropology, community psychology, community organizing, group process, organizational behavior, and clinical psychology. Yet planning programs neglect this territory. The clearest indicator is what most curricula present to students as "methods": ways of doing research, rather than practicing planning (Baum 1997c). Moreover, most research courses teach methods of analyzing quantitative data about people or places, rather than qualitative information about communities collected with community members. In these ways planning programs teach students to keep their distance from communities.

More courses should involve students in communities in ways where they must define problems and identify remedies with community members. They will find that planners' conventional repertoire—mainly physical and economic development programs—will not always respond to people's concerns. They should understand the gamut of amenities that matter in a culture and for which planners might take responsibility—good housing, decent jobs, safe streets, inviting public space, and efficient transportation, for example, but also good schools, affordable nutrition, responsive health care, and dependable social supports. No planner can do everything, but students need to appreciate the range of what planners might do. Even in courses where students concentrate on a few aspects of a community, they should have the experience of struggling to understand how the community thinks and how that thinking shapes what planners are expected to do and what they can do. From such educational experiences, students can learn to plan with a multicultural sensibility.

NOTES

1. The attitude described here is what psychoanalyst Melanie Klein (1952) called the depressive position. It is a developmental stage that may emerge in infancy where a child comes to recognize that the mother is a separate person who is both bad and good and that the child, too, is both good and bad. The child can then recognize similarities and differences with the mother without attaching rash judgments of goodness to the similarities and badness to the differences. This is the beginning of realistic thinking about others and the possibility of empathy.

2. Argyris and Schön (1974, 1978; Argyris 1982; Schön 1983, 1987) offer examples of how professionals, including planners, and their clients resist reflecting on assumptions.

3. Evans and Boyte's (1992) description of "free spaces" uses different language to explain how communities can create the mental and political space to reflection and change themselves. The formulation of the planning process as a transitional space draws on Winnicott's (1953, 1967) discussion of transitional objects.

4. Baum (1997b) describes the planning process and study method in detail.

5. Woocher (1986) describes how federation participants find in their civil activities emotional experiences similar to others' religious experiences.

6. Baum (1997b) analyzes these relationships in detail.

7. Baum (1997b) analyzes the work of the Jewish Continuity Subcommittee in detail.

REFERENCES

Argyris, Chris. *Reasoning, Learning, and Action*. San Francisco: Jossey-Bass. 1982.

Argyris, Chris and Donald A. Schön. *Theory in Practice*. San Francisco: Jossey-Bass. 1974.

Argyris, Chris and Donald A. Schön. *Organizational Learning*. Reading, MA: Addison-Wesley. 1978.

Arnstein, Sherry R. "A Ladder of Citizen Participation." *Journal of the American Institute of Planners* 35, 1969:216–24.

Baum, Howell S. Transference in Organizational Research. *Administration and Society*, vol. 6, no. 2, 1994:135–57.

Baum, Howell S. Community Organizations Recruiting Community Participation: Predicaments in Planning. Paper presented to Association of Collegiate Schools of Planning, Fort Lauderdale, FL, November 1997a:6–9.

Baum, Howell S. *The Organization of Hope; Communities Planning Themselves*. Albany, NY: State University of New York Press. 1997b.

Baum, Howell S. Teaching Practice. *Journal of Planning Education and Research*, vol. 17, no. 1, 1997c:21–30.

Baum, Howell S. "Ethical Behavior is Extraordinary Behavior; It's the Same as All Other Behavior: A Case Study in Community Planning." *Journal of the American Planning Association*, vol. 64, no. 4, 1998:411–23.

Cahn, Louis F. *Man's Concern for Man*. Baltimore: Associated Jewish Charities and Welfare Fund. 1970.

Checkoway, Barry. "Six Strategies of Community Change." *Community Development Journal*, vol. 30, 1995:2–20.

Davidoff, Paul. "Advocacy and Pluralism in Planning." *Journal of the American Institute of Planners*, vol. 31, 1965:331–38.

Elazar, Daniel J. *Community and Policy*. Philadelphia: Jewish Publication Society of America. 1976.

Evans, Sara M. and Harry C. Boyte. *Free Spaces*. Chicago: University of Chicago Press. 1992.

Fein, Isaac M. *The Making of an American Jewish Community*. Philadelphia: Jewish Publication Society of America. 1971.

Forester, John. *Planning in the Face of Power*. Berkeley: University of California Press. 1989.

Geertz, Clifford. *The Interpretation of Cultures*. New York: Basic Books. 1973.

Goldberg, David Theo (ed). *Multiculturalism*. Cambridge, MA: Blackwell. 1994.

Hollinger, David A. *Postethnic America*. New York: Basic Books. 1995.

Kaplan, Mordecai M. *Judaism as a Civilization*. Philadelphia and New York: Jewish Publication Society of America and Reconstructionist Press. 1981.

Kellman, Naomi. *The Beginnings of Jewish Charities in Baltimore*. Baltimore: The Jewish Historical Society of Maryland. 1970.

Klein, Melanie. "Notes on Some Schizoid Mechanisms" in Joan Riviere (ed) *Developments in Psycho-Analysis*. London: The Hogarth Press and the Institute of Psychoanalysis. 1952.

Krumholz, Norman and John Forester. *Making Equity Planning Work*. Philadelphia: Temple University Press. 1990.

Levin, Marshall S. and William S. Bernstein. "Community in Concert: Baltimore's Vision Toward the Year 2000." *Journal of Jewish Communal Service*, vol. 67, 1991:194–204.

Liebman, Charles S. *The Ambivalent American Jew*. Philadelphia: Jewish Publication Society of America. 1973.

Liebman, Charles S. *Deceptive Images*. New Brunswick, NJ: Transaction Books. 1988.

Mandelbaum, Seymour J. "Open Moral Communities" in Mandelbaum, Seymour J., Luigi Mazza, and Robert W. Burchell (eds). *Explorations in Planning Theory*. New Brunswick, NJ: Center for Urban Policy Research, Rutgers. 1996:83–104.

Marris, Peter and Martin Rein. *Dilemmas of Society Reform*. Second Edition. Chicago: University of Chicago Press. 1982.

Medoff, Peter, and Holly Sklar. *Streets of Hope*. Boston: South End Press. 1994.

Parsons, Talcott. *The Social System*. New York: Free Press. 1951.

Schön, Donald A. *The Reflective Practitioner*. New York: Basic Books. 1983.

Schön, Donald A. *Educating the Reflective Practitioner*. San Francisco: Jossey-Bass. 1987.

Seeley, John R. *Community Chest*. New Brunswick, NJ: Transaction Books. 1989.

Stein, Howard F. *The Dream of Culture*. New York: Psyche Press. 1994.

Strategic Planning Committee, Associated Jewish Charities and Welfare Fund. Building a Stronger Community: Toward the Year 2000, vol. I. Baltimore: Associated Jewish Charities and Welfare Fund. 1989.

Thomas, June Manning, and Marsha Ritzdorf (eds). *Urban Planning and the African American Community: In the Shadows*. Newbury Park: Sage Publications. 1997.

Turner, Terence. "Anthropology and Multiculturalism: What is Anthropology that Multiculturalists Should Be Mindful of It?" in David Theo Goldberg (ed). *Multiculturalism*. Cambridge, MA: Blackwell. 1994:406–25.

Wallace, Michele. "The Search for the 'Good Enough' Mammy: Multiculturalism, Popular Culture, and Psychoanalysis." in David Theo Goldberg (ed). *Multiculturalism*. Cambridge, MA: Blackwell. 1994:259–68.

Winnicott, D.W. "Transitional Objects and Transitional Phenomena." *International Journal of Psycho-Analysis*, vol. 34, 1953:89–97.

Winnicott, D.W. "The Location of Cultural Experience." *International Journal of Psycho-Analysis,* vol. 48, 1967:368–72.
Woocher, Jonathan. *Sacred Survival.* Bloomington, IN: Indiana University Press. 1986.

CHAPTER 9

Multiculturalism in Rural America

Mark Lapping

Multiculturalism in rural America has two distinctive but interrelated dimensions. First, there is the matter of the rural itself within an unrelenting urban milieu. Second, there is the multicultural reality in and of itself—rural people are diverse and this diversity is poorly understood and too little appreciated.

THE RURAL AS THE "OTHER"

Everywhere, so it seems, the march of urbanization appears inevitable, entirely desirable, the mark of "progress," the accepted norm. This view is as true among planners and policy makers as with others. A strong urban bias exists within the planning community, and this orientation and worldview sees multiculturalism almost exclusively in urban terms. Either by neglecting or denying the existence of multicultural issues in village and hinterland areas—let alone the importance of rural people and the integrity of rural living—planners and policy makers exhibit a myopia and a certain arrogance of place. This urban bias consistently fails to recognize the great diversity in and among rural people and places and has led to a fundamental unwillingness to treat in a serious and meaningful way the many issues and problems confronting rural people, their families, and communities.

Neglect of the rural, itself a salient dimension of the multicultural problem, is abetted and undergirded by our myths about rural people. On the one hand, we have tended to idealize rural people as virtuous, hard-working, self-reliant, stable, patriotic, and inherently democratic. In a word, they are extolled as being "Jeffersonian." Such people can solve their own problems and, thus, require very little in the way of support and help. It is often remarked of even the rural poor, for example, that "at least they can grow their own food." On the other hand, we have also stereotyped rural people as inbred, intolerant, ignorant, and grotesque. David Bell has accurately labeled this the anti-rural idyll, or the "hillbilly horror and rural slasher" theme (Bell 1997:94–108). Within this stereotype rural people are seen as being fundamentally degenerate and the very best that one can hope for them is as quick a transition to the urban as possible. Only an end to the isolation and depravity of rural life will help. Perhaps, not surprisingly, this has been the direction of many rural development policy initiatives that really sought to relocate people to the cities or to urbanize the countryside (Lapping 1992; Lapping and Fuller 1985).

Both stereotypes see rural places as different kinds of cultural archetypes: one the handsome, bucolic landscape peopled by competent and independent individuals, stable and intact families, and cohesive communities; "the other" the wild, isolated, paranoid, and violent world of Appalachian "Deliverance" or militia America. Neither view accurately reflects the reality, which falls well in between these simplistic characterizations. No matter which myth is purveyed, the same result is achieved: the reality of so much of rural America and its many problems—persistent poverty over the generations; poor-quality housing and physical infrastructure; the lack of adequate health care, policy protection, and educational, nutritional, and social services; the erosion of extended family support systems; self-destructive behaviors; and the overall collapse of economic opportunity—lies hidden away or masked. Indeed, when compared with their urban and suburban neighbors, rural Americans "are far more likely to be poor, less well-served by medical and other health services, less educated, more isolated from economic and social opportunities, and persistently at a disadvantage in accessing governmental, educational, and technological expertise" (Benzinger, Lapping, and Blakely 1994:213)

The marginalization of rural places and people is symptomatic of the hegemonic nature and power of "metropolitanism" throughout American culture. A genuinely multicultural perspective in planning reflects the many ways in which Americans actually live and work. This implies that the authenticity and legitimacy of rural life in its many dimensions is no longer dismissed or ignored altogether.

But this is not enough. It will not do simply to include the rural within a larger perspective. Rather, the very density and nature of diversity that exists in rural areas must also become plain and better understood. Failure to do so results in a loss of both human dignity and human potential.

THREE COMMUNITIES, THREE DIVERSITIES

The very diversity of rural America can best be understood through a discussion of some of the most compelling planning issues confronting several specific rural communities: Native Americans, African Americans, and the Amish. Each of these groups, among the many in every region of the country, gives meaning and definition to the notion of diversity and multiculturalism in rural America. Further, each group confronts problems long associated with planners—land use and land tenure, community economic development, and participation and stakeholdership in public policy issues.

Native-American Communities

Far from being a homogeneous group, the approximately two million Native Americans are themselves very diverse and are diffused across the landscape. As one rural sociologist has accurately noted of them, "although few in number, American Indians have an enduring place in American society" (Snipp 1995:316). Native Americans are found in every state, and in some, such as Alaska, New Mexico, South Dakota, North Carolina, and Oklahoma, they form a numerically significant part of the overall population. Many Native Americans are highly acculturated, while others are not. Some of those in the latter category may not speak English, are active in subsistence forms of economic activity, hold traditional belief systems, and have little contact with the larger metropolitan world. Significant numbers of Native Americans live on reservations, while still others have migrated to towns and cities. The majority of Indians are rural, however, and they are among America's poorest and most destitute populations. A clear majority of them live on reservations, of which there are nearly 300 ranging greatly in size and resource endowment. These reservations have been accurately described as "the Indian ghettos of America, characterized by high infant mortality, ill health, low education, and poor housing" (Durant and Knowlton 1978:159). Native Americans are, moreover, highly dependent upon welfare, transfer payments, and other governmental support programs. In a very real sense, the history of rural Native Americans is one of transition from traditional self-sufficiency and self-governance to contemporary dependency and poverty.

Only recently has this situation changed as both federal authorities and tribal governments are trying to enhance tribal sovereignty and local economic self-sufficiency. The absence of investment capital, business and entrepreneurial skills, and an adequate resource base, among other barriers, have frustrated these attempts. Land, water, timber, and mineral resources are not individually owned by Indians or the tribes themselves, but rather are held in trust by the federal government. This legal condition has made collective decision-making, a tradition among native people, a precondition for planning and development activities. It has also created some degree of friction between Indian and non-Indian communities when conflicts have risen over fishing, resource harvesting, or water rights.

Persistent poverty, lack of job opportunities and adequate educational, social, and health services, high levels of dependence on publicly provided services, and the organizational and administrative context in which reservations exist have led to a degree of individual and communal desperation. This has forced more than a few tribes to accept almost any form of development on their reservations, such as toxic waste dumps and other "not in my backyard" land uses. Not many tribes have been as resilient as the Kaibab Paiute nation in Arizona, which recently rejected such a facility (Flora et al 1992:244). Seizing almost any legal opening, reservations have exploited their tax-exempt status to create smoke shops—where tobacco products are sold tax-free to Indians and non-Indians alike—and to introduce several forms of gaming or gambling. Governed by the federal Indian Gaming Regulatory Act (IGRA) of 1988, gambling has been termed a "remarkable development" that "has generated a stream of cash income that was once unimaginable" for reservation residents and tribal governments and organizations (Snipp 1995:315). Not without controversy, especially between traditionalists and modernizers within tribes, gambling has begun to transform some tribes, such as the Pequots of southern New England, whose gambling and resort facility in Connecticut (Foxwood) routinely grosses well in excess of $500 million annually. The challenges, of course, are not only to create employment and a "high road" to enhanced job skills for tribal members, but also to avoid some of the negative social problems that often accompany gaming, and especially, to capture capital for reinvestment to diversify the economic base of the reservation for future generations.

When the Passamaquoddy nation settled a land claim with the State of Maine in the mid-1970s, it invested a good portion of its capital in a construction company, built new homes on its reservations, established some fishing-related enterprises, and developed a blueberry farm in down east Maine. The goals of such investments remain job creation and greater self-reliance, along with the ability of the tribe to retain its younger members, who have been leaving the community for opportunities elsewhere.

No matter where the tribal organization exists or the location of the reservation, rural Native Americans will continue to engage in planning and community development activities for the very same reasons that majoritarian communities do. The persistent poverty and malaise of Indian communities make the need that much greater and planners will have as their priority the maximization of job-creation opportunities, long-term diversification of the economy, provision of key social services, sensitive stewardship of tribal assets and natural resources, and mitigation of spillover or externality effects. And to the extent possible, Native-American planners will have to aid in the process of selective closure of external forces if traditional options are to exist.

Rural African-American Communities

As with Native Americans, rural African Americans are also caught in a web of persistent poverty and dependency. Unlike Indians, however, rural African Americans tend to be concentrated in pockets of the American South. Though their numbers are far larger than those of Native Americans—perhaps as many as five million people, or 13 percent, of the total Black population of the country—they also seem to be largely invisible to most planners and policy-makers alike. When planners speak about African-American communities, they tend to perpetuate the myth that with the great migrations of this century, all African Americans left the deep South for northern and western cities (Lemann 1991). As Daniel Lichter astutely noted, "Rural Blacks, most of whom live in the South, are more spatially dispersed than urban Blacks, less visible, and apparently easier to ignore" (Lichter 1989:116). The fact remains that significant areas of the South, such as the Black Belt, which includes part of eight states, contain large African-American rural populations. These are overwhelmingly poor communities. Of the 205 counties nationwide classified as "persistent poverty" counties by the U.S. Department of Agriculture for the years 1950 to 1984, all but eighteen were in the South, and most had substantial African-American populations (Bellamy 1988). In the 1990s the 147 Black Belt counties contained nearly 75 percent of the total rural African-American population; all of these counties were classified as "persistently low-income" by the U.S. Census Bureau (Williams and Dill 1995:344).

The impoverishment of the rural African-American community is hardly new. Its roots lie back in slavery and have been reinforced by decades of "Jim Crow" segregation, institutionalized racism, and the conflation of race and class and, to a slightly lesser degree, gender. This is most especially the case, though not exclusively, in the South. Problems have been exacerbated further by the ongoing decline in the number of African-American farmers and the concomitant loss of farmland ownership by Blacks. In 1920 African Americans accounted for 14.7 percent of all American farmers; by the mid-1980s the percentage fell to less than 2 percent (Schulman et al 1985:41; Banks 1985; Hoppe et al 1986; Beaulieu 1988). In an agrarian region, where land traditionally bestows power and provides other opportunities, the decline in Black ownership—precipitated as it was by far too many cases of corruption and racism—is symbolic of the growing peripheralization and marginalization of rural Blacks.

While the ongoing plight of small farmers throughout America cannot be exaggerated, no matter their race or ethnicity, Black Belt counties also lack the sorts of off-farm employment opportunities that have become essential for farm family survival. Economic growth in some portions of the South has been nothing short of spectacular over the last several decades. In those areas where African Americans predominate, like the Black Belt, the lack of industrial development and other forms of economic growth remains a chronic problem that led one student of the situation to talk of the reality of the "two Souths" (Rosenfeld 1988:57). Markusen and her colleagues have documented that high technology firms purposefully avoid locations with large Black populations (Markusen, Hall, and Glasmeier 1986). Two other analysts have labeled this phenomenon of dual southern economies "boondocks capitalism" (Falk and Lyons 1988). In previous years this has meant the loss of the young to urban places in other parts of the country; now the migration is concentrated in the booming urban South (Blevins 1971).

While economic development much enhanced housing and infrastructure, a robust educational system for people of all ages, and a more equitable distribution of land and other resources are all central to any planning strategy for rural African-American communities, there remains the need to confront the residual power and influence of old elites throughout the South (Lapping 1990). Such individuals, groups, and institutions have for too long squelched progress and have employed racism to frustrate the emergence of new leadership and new coalitions. As Williams and Dill (1995) have wisely written, "Attacking the problems of rural African Americans also represents a direct assault on the plight of poor White southerners, who are caught up in an economic and social system that inhibits their abilities to place class above racial interests."

Any agenda for economic and community development for African-American communities must include some emphasis on combatting those social and behavioral factors that contribute to instability and vulnerability, such as single and teen parenting, the erosion of extended family support systems, self-destructive behaviors like substance abuse, and other pathologies of poverty (Fitchen 1995:24–67). Planners will also have to work to reverse those conditions that Hyland and Timberlake call the "ideology of underdevelopment," wherein class, race/ethnic, and gender relations are compromised by a pattern of "paternalism, fatalism, and fractionalism," which is the inheritance of generations of racism and dependency (Hyland and Timberlake 1993:97).

Rural Amish Communities

The case of the Amish represents a different aspect of rural diversity and multiculturalism. Scattered in small community settlements across the country, Lancaster County, Pennsylvania, contains the most dense concentration of Amish congregations in the United States. A religious community reinforced by ethnic and linguistic attributes, the Amish, or "Plain People," constitute a faith community that is often at odds with the nature, texture, and direction of contemporary mass society. The Amish are one of the few functional examples of sustainable rural development in North America (Lapping 1997:29–39). They are predominantly farmers, though in recent years they have also established a number of micro-enterprises based on crafts, furniture making, construction, food preparation, and blacksmithing—traditional rural pursuits (Kraybill and Nolt 1995). Living among the non-Amish, they seek to remain aloof but not entirely detached from the majoritarian culture. Theirs is a "struggle with modernity," as two scholars have noted, rather than a struggle against modernity (Kraybill and Olshan 1994). The distinction is an important one because the Amish are not separatists in the conventional sense of the term. Rather, they seek selective cloture and to retain the ability to determine what from the larger society they will integrate into their faith-community and lifestyle and what they will reject. The foremost modern student of the Amish, Donald B. Kraybill, astutely writes of them that "the hallmark of Amish culture has been its highly integrated community where all of the bits and pieces of social life, from birth to death, are gathered into a single system." This has allowed them to "avoid the fragmentation that accompanies modernity" (Kraybill and Olshan 1994:33).

Natural growth within the Amish community has made farming increasingly difficult for all who would like to engage in it. As one analyst has put it, "the Amish population is burgeoning at a time when affordable farmland for the upcoming generation has become scarce" (Place 1993:192). The absence of land has, in fact, forced some Amish families to relocate elsewhere. The recent establishment of some Amish businesses has created some planning conflicts between the Amish and non-Amish communities. The same zoning and planning ordinances that were developed to protect and preserve Amish farmland now make it difficult for some Amish to establish businesses on or near their home farms.

"Especially where farmland is scarce," notes Elizabeth Place, "cottage industries in rural areas provide necessary employment for the Amish, who prefer to work at or near their homes and within their ethnic group. To protect the cohesion of their community in this manner, the Amish have approached local authorities, seeking accommodations between their lifestyles and zoning ordinances" (Place 1993:200). Additionally, the environmental consequences of some Amish agricultural practices, such as the land spreading of manure, have been identified as a substantial source of nonpoint water pollution. All about them, then, the Amish face important challenges to their very way of life. Given their reluctance to involve themselves in governmental affairs and their faith's prohibition against membership in organizations, it is exceedingly difficult for the Amish to participate in the local planning process.

Unfortunately, the Amish have become something of a cultural curiosity. Their distinctive dress, style of living, mode of transportation, and overall "otherness" have led to their commodification, especially by the growing tourist sector, which has capitalized on everything that is "Pennsylvania Dutch"—cuisine, crafts, dress, and landscape. The growth of the tourism sector has led to sprawl and incomplete land development. In a very real sense, parts of Lancaster County, as well as other areas where the Amish live, have begun to exhibit some of the same characteristics and problems that other gateway communities encounter (Howe, McMahon, and Propst 1997).

How and in what ways planners can represent the interests and needs of the Amish, harmonize them with those of the larger community, preserve a landscape under very heavy pressure, and provide the appropriate balance between economic connection and social disengagement constitute their own challenges. Planning to preserve the options of those whose relationship to the process is ambivalent, at best, should not present an obstacle to the profession.

CONCLUSION

Ethnic and racial diversity in America's rural areas and hinterlands abounds. In addition to those diversities mentioned above, Latino communities, Asian-American populations, distinctive regional cultures, such as in Appalachia and the Ozarks, Franco-American areas, and others, can be found across the American landscape. Likewise, rural America is home to those with diverse sexual orientations and gender preferences, a not insignificant number of people with disabilities for whom rural living constitutes a particular set of problems, and people of all age groupings, belief systems, and ideas. In short, rural America is diverse, textured, and highly idiosyncratic. The practice of planning in such places must increasingly reflect these facts. Most importantly, however, planners must come to take rural people and their needs seriously. They are not simply the "people left behind," as one government report in the 1960s labeled them. More appropriately, they are, in the words of the late Michael Harrington, part of "the other America" (Harrington 1971). Planning has always been about meeting the needs of these people and communities. It could not be otherwise if it is to fulfill its role in strengthening the fabric of the nation's civic culture and pluralist character.

REFERENCES

Banks, Vera J. *Black Farmers and Their Farms.* Washington, D.C.: U.S. Department of Agriculture. Rural Development Research Report No. 59. 1985.

Beaulieu, Lionel (ed). *The Rural South in Crisis.* Boulder: Westview Publisher. 1988.

Bell, David. "Anti-Idyll: Rural Horror" in Cloke, Paul and Jo Little *Contested Countryside Culture: Otherness, Marginalisation, and Rurality.* London: Routledge. 1997.

Bellamy, Donald L. "Economic and Socio-Demographic Change in Persistent Low-Income Counties," a paper presented at the Annual Meetings of the Southern Rural Sociology Association. New Orleans. 1988.

Benzinger, Nancy, Mark Lapping, and Edward Blakely. "Rural Diversity: Challenge for a Century" in *Planning and Community Equity.* Chicago: The Planner's Press. 1994.

Blevins, A.L. "Socio-economic Differences Between Migrants and Non-Migrants," in *Rural Sociology,* vol. 36, 1971:509-519.

Durant, Jr., Thomas and Clark Knowlton. "Rural Ethnic Minorities: Adaptive Response to Inequality," in Ford, Thomas (ed), *Rural USA: Persistence and Change.* Ames: Iowa State University Press. 1978.

Falk, William and Thomas A. Lyons. *High Tech, Low Tech, No Tech: Recent Industrial and Occupational Change in the South.* Albany: State University of New York Press. 1988.

Fitchen, Janet. "Why Rural Poverty is Growing Worse: Similar Causes in Diverse Settings," in Castle, E. (ed.), *The Changing American Countryside.* Lawrence: University Press of Kansas. 1995.

Flora, C., J. Flora, J. Spears, L. Swanson, with Mark Lapping and Mark Weinberg. *Rural America: Legacy and Change.* Boulder: Westview Publishers. 1992.

Harrington, Michael. *The Other America.* New York: Penguin. 1971.

Hoppe, Robert, et. al. *Social and Economic Environments of Black Farmers.* Washington, D.C.: U.S. Department of Agriculture. Rural Development Research Report No. 61. 1986.

Howe, Jim, Ed McMahon, and Luther Propst. *Balancing Nature and Commerce in Gateway Communities.* Washington, D.C.: Island Press. 1997.

Hyland, Stanley and Michael Timberlake. "The Mississippi Delta: Change or Continued Trouble" in Lyson, Thomas A. and William Falk (eds), *Forgotten Places: Uneven Development in Rural America.* Lawrence: University Press of Kansas. 1993.

Kraybill, Donald B. and Steven M. Nolt. *Amish Entrepreneurs: From Plows to Profits.* Baltimore: Johns Hopkins University Press. 1995.

Kraybill, Donald B. and Marc A. Olshan. *The Amish Struggle with Modernity.* Hanover: University Press of New England. 1994.

Lapping, Mark B. "Among the Poorest of the Poor: The Economic Development Imperative for Rural African Americans." Working Paper No. 23, Center for Urban Policy Research, Rutgers University. 1990.

Lapping, Mark B. "American Rural Planning, Development Policy, and the Centrality of the Federal State." *Rural History,* vol. 3, no. 2, 1992:219–42.

Lapping, Mark B. "A Tradition of Rural Sustainability: The Amish Portrayed" in Ivonne Audirac (ed.), *Rural Sustainability in America.* New York: John Wiley and Sons. 1997.

Lemann, Nicholas. *The Promised Land.* New York: Alfred A. Knopf. 1991.

Lichter, Daniel T. *Underemployment and the Utilization of Labor in Rural America.* Washington, D.C.: Aspen Institute. 1989.

Markusen, Ann, Peter Hall and Amy Glasmeier. *High Technology America: The What, How, Where, and Why of Sunrise Industries.* Boston: Allen and Unwin Press. 1986.

Place, Elizabeth. "Land Use" in Kraybill, Donald B. (ed), *The Amish and the State.* Baltimore: Johns Hopkins University Press. 1993.

Schulman, Michael D. "Problem of Land Ownership and Inheritance Among Black Smallholders." *Agriculture and Human Values.* Summer 1985.

Snipp, C. Matthew. "American Indian Economic Development" in Castle, E. (ed), *The Changing American Countryside: Rural People and Places.* Lawrence: University Press of Kansas. 1995.

Williams, Bruce B. and Bonnie Thornton Dill. "African Americans in the Rural South: The Persistence of Racism and Poverty" in Castle, E. (ed), *The Changing American Countryside: Rural People and Places.* Lawrence: University Press of Kansas. 1995.

CHAPTER 10

Multicultural Planning in Deed: Lessons from the Mediation Practice of Shirley Solomon and Larry Sherman

John Forester

> Respect conceived as the mere acceptance of difference stymies interaction, dialogue, and mutual learning. It enjoins us to appreciate others but not to engage them in mutual critical reflection. The end product of multiculturalism misinterpreted as mere acceptance can thus be isolation (We're us and they're them). This is not respect but neglect.
>
> —Fay 1996:240

Planning conflicts often involve not only resources like land and money, but relationships that involve personality and politics, race, ethnicity and culture, too. In part, this is one of the challenges of a multicultural planning practice—the ability to anticipate and respond sensitively and creatively to complex differences of standpoint, background, race and gender, cultural, and political history. Burayidi put the challenge succinctly in chapter 1 when he wrote, "For planners, the practical imperative is no longer whether planning ought to be culturally sensitive, but how (it can be so)? How do planners accommodate one group's view of the physical environment when it conflicts with that of another group? More importantly, the question remains whether . . . planning can be sensitive to diverse cultures and yet maintain a unified public realm?"

This chapter takes an unconventional approach to these questions by examining planning practice not across types of cases or across regions or even types of problems, but from the inside of the practice of environmental and community mediators who have squarely confronted practical questions of multicultural difference. This analysis is just one part of the author's work in progress studying planners' and mediators' responses to challenges of ethnic, racial, and cultural difference.[1]

By considering the accounts of mediators, facilitators, and planners who have worked in the face of multicultural challenges, we can explore the demands of such practice. Perhaps we can improve upon the accounts we review, but more likely we will find many suggestions for improving current planning practice. The point throughout will not be that planners should become formal mediators, but that planners in multicultural settings can learn a great deal from skillful and insightful mediators.

The accounts from which the following excerpts have been taken were collected through a research project involving focused telephone interviews with planners identified and recommended by colleagues as being thoughtful and experienced in the face of ethnic and multicultural disputes. These accounts, of course, do not provide recipes for the cure of ethnic tension, racial hatred, and/or cultural animosity. But the accounts, and the commentary that follows, do provide suggestions, insights, practical reflections, and elements of a multicultural repertoire of skills and capacities that the planning profession can consider and build upon.

In what follows we consider most closely the extended comments of two planner-mediators facing environmental and community disputes involving, in turn, ethnic and gender differences as well as conflicting interests, histories of suspicion, power imbalances, and opportunities for learning and collaboration, too. Having moved from South Africa to the rainy Northwest in Seattle, Washington, Shirley Solomon describes her work of bringing together Native Americans and non-Native county officials in Skagit County, Washington, to settle land-use disputes over issues of growth control, sovereignty, and land use more generally. We consider, too, excerpts from the practice story of Larry Sherman, a city planner turned mediator, who provides instructive comments about dealing with difference in the context of a dispute among Toronto schools involving issues of gender and power. Along the way, we will consider the reflections, too, of Gordon Sloan and Wallace Warfield, thoughtful and experienced mediators with long histories of work on public disputes.

DISPUTES ARE ALWAYS ABOUT MORE THAN THEY SEEM: SAVING FACE AND THE NECESSITY OF ACKNOWLEDGMENT

In complex planning disputes community members often contest relationships as well as resources. Not only do parties worry about gaining resources, but they also worry about being exploited, taken advantage of, accepting an explicitly subordinate position. They worry, too, about public perception. Will a decision or agreement mean that their community looks weak or humiliated, vulnerable or worthless? Consider the comments of Wallace Warfield as he reflects on his mediation of contentious community conflicts (Forester 1994):

You have to understand, for the African-American community organization's representatives, for their community, and from the standpoint of the people they feel they represent, their coming to a joint problem-solving process can almost be viewed as a sell-out. And so it's almost important for them to take a position and stance that's very positional, very argumentative, if for no other reason than, at least symbolically, to send a signal back to their communities that they purport to represent "We're not selling you out."

When relationships matter in these ways—as they often do—creative and rational solutions to problems may never be explored if one or more parties feel that they will look stupid, weak, or vulnerable as a result. If they cannot save face, then, by having the seriousness of their concerns acknowledged, they may quite understandably resist what otherwise seems to be good solutions (Forester 1999a).

Listen, too, to an experienced Canadian mediator, Gordon Sloan, who had recently completed an eighteen-month mediated-negotiation process to devise a land-use plan for Vancouver Island. Sloan tells us how such acknowledgment can facilitate the ongoing conversation of parties by freeing them up from more rigid and defensive positions and so enabling more flexible and fresh statements of underlying interests they hope to serve (Forester and Weiser 1996):

Acknowledgment is important for the mediators, but it's also important for other parties in disputes to acknowledge something that someone else has done, in this case to articulate their interests rather than hammering away at their position. It's then possible for the person who's just made the movement to see that they haven't compromised. They haven't been seen to have given something up.

Without that acknowledgment they're just making that change and shifting from positions to interests against a brick wall. It's a tree falling in the forest and there's no one there to hear it. So they have to have acknowledgment. Typically, in a multi-party table, they get it from those at the table. The mediators don't have a whole lot of work to do in acknowledging because there are so many others there who have done their courses that they know that it's worth doing that. They're inclined to anyhow because they're relieved. But the mediators also have an important role to play.

The mediators, and planners playing de facto mediating roles, have an important role to play, in part because every negotiation is really two negotiations in one. First is a negotiation about content—the issues at hand. Second is a negotiation about relationships—how the parties will continue to relate to each other as they move forward. Both are within the negotiation process and in the eyes of the larger community as well.

That double structure of all negotiations, as we shall see, has important implications for the kinds of doubt, and the kinds of explorations, that negotiators and planner-mediators need to do, too. For if future events will be uncertain as long as our abilities to predict the future remain poor, the quality of parties' relationships and the meaning of participants' moves promises often to be significantly ambiguous, which turns out not to be such a bad thing!

AMBIGUITY

Little may be certain in a multicultural world, but the pervasiveness of ambiguity seems to be uncontroversial. In multicultural settings parties may talk past one another, misread cues, fail to understand what the other finds significant, and fail to understand how even the most apparently innocuous procedural rules may privilege some cultural backgrounds to the detriment of others. Nevertheless, ambiguity in multicultural settings should be explored, not minimized. If the issues are too clear, little room for negotiation may be possible. Not surprisingly then, mediators, like many planners, can find the very ambiguity of issues to be a real practical source of opportunity (See Krumholz and Forester 1990). Working on tribal-county government negotiations in Skagit County, Washington, for example, Shirley Solomon tells us:

There was just enough "grey" attending all these issues at that point in time that we could go ahead. I like ambiguity. You can do a lot with ambiguity. My feeling is that there's no such thing as black and white anywhere. Life is, in fact, shades of grey. Not everybody thinks that, but I do. We worked very effectively in that grey area, suggesting to the county that the tribes had rights and interests, and that it behooved the county to get into some collaborative mode with the tribe, as a partner, not trying to prevail in a hierarchical way with the county being on top, so to speak. They were quite willing to listen. I never ever had a door slammed on me. They were reluctant to a certain extent, but reluctant only because of the appreciation that it was a volatile undertaking, that it involved political risk, would take forever, and because they had no real sense of what would come of it. They were not at all resistant to the idea of partnership. (Personal Interview with Shirley Solomon)

Ambiguity, she suggests, may raise doubt, but through that doubt we can learn. Maybe there is something here that we can work out, the sentiment may be. When the issues and interests and desires and obligations of parties are not clear, those parties may be more, rather than less, willing to meet and to listen, discuss and explore issues.

CREATING SAFE SPACE

But those discussions can, of course, be volatile, risky, time-consuming, and threatening, too. Thus, the theme, noted again and again by professionals who work on public dispute resolution of creating safe spaces in which parties can meet without fear of exploitation, attack, or even violence. Listen to Solomon's account of creating safe spaces in which public conflicts can be explored:

If you can create a safe place, wherein people can just talk about things without it being product-driven or where there are no specific stakes, where you can just come together, talk about things, weigh some options, test out some ideas, you can do a lot. That was really what the first phase was all about—to create that safe place we carried messages back and forth between different people in county government and different people in tribal government. We engaged both the elected officials and the key policy staff people. One county commissioner, in particular, was willing to talk about things. The planning director was willing to talk about things. A couple of his staff people were willing to talk about things. On the other side, the general manager of the tribe and several of the senators were interested in just testing the waters and seeing what could happen.
We began laying out the premise that given the underlying land ownership pattern, no one could act unilaterally. Things were stalemated. The county had constituents on the reservation. The county felt that they had jurisdictional authority on the reservation. The tribe certainly had what they felt was jurisdictional authority. Both were essentially saying the same thing. So there was a conflict. These were initially very informal get togethers, the tribal government and the county meeting face-to-face. It was people with the cloak of office. It was not a formal get together between two governments. It was the county commissioner and a couple of people from the tribe just playing around with notions of what

could happen. We had quite a number of meetings and finally they had the sense that they probably had talked through things sufficiently and they were ready to put together a Memorandum of Understanding. The Memorandum of Understanding said that the tribe claims jurisdiction over the whole reservation and the county claims jurisdiction over the non-Indian owned land on the reservation. That's the way it was. They weren't going to dispute that. No one was giving up anything, but they felt that if they spent some time engaged with one another, they could, in fact, come up with something. (Personal Interview with Shirley Solomon)

Solomon teaches us that safe spaces are not found; they are created. They depend on the qualities of the participants and the prior work of finding interested parties willing to discuss their commitments and interests, either willing or perhaps, in more cases, needing to meet with others and listen. Then, parties cannot just talk about things, they can weigh some options and do still more together, too; test out some ideas together that otherwise would be mere speculation by each party about what they (the others) think and would consider.

The back and forth movement is crucial too, for here is a process of checking with the parties, aligning a quality of participation that will allow actual conversation, a reprieve from being so product-driven that broader issues and concerns could hardly be explored. Similarly, the back and forth movement between parties enables mediators and planners to match parties who can bring some authority or knowledge to the table together. Both parties here were interested in testing the waters. Both parties knew and were willing to acknowledge to one another that they had something to learn together.

Solomon suggests, too, that the very lack of formality helped their discussions—even while representatives having formal authority were present together. In this meeting, which was not held as a formal get-together between two governments, the parties were all the more able to spend their time just playing around with notions of what could happen. But that playing, of course, was crucial to exploring new options and new solutions that this tribe and county government had not devised before. That playing was not entertainment, but creative exploration, the play of design. That play allowed not just exploration and testing, but the development over time of understanding, an understanding that subsequently became formalized into a Memorandum of Understanding between the tribe and county officials.

Creating safe spaces for discussion involves more than good intentions, more, too, than the back and forth aligning and matching of parties' temperaments. In many settings just because the conventional settings of public hearings or courtrooms are so adversarially aggressive, the ceremonial design of innovative public policy conversation can be an important signal to all parties that they are about to engage in a different—fresh and nonthreatening—kind of exploratory conversation in a different, deliberately designed setting. Solomon shows us how she signalled that shift to a different kind of conversation as she worked with the county and tribal governments:

How did we accomplish that shift, from their place, within that place, to their place together? We ceremonialized the activities. To the whole concept of open space, safe space, we added

sacred space. There was the whole notion of getting to higher ground. There's got to be a
call to common purpose or to higher purpose, and what better to use as the galvanizing force
or the underlying connection as your place? If you cannot think in terms of protecting your
place and of making your place better, not only for yourself but for those who will come
after you, your family and the family of your neighbors, then I can't think of a better
connector myself.

We've done a lot of convenings and gatherings and, by and large, one always gets into "my
view versus your view," and "my needs versus your needs." What we did here was sweep
that aside and have people talk about what that place was to me, for me, and how my life and
the life of my family both before me and after me, are in that place. I was surprised at the
history that the vast majority of people had there. For instance, the one county commissioner
who proved to be a real leader in this effort was third or fourth generation. His people had
come there as farmers way back when.

He felt close to the land. He characterized his feelings differently from a tribal leader, but
you began to see the similarities and the common ground. Perhaps not the common ground
per se, but the opportunity to find the common ground. I think the video we did captures
it really quite beautifully, people talking to one another, and people just talking about what
came out of it all for them. We used a talking circle, with different people opening the
circle. (Personal Interview with Shirley Solomon)

Here we see that the ceremonial aspects of the conversation enabled a quality of
thought and revelation that a formal public hearing could hardly have achieved. By
invoking a notion of sacred space, without pushing any particular theology to be
sure, the mediators and parties alike found a way to discuss the meaning of the land
whose multiple and conflicting uses they were ultimately to resolve. By first
shifting the conversation away from the conflict of goals and objectives, away from
particular disagreements, to underlying issues of how the parties had come to value
that place, the parties were able to begin to see the similarities and the common
ground. Again, perhaps not the common ground, *per se*, but the opportunity to find
the common ground.

THE INDIRECT PEDAGOGY OF STORY-TELLING

We can think of this as taking a step to the side to allow three steps forward;
stepping aside to discuss personal histories (how my life, and the life of my family,
both before me and after me, are in that place) that in turn opened surprising
connections to be explored between the parties. The facilitator describes the
simplicity, but also the surprising power, of such story-telling.

So the objective of this was to create a dialogue and a sense of community that would
forward the way that people did governance together. This happened . . . in four different
activities.

The first was to get familiar with one another, to learn something about one another as
individuals and then learn something about your place within this place. Because your place
in a place is quite different, everybody's perspective of place is quite different. There were
a number of other activities. One activity after the two presentations, after the two sets of
storytellings really, was to take historical and present day slides gathered from all over the
place, also from participants, and just put the slide up and ask people to talk about what

feelings and stories, and histories and what have you, were triggered by those particular images. That was just a phenomenal activity, just an amazing activity. (Personal Interview with Shirley Solomon)

We can begin to see an important lesson about negotiation and conflict resolution. In many cases, backing up or stepping to the side may be necessary before pushing ahead will be possible. Practically, it seems the most straightforward thing to do, many times, to make progress between conflicting parties will be not to go straight forward, but to step aside, to consider issues and histories from a new angle, then to move forward after that, with new insights into the issues, the other parties, and the practical options that may be created.

But this stepping aside will be confusing to some, all the more when appearances are deceptive. Oftentimes the sentiment will be one of: "Let's get down to business! Time is short. What's all this process stuff? Let's deal with the issues!"

APPARENTLY NEUTRAL PROCEDURES ARE REALLY SUBTLY SELECTIVE FILTERS

This sounds rational enough, certainly direct enough, but it may be culturally constructed, too, in a way that does not help parties actually to resolve complex, multicultural disputes. Too often such directness can, deliberately or inadvertently, become a power play in itself, an attempt to control the agenda and style of discussion, the timing and procedures; and thus, in effect, not just the rules of the game, but possibly the outcome of the game itself. All this, at times, may be tucked into an apparently simple request for getting down to business! Listen again as Shirley Solomon reflects both on her work with Native Peoples and on her experience as a woman sensitive to the shaping of rules of conversation and public discourse:

What you had here was essentially two worlds, two cultures. People will say though, "Well, hell, you know, I mean that's nonsense, because Indian people have been around White people for a century or more. They run their governments. Their governments look very similar to any other form of government. They know how to conduct meetings. They do Robert's Rules, all these things. What are you talking about, two worlds?"

But the fact of the matter is, an Indian world view is fundamentally different from a Western world view and the structures that we brought with us are those that have been super-imposed over Indian peoples, like it or not. Now you've got a real and pretty hefty callous that has built up. If you want to shape-shift things, if you want to shake them around and have different outcomes, then you've got to come at it differently. You've got to allow that which is not much prevalent in the way we do things—you've got to allow that forward.

I also, as a woman, have had great resentment, over time, to the way in which conversation and dialogue has been just obliterated from the way in which we conduct our business. The whole relational aspect of our work has been neutered, just sterilized, I think. There's no opportunity to do anything other than speak to the topic at hand. Our public engagement processes are just criminal in my mind. A public hearing, for instance, is just an abomination because it requires people to indulge in hyperbole. You've got two minutes to speak and you've got to be as rash as you possibly can in order to make a point. There's no opportunity for discourse. (Personal Interview with Shirley Solomon)

Solomon poses a deep challenge here for planners and public administrators. She links the design of public processes—here, the conventional public hearing, for example—to the quality of the resulting public intelligence we achieve through such designs. In many public hearings we produce less listening and learning than hyperbole, she argues, and we find that instead of cultivating attitudes of practical exploration of joint options, we have strategies likely to engender anger, distrust, and defensiveness—to be as rash as you possibly can . . . to make a point. These observations are similar to the point Burayidi makes in chapter 1 regarding the challenge, in part, to understand how an apparently neutral, formal set of procedures can be experienced as so completely not neutral at all. As Solomon illustrates with a powerful account of one participants' discomfort, if not humiliation, when faced with the restrictions of Robert's Rules of Order, she goes on:

That is what we were trying for in this fellowship circle thing—thoughtful discourse—where I had the opportunity to tell you something about me, the way I see the world, the way I think about things, and you not being in rebut mode, waiting to say, "Yes, but . . . " Or poised to use what I am saying as a way of making your own point better, but instead to really see my world, see things from the vantage point that is mine and mine alone. People on the video talk to this.

There's one piece that just brings tears to my eyes every time I hear it. It's one of the tribal leaders, who you have to sort of bend forward to hear because he doesn't articulate, he doesn't move his lips in a way that helps you hear very easily. But what he says is, "In those meetings where it's Robert's Rules of Order, I know that I either have nothing to say, or what I have to say counts for nothing."

It just pierces me every time I hear it. That is, by and large, the world for Indian country and Indian issues. There is not the opportunity to bring forward who and what they are in totality, so what you have are what are derogatorily termed the "thousand year speech," where an Indian person will stand up and talk about what and who they are, how they see things, what has happened to them, and people tune them out because the "thousand year speech" is an attempt to gain standing and status. It's in an environment that is unsympathetic. It's "Out of Order," so to speak. It's not part of the agenda, but it *is* a valiant and courageous attempt on the part of that particular Indian person, taking on the role of spokesperson, to let all these uncaring others hear just something that is different. But it's ineffective. (Personal Interview with Shirley Solomon)

Solomon teaches us that formal rules become less abstract when they are put into practice in specific instances. In an actual meeting the use of such rules subtly privileges some styles of conversation and discussion over others, honors and values some qualities of exposition and representation, of accounts and stories, over others. When parties have adopted the rules themselves, of course, this may be unobjectionable. When such use of rules becomes a deceptive means of control and devaluation of one group by another, public deliberation is in trouble.

THE MOVEMENT TOWARD COLLABORATIVE INQUIRY: LISTENING TO AND SEEING MANY DIFFERENCES

Solomon goes on to describe an alternative metaphor the parties used in this case, the metaphor of collaborative learning:

In our case, the intent was to get more familiar. That was the whole and sole purpose of the undertaking. How did we get people to not turn off? It involved the whole notion of collaborative learning. There's a wonderful image. I've never seen this, but I've heard several people talk about it. There's a temple in Japan with a garden. The rocks are arranged in such a way that one has to walk all the way around in order to see every aspect of it. The principle is that no one individual could possibly know all that there is to know about anything, about this piece of art, let alone anything else. So in order for the larger truths to be revealed, all the voices, that are part of whatever it may be, need to be present and need to be heard. (Personal Interview with Shirley Solomon)

But what guiding role did the conveners of the meeting play? When planners convene similar exploratory meetings, what qualities of discussion might they cultivate? Listen as Solomon describes her work as the facilitator of the county-tribal government conferences:

Then we did role play exercises—an entire day taken up with that. The third day was beginning to talk about all sorts of aspects of the particulars of Skagit county from, again, the different perspectives. It was quite directive in some instances, having free-flowing conversation some and in more facilitated conversation so that you're essentially being asked to think about specific issues and to think about how to talk about those issues in ways that press things forward. We asked them to be mindful of time constraints and how to get the most out of discussion, how to put forward your issues in a way that enables others to better hear and better address them, and then in ways that sift out common concerns and common ground.
  I think what people also understood was that there is no requirement that the county and the tribe get into lock step over anything. They understood that there are differences that are enduring differences, and that there are differences that make not a whit of difference to collaborative endeavors. (Personal Interview with Shirley Solomon)

Here we begin to see the mediator's encouragement of several different kinds of conversation— sometimes free-flowing, but sometimes directive—to think about specific issues and to think about how to talk about those issues in ways that press things forward. Here the mediator is trying to cultivate not argument but more perceptive judgment in a diverse group, enabling others to better hear and better address issues, in ways that sift out common concerns and common ground.

INTERDEPENDENCE CREATES OPPORTUNITIES

Solomon continues, telling us both about simple strategies and strikingly successful results:

But it's finding those places that are potential hot spots, or that are fertile opportunities for collaboration. We had to figure out what to do in those instances where they may be problems. It could be something as simple as, "Don't ever go off half cocked over something. Always check in with your counterparts, or with others, to find out what the specifics are. Do not accept on face value what you read in the newspaper, what you hear from people, but rather get to a reasonable fact-set before you decide on what it is you need to do." Many, many, many opportunities came as a result of that one particular day.

Then the last day was, "Okay, what are we going to do now?" I had hoped for a concurrence that they would continue with the process and agree to meet, agree to do some things and then meet in the future. What they wound up doing was writing an open letter to the community. First the mayor, then another city person, and then the county, offered a resolution acknowledging the tribe as rightful government and pledging a cooperative mode of dealing and being. I never would have thought of that. It was far, far beyond what I would have hoped for. It was bigger than anything I would have hoped for. Then there was just talking about very concrete things that they would want to do with one another in the interim. It's made a difference to intra-governmental carryings-on in Skagit County. I mean, it's one of those events that stands tall. (Personal Interview with Shirley Solomon)

THE CHALLENGE OF CREATING PRACTICAL FUTURES FROM PAINFUL PASTS

We should hardly think that this work is easy, just a matter of convening reasonable people to talk about public disputes. The conditions that mediators and planners face are anything but simple, anything but simply rational. Especially when cultural and ethnic difference is involved, deep histories of identity and domination can provide the context in which the affected parties see today's dispute. Painful histories provide complex challenges to planners and mediators alike. Too much attention to these histories can escalate or polarize public conflicts further, or turn their discussions into improvised therapy sessions. Too little attention to these histories, certainly, will provoke more rage than understanding, more suspicion than trust (Herman 1992; Rogers 1990).

Solomon's story can teach us not only about caution in the face of explosive histories, but also about the place of storytelling in setting the stage for beginnings of reconciliation. Her account finds echoes in others (Forester 1999a,b; see profiles of Hughes and Sobel in Forester and Weiser 1996):

From the way people asked questions, you could just see that it was mesmerizing, with people becoming engaged in that story and beginning to think about what life was like there for those people. But the whole thing needs caution. You've got to be really careful. You have to look for certain people to make these presentations—people without baggage. It certainly cannot be someone who has been in conflict with some of the participants at the time. It's very delicate because, again, you're dealing with a great power imbalance—great loss, great change, guilt, fury, lots of things. I mean there's a cauldron under this that you're trying to help release in a way that doesn't just blow you all to hell but starts the siphoning off of all this torture and pain.

We had the professor that came from the community college in the area talk about when the White settlers came—so it was historical. But his manner was just a little more abrasive than the first speaker on pre-settlement history, so he was harder to deal with for the participants. But the story he told is a story that needs to be told. When White settlement occurred, the environment of Skagit county changed dramatically. There had been spruce marshes and cedar marshes, and all those ancient, ancient, ancient trees got cut down and the area was drained and diked, and it became farmland. That brought prosperity to those who moved in and usurped Indian land, and it brought extreme dislocation to those who were displaced.

That's a story that needs to be conveyed. It needs to come out. It's the history of the place, and it's in the recognition and the appreciation of that that reconciliation occurs. Stories have to be told in order for reconciliation to happen. (Personal Interview with Shirley Solomon)

Solomon teaches several lessons here, that we need to consider in more detail. She tells us that our history is not simply past, not just gone before, but with us today in pain and suffering for some, fury and anger, a cauldron that constantly threatens to simmer, if not boil over. Clearly, she suggests that planners and mediators alike ignore these painful histories at their own risk. She also suggests that these stories of extreme dislocation need to be conveyed. They have to come out not simply for educational purposes but for deeper reasons tied to redemption and reconciliation. In the stories of the dislocation and suffering, the past losses suffered and defining identity today, can recognition and appreciation of trauma lead to reconciliation (Forester 1999a; Herman 1992). She puts the practical point squarely: stories have to be told for reconciliation to happen.

Of course this does not mean that stories automatically produce recognition, appreciation, and reconciliation. But Solomon's mediation experience does suggest that when parties bring histories of victimization and pain they are likely to do better. They are able to act more effectively with others, when their histories are acknowledged rather than ignored, when their particular identity is recognized rather than swept under the rug, when the participants are treated as the particular people they are, rather than as some typical, generic citizen without the distinctive history that they have—the particular history that their parents and grandparents, and their parents before them, lived.

TELLING DETAILED STORIES CAN HAVE MANY PRACTICAL RESULTS

In practice settings, the stories of what has happened to my land and my family, the stories of my hopes for my land and my family's future are not just mere stories, for in telling these stories, parties do a great deal of work. Most importantly, these stories tell as much about the teller as the teller tells about events. These stories produce surprising details, and so help to clarify and identify problems and opportunities. These stories provide descriptions of character that inform reputations, too. They invoke values and so raise questions of obligations and responsibilities. In facilitated negotiations, storytelling often becomes the source of a good deal of learning (Forester 1999a; Susskind and Field 1996 and 1999). Solomon suggests that the parties learned a good deal from one another and through the workshop process, too:

But there's more than skills-building going on. Certainly people were able to talk about past experiences. What they wound up saying was, "Knowing what I know now, I know now more than I knew four years ago. Had I had that information, we could have strategized internally and handled X, Y, Z situations somewhat differently. There are some tenets that I can carry forward and that I can start institutionalizing."

That was, in fact, what people did and said. "You know, I can think about these things in a slightly different way. If I want to be able to work with you, and if we want to be able to clean up Skagit Bay, or if we want to be able to get that new road in, or whatever it is, then we better strategize and figure out some institutional approach here that accommodates and attends to and addresses all these potentially polarizing circumstances." (Personal Interview with Shirley Solomon)

Solomon's comment is striking not simply because it reflects the parties' appreciation of new information, but because it suggests a shift by the same parties from a perspective of what are *my* problems to what are *our* problems, a shift from thinking about *me* to thinking about *we*. The more interdependent the parties, the more crucial is the recognition.

LEARNING THROUGH DOING AND THE WORK OF IMPROVISATION

But the work of facilitating or mediating land-use and environmental conflicts is always challenging. We need to learn from mistakes, as well as to appreciate successes. Consider this account of running into big problems:

We were coming at it from a number of different perspectives and then trying to build a bigger truth, if you will. We had a hell of a lot of trouble that day. It just went quite poorly for part of the day. Part of it is that someone that we had invited in as a process person put together a role play and what she came up with just didn't fit. It didn't fit right. Several of the people couldn't get into it because they just wanted to be themselves. They wanted to talk about their perspectives, their issues from their perspectives and represent themselves. So we labored and looped and had just a very difficult time and finally, we stopped that and got into: "You as you," and "You as who and what you were," and talking about your issues, as opposed to taking these roles.

How did we realize that something was wrong? There's a feel out of a group. You know all the non-verbals, all the weird energy that starts coming up. You lose people. They get up. They walk around. They shake their heads. They do all the things that you'd never want to see your group doing. It was an excruciatingly difficult time; what I did was that I just took the group back, I guess. It was awful. It was a very delicate thing. What I felt I had to do was to re-direct the group. But the only way I could re-direct the group was to take charge of the group. And in doing so, we had to pass the baton from one facilitator to the other and do it in a way that was affirming in some way.

All this is experimentation. It's not like there's a prescription and there's a cookbook, and you're following it, and it all goes the way it should go. (Personal Interview with Shirley Solomon)

Even with invited experts or process people, things go wrong. The planners convening and facilitating contentious meetings must be able to improvise and adapt. Here we see the cues and clues: not explicit complaints listened to and acted upon, but a perception that you lose people—they get up, they walk around, they shake their heads, and we get a glimpse of how it felt to be managing all this as it went wrong. It was an excruciatingly difficult time before this facilitator took the group back, redirected the group in a delicate way to shift the leadership from the invited facilitator, and to do that in a way that was affirming rather than negative, forward- looking rather than recriminating. This facilitator leaves us with a crucial lesson about managing conflict-resolution processes. All this was experimentation, a matter of being pragmatic in real time and being critical, too, recognizing clearly that there was no pre-defined prescription, no simple steps to follow to guarantee that the process of dealing with differences would all go the way it should go, in the cookbook.

As she explained the failure in this case, Solomon helps us to be more sensitive to the interplay of culture and process, procedures that seem quite neutral on substance. Switching roles, for example, might be culturally more difficult for some groups than others, within broader ethnic groups, tribes, local communities too:

> The role play just was not the right technique to use because all these people are very much engaged in these issues, and it's passionate for them. They learned not at all from having to take the other's role. For instance, the Swinomish general manager was asked to be a developer. He just didn't want to be a developer. So he tried to do it for a while and then just got aggravated with it. One of the tribal leaders never got it, couldn't get into it, and just couldn't believe he wasn't able to represent who he was himself. Maybe if it had been outlined in a way that they could have seen where they were going with it, it could have encouraged some perspective taking and appreciating the other's positions, but it just didn't get there. It didn't get there, and it didn't get there, and finally you had a choice, just continue to let it go and maybe it will come out the other end, or you can start to paddle, you know. (Personal Interview with Shirley Solomon)

Seeing the difficulties of the role play, understanding that the perspective-taking goal that can often be achieved in similar situations was not going to be successful here, Solomon started to paddle, to change course. Perhaps these initial difficulties fueled some of the constructive efforts that followed:

> So, then we switched gears and moved it to them talking from their hearts, from where they really were at. We started to really get to some of the things that they felt they should be doing together. What we wound up doing was still talking about the river, but talking about it from people's experience with specific issues they wanted to think about and talk about, including the river from their perspective.
> From there it got bigger. What they wound up doing was exactly what we had hoped they would do, and that was to start bringing it down to the ground. What opportunities were there to be more collaborative? What were the specific things that they needed to begin to work on, because not only were there opportunities there, but things that could really cause great difficulty if they did not come together. (Personal Interview with Shirley Solomon)

Here we see a crucial shift in the process of recognizing issues and others. The parties moved from the virtual recognition of another's perspective, the imaginary work of seeing issues as someone else might to the immediate recognition of felt experience, as parties began talking from the heart about what mattered. Rather than considering imaginary viewpoints, this began to disclose where the tribal leaders and county officials really were. In doing so, they became less hypothetical and more directly attentive to some of the things that they felt they should be doing together, moving then to the exploration of real opportunities to be more collaborative. Here were the crucial questions. What did they need to begin to work on—not just objectives to accomplish, but threatening difficulties to prevent?

MODELLING A NEW APPROACH: MEDIATED NEGOTIATIONS AND COLLABORATIVE PROBLEM-SOLVING

Exploring collaboration between conflicting parties, of course, works against the grain of initial suspicions, histories of distrust, presumptions that others will never be reasonable, and so on. Listen, now, to another mediator, Larry Sherman, originally trained as a city planner, as he describes the initial resistances to collaborative work and the subsequent possibilities for getting more information, for education about the process, for training that can help parties take better advantage of their negotiations with others (Forester and Weiser 1996):

In the first instance, people's response to collaborative problem-solving is disbelief. People do not believe you are offering them another process that actually works the way we say it works. But, once they've understood that we really mean business, there's then a tremendous surge of need for more information and more education, and they're willing then to equip themselves much better. They first want more information about the problem.

The second reaction of people is, "Oh my goodness, we need a lot more information." They're much more willing, then, to sit and be told things by others than they were before, because it's not an authoritarian thing any longer. They now realize that they're in part of the driver's seat and that they need that information.

The third step is the bargaining and the collaborative problem solving, where they really need the skills, and they are willing to acquire more of them. So I find that the desire for training doesn't come until farther down the line. (Personal Interview with Shirley Soloman)

INTERVENTION AND EMPOWERMENT: CREATING THE CONDITIONS FOR COLLABORATION

The interest in collaboration depends on the conditions of safety and protection, however. The more that parties feel that they must work actively to defend interests from opposing claims, the more parties feel that they must defend themselves from personal attacks, the less likely they are to feel free to explore mutual gains and collaborative relationships. As we proceed we will consider how the basic elements of collaborative problem-solving and mediated negotiations may pertain to public dispute resolution and multicultural differences more generally. Referring to a dispute between boys' and girls' private schools in Toronto, Sherman tells us how he created the conditions for collaborative inquiry in a conflict involving students and principals negotiating over issues of gender, administration, and policy:

How did I enable the students to feel empowered enough to confront the administration as they did? That was the profound nature of that comment directed to me that "This discussion wouldn't be happening if it weren't for you."

The role of the mediator, or whatever we're going to call this person, is absolutely essential to creating a safe place for dialogue. I think the primary thing for a mediator to do is to create a place that is safe for the parties who don't agree and who are not used to talking to one another so they can do that. If the mediator can get the people to feel that it's safe to say something that is relatively untested, particularly when there's not a power balance (which there wasn't certainly in this case) that's very important. I think that happened here. The students actually learned not only that it was okay for them to say those things, but that, having said them, they were respected. (Personal Interview with Larry Sherman)

Sherman signals several issues here that deserve a great deal of attention. Echoing Solomon, he suggests to us that creating such safe places can happen in several contexts. He does not imply that only mediators, narrowly defined, can create such safety for parties. When he speaks of the role of the convener, he immediately suggests other possibilities by referring to the role of the mediator, or whatever we're going to call this person.

Sherman suggests, however, that the role of the convener is absolutely essential to creating a safe place for dialogue. The parties come, he suggests, without agreement, antagonistic, and not used to talking to one another. He suggests, though, that the parties can indeed come to talk and explore issues and options, but left to themselves, they may simply begin to argue. Crucially, this planner-mediator helps us to see that power and inquiry are intimately connected. With power differences, weaker parties may not only feel disrespected, they may also feel they are not treated as equals. They may feel unable to ask questions and explore issues that are central to the disputes at hand.

But what enables mediators, or planners, or whatever we're going to call this person, to create that safe place, that safe space for conversation and collaborative inquiry? Sherman suggests that his power to do that came from several sources:

How'd I make that safe space? I become very active in giving respect to things that are said. I respond, often before the other party responds, by saying, "Oh, that's interesting" or "What do you mean by that?" or "Can you elaborate on that?" or "I could imagine the other party might be asking you this question," which makes it a little easier on the other party.

So I could say, "Gee, I could imagine that some parents might be saying to you, 'Well, there's no way you're going to spend another fifty dollars on a fee'" or something, and it might be easier than the principals saying that. I would say sometimes to the principals, "Well, wait a minute. If I were a young person, a young student in your program, this would be my reaction to what you just said." It makes it a little easier then for the students to come back and reinforce that, if it's true. I might turn to the students and say, "Is that right?" So I try to animate a discussion that gives that balance on the one hand, and makes people feel easier about having a discussion. It's okay. It's not an argument—it's a discussion.

I'm balancing the power by interjecting into the conversation, in the beginning, things that one side might be saying to the other. If it was coming from the other side, it would likely be received as more confrontational. It's attenuated through me; therefore, it's more benign and that's why I like that whole issue of contextual knowledge, because a mediator can't do that without knowing something about the subject. (Personal Interview with Larry Sherman)

As a land-use planner with broader mediation experience here, Sherman shows us how his role as a third party between disputants might help to role-model a quality of conversation by interjecting questions of his own, by providing a bit of balance, reinforcing a reaction or line of questions that the weaker party may have been reluctant to air, raising a concern to make its exploration less confrontational than if one party or the other had raised it. Sherman focuses on the quality of inquiry and the exploration of options; the parties are worried about one another and protecting themselves. So Sherman not only tries to animate and embody a quality of inquiry, then, but he tries to make people feel easier about having a discussion. He tries to change the expectations, and the fears, of the parties by trying to show them that it's okay. It's not an argument. It's a discussion.

So the confrontational quality of the conversation is attenuated and more benign because the mediator can, in fact, raise an issue of concern gently as the third party. Doing that is delicate, of course, for the mediator can be challenged, too, for bringing up extraneous concerns. Thus, we see this mediator's checking with the other party, "Is that right?"

He tells us that raising an issue in that way takes more than delicacy or good judgment. It takes contextual knowledge of the field as well. That knowledge required seems a good deal less than the expertise of insiders, but a good deal more than ignorance of the issues altogether. Increasingly it seems, public dispute mediators recognize that they, singly or in teams, must have enough knowledge of the dispute at hand to be able to ask good questions and to follow the parties' conversations. They acknowledge, too, that a complex public dispute may call for such a wide range of expertise—from law and finance, to toxicology, to marine biology—that the mediators can hardly be expected to have substantive expertise in each of the relevant fields.

WHEN TO MEDIATE YOUR DISPUTE? WHEN YOUR ALTERNATIVES ARE EVEN MORE UNCERTAIN!

But how, in situations of local political conflict over land or other resources, policies or regulations, can mediators actually help parties, at times, to turn the corner from confrontational arguments to exploratory discussions? Mediators can do this, in part, because the parties have little to lose in mediation and a good deal to gain. Without the mediator, they face business as usual, which means not just power relations and antagonism as usual, but also the usual uncertainties of knowing when anything will be settled, and whether anything apparently settled will last or be opened up once again. The promise of the mediation process, for all parties, is to do better than that. Many parties may give a third-party facilitator or mediator a try, especially if they can do so without giving anything up in the process—by keeping the option to leave that process if and when they wish. This means, of course, that joining a process of mediated discussions, or whatever we may call it, must not require any of the parties to look weak, to be unable to save face, to be publicly humiliated just by appearing to join these discussions. Sherman teaches us that the beginning of the promise of mediation comes when parties recognize their interdependence:

The same kinds of things that happened in this little session with the schools reflect the same principles that apply in much larger kinds of cases. It's about solving problems collaboratively and it's about reforming conditions. We accept so many of the conditions because we can't get the parties to sit down in the same room and exchange ideas. I'm sure it's the same in volunteer-mediated community disputes, because these people are neighbors. I find those kinds of disputes fascinating because it doesn't occur to them when they come in that they're neighbors, what it means to be a neighbor, and the interdependency that is implied in being neighbors. (Personal Interview with Larry Sherman)

FACILITATING COLLABORATIVE INQUIRY: ASKING QUESTIONS, BUILDING TRUST, AND MAKING IT WORK

How can mediators work with the parties to explore that interdependence, that need to work things out together, and the ways of doing that that can be better for both that can realize mutual gains for both parties? Sherman provides a strikingly instructive account:

I'm pretty active in the discussion as a third party and I ask people what they really mean, to clarify what they've said, or I sometimes inject an assumption. I say, "Let me assume that somebody could read something into this." In other words, I'm always probing to make sure that everybody has a clarity about what it is they're agreeing to. As a rule, I never allow minutes to be taken or tapes to be made. I rely totally on the flip charts and I tell people that this is the group memory and that if it's wrong, it's got to be corrected, and very often it is. Very often people will say, "Don't use that word. Use some other word," or "That's not what I really said," or "That's not what I really meant." They see me cross it out and change it. Everybody does. I think that helps a lot. That helps you build trust, and then confidence, among a group of people who felt dis-empowered. (Personal Interview with Larry Sherman)

Here we see a few of the nuts and bolts of third-party intervention, of dealing with differences and creating a shared aura and reality of respect and recognition. This planner/mediator tells us not just that he probes actively to clarify issues and intentions. He does not interpret neutrality as the lack of such probing. He takes the role, at times, of a virtual interested participant who could understand or misunderstand a party. He draws out a possible proposal or refusal or implication with "Let me assume that somebody could read something into this," could understand what's just been said in this or that way. By doing so he explains, he helps everyone to make sure that they know just what they are agreeing to—thus strengthening not only the durability of agreements, but the confidence of the parties as they go.

HONORING ADVERSARIAL PARTIES WHILE CREATING A
COMMUNITY OF COLLABORATIVE INQUIRERS

Sherman teaches us more, too, by telling us that he gives up the deceptively easy conveniences of taking minutes or using tape recordings in favor of constructing on flip charts a common record then and there with the group, a group memory that is theirs. If it's wrong it's got to be corrected, and very often it is. Of course, there is no simple matter of correcting grammar, even though he tells us that very often people will say, "Don't use that word. Use some other word." They say, too, "That's not what I really said," or "That's not what I really meant," and then as importantly he tells us, "and they see me cross it out and change it. Everybody does. I think that helps a lot."

Here we see not just the creation of a group memory but the creation of a group itself, a working group in which everyone is respected, one in which everyone sees that their words are taken seriously and not just their words, but what they meant, what they intend. They come to see that together, as a group, they can work with the mediator/facilitator to explore issues and proposals for action. This is about power as much as about group process, though, Sherman explains. Everybody's seeing that they can change the record. This helps you build trust and then confidence among a group of people who felt disempowered. How does that trust and confidence get built? His lesson is worth repeating: "Both writing down what they say and feeding it back to them is very important, particularly in the beginning, until they are convinced that what they're saying is really being registered and that there's some respect for what they think. That's the device for doing that" (Forester and Weiser 1996).

What we have seen in these extended excerpts from Shirley Solomon's and Larry Sherman's accounts of their mediation practice can help us in several ways (see Forester and Weiser 1996; Susskind and Field 1996, 1999). First, we have these practitioners' substantive lessons and insights to consider. We need to assess carefully the importance of setting ground rules, assuring safe spaces for participants, building confidence and trust, developing recognition and respect, as well as collaborative inquirers within the conflict resolution process itself.

Second, we have been able to consider an ethnographic approach to these same questions. By taking the reflective accounts and practice stories (Forester 1993) of practitioners seriously, we can try to stand on the shoulders of practitioners to see further than we can by ourselves. We can try to take the friction of the practitioners' efforts as touchstones for our own challenges—so that we may anticipate our challenges better, developing insight into our practice settings and their requirements. This double-vision, a substantive focus upon the problems of dealing with differences and a strategic, practical focus upon the interpretation of skillful practitioners' stories, can help us learn about the challenges of multicultural theory and practice alike (Sandercock 1998).

We can close with a striking passage in which Larry Sherman suggests the promise of mediation for planners facing value and cultural differences. Contrasting the conventions of planning with those of mediation, Sherman reflects here upon the ways that his mediation practice makes him more effective as a planner. In so doing, he provides a promising avenue for all those of us interested in the actual practice that might reflect the more abstract theory of multicultural planning. He tells us:

What have I learned over my years as a planner using mediation? I've learned that mediation is an incredibly powerful tool. It certainly has humbled me a few times. I have learned as a professional planner that I would never have achieved as much planning, that is, the implementation of as much planning, in any other way.

Over the years I have learned to magnify that whole point I made about the school—just how very much people know that they don't share about whatever the subject is and how very creative they can be. The power of creativity of people and the amount of knowledge they have is just not normally uncorked. This is a process that does that. (Personal Interview with Larry Sherman)

Sherman also tells us more, finally, about the integration of planning with implementation, the integration of thought with action, recognition with real response:

I've always been concerned as a planner, as I hope most are, with results, with implementation. It's not enough to have a beautiful design or a beautiful plan on the wall. As life in cities gets worse instead of better, we should be blamed for all that planning that never came to anything; or, in fact, that in many cases created worse problems. Over the years, it's become more and more important to me to find ways of implementing plans.

Now I find that you can pretty well forget the act of planning as a prerequisite to implementation. You can put that aside. If you get into the implementation of problem solving, you will find that the folks who are going to implement it will solve the problems; i.e., they will do the planning. That's what makes sense, too, you plan in the process of implementing. I find that to be fascinating because now I don't have to sit there and do all that boring stuff. I can actually get in there and help people to agree to do things. I find planning and design more exciting than it ever has been for me. Even in the great days of urban renewal, when there were enormous amounts of money and legislative power for the planner to use, it wasn't as much fun as it is now because of the avenue that mediation provides. (Personal Interview with Larry Sherman)

Larry Sherman concludes with a note about power and possibility, the power of people to solve the problems that we, the planners, can't solve—the power of a planning practice that is multicultural in practice as well as in intention:

The opportunity for empowering people to be creative in solving their problems is much greater than the ability of a mediator simply to go in and get people to shake hands and not shoot one another. That's what planners have always wanted to do—solve people's problems—big, public, social problems. What we're now finding is that if you get the right people together, you can actually act on these things. If they are empowered with a process, they can solve problems that we can't solve. (Personal Interview with Larry Sherman)

But let us give the last word to Wallace Warfield, who illustrates Sherman's insights by referring to a racially charged police-community relations dispute settled through Warfield's mediation intervention a year before:

What I found to be most satisfying, beyond the specific outcomes, were the new relationships that had been built and the sense of trust that I felt had been built. We came back a year later to do a follow-up process and the same groups were still intact. All parties—city officials, community representatives, both Black and White—felt that the process had brought them together in a way that they had not been together before. They felt they were stronger now for it, and that they would be able to go on to handle disputes themselves. They now had a mechanism to deal with disputes and conflicts. (Forester 1994)

This brief consideration of mediators' practice seeks not to resolve, but rather to open up a way to explore practical questions of multicultural planning. If the work of Shirley Solomon and Larry Sherman are even close to the concerns of planners dealing with complex cultural differences, we may learn a good deal about multicultural planning by taking a close look at the practice of—and listening closely to— community and environmental mediators who have handled diverse public disputes involving issues of race, gender and ethnicity, and community members rooted in diverse cultures.

CONCLUSION

The reflections of these mediators do not provide recipes for multicultural planning. They do not even suggest that mediation should always be the strategy of choice—that planners can work as official mediators; for example, on projects in which diverse cultural influences come into play. They do suggest a range of skills and sensitivities that planners can put into practice in multicultural situations. Without pretending to be mediators, planners certainly can and should learn from mediators who have worked skillfully in the face of cultural difference and conflict.

Planners can learn, we have seen, about the importance that saving face can have to parties; thus, the importance of enabling the acknowledgment and recognition of the seriousness of parties' problems, even if other parties' agreement with their original positions is not forthcoming. Planners can learn, too, of the importance of ambiguity as a source of opportunity to redefine concerns, rather than as a source of confusion. Planners can learn, very practically, how they might establish consensual and shared ground rules, how they might help to create safe spaces for discussion, spaces in which parties can learn about each other and the issues before them, and explore options in creative ways, too.

From the details of the mediation processes, planners can come to see the rich complexity and practicality of storytelling in multicultural situations; for in telling stories, parties tell who they are, what they care about, and what deeper concerns they may have that underlie the issues at hand. Attentive planners can learn, too, that without emerging forms of recognition of the past losses of some parties, losses that partially define who they are today, planning for any future gain may be impossible. Taking the lead from Shirley Solomon's insight, we found that stories have to be told in order for reconciliation to happen. We need to explore together how our recognition of past loss can help us move forward together pragmatically.

Planners can also learn about the need for sensitive improvisation in the face of multicultural disputes and complex relationships. Perspective-taking and listening will always be important to parties who meet each other and find each other strange or frightening (National Hunger and Poverty Resource Guide 1998). How to encourage such listening and perspective-taking is a matter not of recipes, however, but of fitting a variety of strategies or techniques to the practical situations at hand. Many times, role-playing will be crucial, so that one party is able to imagine the perspective and concerns of another party. Sometime, however, as we have seen, role-playing may not work on a given day, and then other group processes can be called into play. What matters most, here, is not that planners look for simple solutions, but that planners become familiar with the range of situations they will face, the range of situations to which they can come to respond, sensitively and productively.

Finally, Larry Sherman's striking point to integrate planning and implementation through mediated negotiations demands attention. Sherman asks us to recognize that implementers have a special power, a power we ignore at our peril if we pay so much attention to planning analysis that we fail to ask carefully how that analysis will be put into practice. However, Sherman is not telling the dispute resolution joke that recounts how the lion and lamb lay down peacefully together every evening, even though the lion always needs a new lamb in the morning. Collaborative problem-solving only can be truly collaborative when the power of parties is balanced enough to make them interdependent, to make their problem-solving a joint enterprise, not the decisions of one party visited upon the others. If any party can prevail on its own, collaboration is likely to be a sham, and the weaker parties may well need the protection of courts or legislatures, not mediated negotiation processes in which participation is ostensibly voluntary.

This point is crucial in multicultural settings: mediation practices by planners may enable parties to resolve disputes productively only when the parties are interdependent enough to negotiate, interdependent enough to need to listen to one another. Mediation processes can complement, but not substitute for, legal and political processes in which weaker parties might gain real protections of their resources or entitlements (Susskind 1999). The purpose of this chapter has not been to recommend mediated negotiations as a cure-all for political inequality, but to show how the practical experience of environmental mediators provides insights and lessons regarding the complexity and actual practice of multicultural planning processes.

NOTE

This chapter contains interview material from Shirley Solomon and Larry Sherman. The complete interviews can be found in *Mediation in Practice: Profiles of Environmental and Community Mediators* edited by John Forester. This teaching material is a compilation of interviews available at the Department of City and Regional Planning, Cornell University, Sibley Hall, Ithaca, NY 14853.

1. Support for this project has come from a USDA Hatch grant, administered through the Cornell Community and Rural Development Institute.

REFERENCES

Fay, Brian. *Contemporary Philosophy of Social Science*. Malden, Mass: Blackwell. 1996.

Forester, John. "Learning from Practice Stories: The Priority of Practical Judgment," in Fischer, Frank and John Forester (eds). *The Argumentative Turn in Policy Analysis and Planning*. Duke. 1993.

Forester, John. "Joint Problem Solving and the Challenges of Cultural Translation: A Profile of Wallace Warfield," typescript. Ithaca: Department of City and Regional Planning. Cornell. 1994.

Forester, John. *The Deliberative Practitioner: Encouraging Participatory Planning*. Cambridge: MIT. 1999a.

Forester, John. "Dealing with Deep Value Differences: How Can Consensus Building Make A Difference?" in Susskind, Lawrence *et al* (eds). *Handbook on Consensus Building*. Los Angeles: Sage. 1999b.

Forester, John and Irene Weiser. "Making Mediation Work: Profiles of Community and Environmental Mediators," typescript. Ithaca: Department of City and Regional Planning. Cornell University. 1996.

Herman, Judith L. *Trauma and Recovery*. New York: Basic Books. 1992.

Krumholz, Norman and John Forester. *Making Equity Planning Work*. Philadelphia: Temple University Press. 1990.

National Hunger and Poverty Resource Guide. http://www.iglou.com/why/resource/index.shtml. 1998.

Rogers, Mary Beth. *Cold Anger*. Denton, Texas: University of North Texas Press. 1990.

Sandercock, Leonie. *Making the Invisible Visible: A Multicultural Planning History*. Berkeley: University of California Press. 1998.

Susskind, Lawrence and P. Field. *Dealing With An Angry Public*. New York: Free Press. 1996.

Susskind, Lawrence et al. (eds). *Handbook on Consensus-Building*. Los Angeles: Sage. 1999.

CHAPTER 11

Planning for an Ethnic Minority: The Bedouin Arabs of Israel

Steven Dinero

This chapter discusses and evaluates the Israeli Government's Negev bedouin resettlement program from the State and target community perspectives. The role of planning and its impact upon indigenous peoples and the ability to quantify and qualify these impacts are the central themes of the chapter.

Development planning among indigenous Fourth-World communities is notorious for its cultural shortsightedness, ethnocentric and/or western biases, and a seeming disregard for the views of those for whom the planning is being undertaken. Instituted in the mid-1960s, Israel's bedouin resettlement program has long been the subject of such criticism and debate. This is due primarily to the fact that the program has been designed and implemented by Israeli Jews for the minority bedouin Arabs with little, if any, input by the bedouin in terms of their needs, attitudes, or interests.

Using primary data gathered in one bedouin town in 1993 and 1996, the public service planning program is evaluated, and gaps in user access of services are measured and analyzed. The overall effects of urbanization upon the bedouin economy and social structures—as seen, for example, through the changing communal identity and politicization of the post-nomadic community—are also addressed.

Analyzing, measuring, quantifying, and defining the successful implementation of any planning project is not always easily accomplished. These tasks are all the more difficult when the planning project in question is plagued by political intrigue and the fact that the group for whom the planning is being carried out differs from the governing planners in terms of religion, ethnicity, economy, and lifestyle. Such is the case of a planning project to resettle the Negev bedouin, a minority population of about 120,000 Arab Muslim nomads living in the barren desert regions of southern Israel.

The impact of Israeli Government provision planning and resident access to public services in the bedouin resettlement sites was first measured in one of the planned towns, Segev Shalom/Shqeb,[1] in 1993 (Dinero 1996a). The study sought to determine the degree to which the bedouin have succeeded in acquiring and enjoying some of the basic elements of modernity in the planned urban environment.

This chapter will provide an update of planning efforts made in Segev Shalom since 1993, including data gathered via a public opinion survey in 1996. A number of concerns will provide the framework for the present study: Have bedouin town residents' attitudes toward living in the settlement changed since 1993? Has access to the provision of modern services improved over the three years that passed between the initial study and the follow-up evaluation? Are there new concerns or complaints concerning planning and development in the town? To what degree has planning succeeded in absorbing the bedouin population into the mainstream of Israeli society? And lastly, what can the Israeli government do to improve planning in this particular minority sector in the years ahead? Before addressing these questions, however, some background context to bedouin society and the resettlement initiative will assist in measuring if, and in what ways, such a program can be deemed a "success."

THE SOCIETY OF THE PRE-SEDENTARIZED BEDOUIN OF THE NEGEV

As pastoral nomads, the bedouin of the Negev were unique not only in the sense of being nonsedentary, but due to the fact that their primary mode of social and economic production stemmed from animal husbandry. Pastoral nomadism may be seen as "an adaptation of people with an underdeveloped technology to the scarcity of water in the dry season . . . when the reserves are exhausted in one place, pastoral nomads move to another site, usually in a fairly regular annual cycle" (Marx 1978:46). Climatic conditions, shifts in weather patterns, and other natural developments dictated the productive capacity of the community, as herd size was a direct outcome of pasture availability. This, in turn, impacted one's role and position in the community, where control of cisterns and other water sources gave one increased power in the extended community.

Another defining characteristic of nomadic communities, like the Negev bedouin, is the centrality of land in economic, political, and social exchange. Though they traditionally lived in temporary, mobile camps of goat-hair tents and owned few material possessions, the Negev bedouin held a very strong attachment to the land. It provided their primary resources in terms of water, pasturage, fuel for fire, materials for clothing and shelter, and fields for crops.

The importance of land in nomadic cultures typically fosters a mutual respect for, and communal control of, this most precious of resources. In the Negev control over land also contributed to a family's power and prestige. Unlike Western societies, which tend to view land as a commodity, indigenous societies in general view land as inalienable and a trust to be handed down from generation to generation (Berger 1985).

In terms of social structure, individualism was an alien concept in traditional Negev bedouin society, for individuals acting alone hold no independent role or status in environments in which mutual support is essential in accomplishing even basic tasks. Ties to family and social interaction between groups are, therefore, necessary components that contribute to the economic and social survival of the individual, as well as to psychological, well being (Meir 1992).

Thus, despite the prevalence of modern social, economic, and political systems in Israel, pastoral nomadism as a way of social and economic interaction has continued to function in the Negev to the present day. To be sure, the persistence of nomadism, or rather semi-nomadism, as pure nomadic activity ceased in the region decades ago, can no longer be attributed to its economic value in harsh environmental circumstances.

While environmental factors were the initial impetus for the development of pastoral nomadism in the region, today a whole culture remains that has developed and formed around this system. Spatial mobility, a geographically dispersed housing pattern, and the development of small, monogenous, well-defined coliable groups with specific rules of behavior and social interaction each typify the traditional bedouin lifestyle. Thus, the retention of flocks, though seemingly irrational from the perspective of Israel's planners are still undertaken by the Negev bedouin for purposes of sacrifices and other celebratory events, or simply as part of one's identity as a bedouin (Abu-Gardod, Nov. 20, 1992).

State involvement in planning and development in areas populated by nomads such as the Negev bedouin must take the above concerns into account. The issue of land-use planning alone is significant, and almost always entails a conflict between the community and the State. In addition, there are inherent difficulties in planning public services for nomads, which, though less politically charged than land-use concerns, still impact effective use.

This is due to three related considerations: (i) nomads are a mobile population, whereas services are usually geographically fixed; (ii) nomads generally occupy remote or peripheral regions, making it difficult to reach them; and (iii) nomad settlement systems are geographically dispersed, requiring more of a given service (health clinics, for example) than concentrated populations and, therefore, poorer economies of scale. Moreover, service provision in developed societies usually relies upon a needs assessment of potential users before being implemented. Rarely is this assessment determined for potential nomadic users, but rather, use is predicted based upon created, rather than effective, demand (Massam 1993).

Cultural barriers sometimes present themselves as well. These include unfamiliarity with a service, belief that a service contradicts existing societal norms, a refusal to rely upon external providers (i.e., the State) to address internal communal needs, or various other fears of what a service's use might entail. Sometimes, the psychological costs of using a service (social welfare services, for example) are viewed as a higher cost by indigenous populations than that of going without the service altogether (Brennen and Berman 1988).

The culture of Israel's planners, most of whom are Israeli Jews schooled in Western views and attitudes, is also a relevant factor. Much of Israel's planning for the bedouin stems from the contention that the State is acting for the bedouins' own good, even if they don't presently appreciate the effort. As one Land Authority planner put it:

[The bedouin] live in illegal structures, stealing water; they have no address. Their kids have to walk ½ km to the bus stop, or 4-5 km to the school itself. They have no clinics. So we bring them everything they need.
  I know the tent is good for them; I know they are happy there. We don't try to tell them that the tent is bad; we only try to show them how living in the town is good...If we must, we will take them to court to remove them from the land that is designated as part of the towns. Democracy is democracy, but we have to find a solution...
  We try to see things through their eyes—not through their minds—for that isn't the goal here. But to understand how they see things helps us to plan for them. (Shapira, Nov. 24, 1992, *personal communication*)

In the final analysis it is clear that the culture and society of the Negev bedouin is quite different from that of the dominant Jewish culture around them. As a product of Jewish planners and State officials, Israel's bedouin resettlement project must be placed within this context in order to appreciate the difficulties in developing and implementing effective planning amid this formally pastoral nomadic population.

BACKGROUND TO THE NEGEV BEDOUIN RESETTLEMENT PROGRAM

Israel sought to resettle the bedouin of the Negev (Figure 11.1) for a variety of social, economic, and political reasons. In the mid-1960s these efforts were formalized through the creation of a new town program, with the ultimate hope of permanently settling the bedouin, bringing to an end their pastoral-nomadic practices, and providing social development services to the community (Boneh 1983). These included electrification, running water, schools, health clinics, and social welfare programs. The State rationalized this argument further by contending that, as Israeli citizens since the early 1950s, the bedouin had a right to these services, and that the State was obligated to provide them (Gur, Nov. 17, 1992, *personal communication*).

Initiated with the construction of the town of Tel Sheva (Figure 11.2), the project initially proved to be a failure according to many observers (see, for example, Boneh 1983; Horner 1982). This was due to an overemphasis upon physical planning at the expense of social planning, and other design features that were inappropriate for post-nomadic populations. These weaknesses in the planning of the town, combined with a variety of politically based conflicts between the community and the state over land ownership and control, led initially to an inability to attract immigrants during the early phase of the program (Maddrell 1990; Falah 1983, 1985, 1989).

These difficulties did not serve to discourage the further establishment of other bedouin new towns in the region throughout the 1970s and 1980s. Today there are a total of seven planned communities.[2] Although living outside of the towns is illegal and grounds for forced relocation through physical means, the Government's approach throughout the 1990s primarily has been to rely less upon the policing mechanisms of the Ministry of Agriculture's "Green Patrol" as it did in the 1970s and 1980s, and instead to use the "carrot" of service provision and the promise of modern amenities and lifestyles as inducement for relocation. The State's unwillingness to provide certain services to the unplanned settlements (roads, electricity, water), as well as an inability to provide adequate coverage for those services that are provided (health, education), has contributed to this process as well.

In the early 1990s, 45 percent of the total bedouin population of approximately 90,000 had settled in the seven officially recognized towns (Maddrell 1990). More than half of the community (55%) had yet resisted relocation to one of the government-built towns, remaining in spontaneously created settlements, approximately 45 percent living in wood or tin shack settlements, and 10 percent living in traditional tents. By the late 1990s these statistics had reversed, with 55 percent of the population of nearly 120,000 having relocated to one of the towns, and the other 45 percent remaining in unplanned settlements (Masos and Shoket Regional Council and Rahat and Tel Sheva Local Council population figures, August 1996; Green Patrol State figures, August 1996).[3]

The town of Segev Shalom, for example, grew from 200 to 300 families numbering 1,500 to 1,800 residents in 1993, to a population of 2,500 by 1996 (Masos Regional Council statistics, Aug. 1996). Located about four kilometers southeast of the city of Be'er Sheva, the town experienced difficulty in attracting residents when created in 1979 and only began to grow after a recommitment to its development was made with the founding in 1986 of a governing body, the Masos Regional Council. Even today the residents comprise only a small minority of the El-Azazma tribe and related 'Abid bedouin (former Black slaves of the El-Azazma) for whom it was built, as the vast majority of the El-Azazma remain in spontaneous shack and tent settlements south of Be'er Sheva, numbering perhaps 10,000 to 12,000 people (El-Hamamdi, July 2, 1996, *personal communication*).

PRELIMINARY OPINION SURVEY OF RESPONDENTS

In early 1993 I was commissioned by the Masos Regional Council that governed Segev Shalom at the time to evaluate the effectiveness of the planning programs in the town (see Dinero 1996a). The main data collection tool for the study was a public opinion survey I designed with contributions and suggestions from a number of concerned bedouin and non-bedouin academics and government officials (Dinero 1996b).

Figure 11.1
Location of the Seig in the Northern Negev Desert

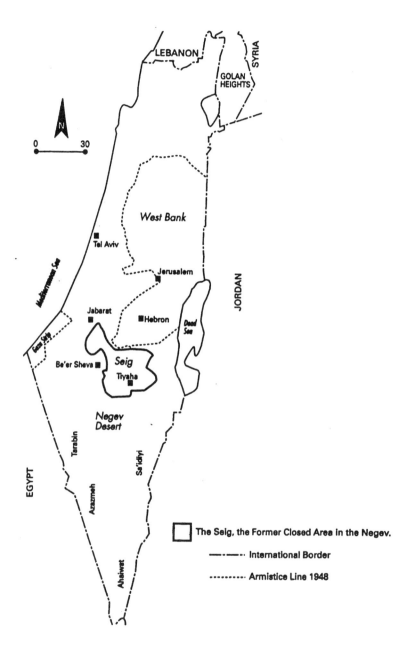

Source: Penny Maddrell, Bedouin of the Negev, 1990:6.

Figure 11.2
Bedouin Spontaneous and Planned Settlement Distribution Within the Seig

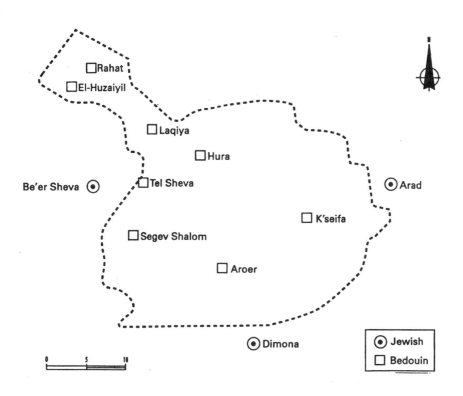

Source: E. Stern and A. Meir, The Negev Atlas, Part A, 1981.

I hired and trained four students, three bedouin and one Arab from the Galilee, to undertake the house-to-house survey. One of the four, a bedouin woman from the El-Azazma tribe, was hired specifically to survey the female heads of household. It was my goal to obtain an even representation of male and female views, a hope that was nearly accomplished (see Table 11.3). To facilitate trust in the survey process, I met with several members of the town's formal and informal leadership prior to the interview period, both to introduce myself and to discuss the project's goals. These men were asked to spread this information by word of mouth to their family, friends, and neighbors (still one of the most effective means of disseminating information in the bedouin community), and to request their cooperation.

The sampling frame for the random sample was comprised of the 215 households that existed in the town at that time. Lot numbers, which also serve as addresses, were selected to form a single random sample of 110 households (Bailey 1987). Eighty-one of the 110 household heads visited—about 75 percent of those approached—agreed to speak to a member of the survey team. Thirty-eight percent of all households in the town were represented in the 1993 survey results.

The majority of survey questions were closed-ended. The last three questions were open-ended to provide respondents with the opportunity to give their views on any topics of concern. Respondents were allowed and encouraged to speak for themselves about those planning issues *they* believed were of the greatest relevance in Segev Shalom.

Upon completion of the survey and follow-up focus-group interviews, each of which I personally conducted, all survey data were coded, entered into the computer, and statistically analyzed using SPSS/PC+. Chi-square tests were carried out in cross-tab format to determine areas of significant statistical correlation ($p<or+.05$). Answers to the open-ended questions served to further elaborate upon the quantitative data gathered.

Based upon the results, resident access and use of modern facilities and services (Table 11.1) and satisfaction with those services (Table 11.2) were measured in an attempt to determine the degree to which the resettlement project was succeeding in its service delivery efforts. The results suggested that the resettlement program had achieved some success in terms of service delivery and use, but also reflected the fact that the process was yet incomplete and that not everyone had succeeded in fully accessing and enjoying State provisions. The primary access and satisfaction correlates found were gender, age, education, and length of time one lived in the town (Table 11.3).

Those who lived in the town for less than five years, for example, were less likely to be living in permanent dwellings (houses) than more veteran residents, were less likely to be hooked up formally to the electric utility, and were less likely to be employed in wage labor. Younger residents also were more likely to be living in temporary housing than residents over forty.

The study also found that women, older residents, and the less educated tended to be most satisfied with urban living. Young educated males, on the other hand, were least likely to express satisfaction, as they were more likely to still reside in temporary housing and to be experiencing acute financial problems, making many resentful and uncertain of whether relocation to the town had been worth the disruption it had brought to their families' lives.

In short, the survey data revealed that those residents who had the highest hopes and expectations—further compounded by exposure to Jewish Israeli urban environments and by government promises that they, too, would enjoy similar provisions and lifestyles—were most critical and least satisfied with the town's services and other provisions. Given that it is the young, educated, and male town residents who may be considered the spearheads of future bedouin social and economic transformation, it was concluded that their inclusion in future planning and project implementation is crucial to the overall success of the resettlement project in the long term.

Table 11.1 Percentage of Segev Shalom Residents Accessing Public Services 1993 and 1996		
Service	**1993**	**1996**
Hooked to Water System	96%	99%
Have Standard Toilets	74%	81%
Live in Standard House	70%	75%
Hooked to Electricity via Public Utility	50%	51%
Children of Respondences (Age 14-17) Attending High School	73%	92%
Use Social Welfare Services (stated usage)	10%	5%

Sources: Dinero 1996a; 1996 Segev Shalom Survey.

THE FOLLOW-UP SURVEY OF RESIDENTS

In the summer of 1996, I returned to Segev Shalom in order to implement a follow-up survey to determine if, and in what ways, resident access and use of provisions had changed over the three-year period. The methodology for the 1996 data collection and analysis was virtually identical to that used in 1993. The sampling frame for the random sample was comprised of the 280 households existing in the town. Of the 140 lot numbers selected, 102 households (73%) were available and willing to provide information for the survey. Thus, 36 percent of Segev Shalom's 280 households are represented in the 1996 survey results.

I again hired and trained four bedouin students, two males and two females, to assist me in carrying out the house-to-house data collection as I had in 1993. Once again, the women were chosen especially for their ability to speak with younger female respondents who are prohibited by their husbands, fathers, or brothers from speaking openly with male strangers, such as myself.

Some descriptive statistics were gathered to provide general background information on the participants of the study (Table 11.4). These data did not differ greatly from those gathered in 1993, with one noted exception concerning marital status. While the percentage of married respondents remained consistent, the percentage of those practicing polygyny rose substantially over the three years to nearly 30 percent.[4]

Though seemingly counter-intuitive, the continuation or even increase in polygyny levels in the towns, a sign of weak social development by Western standards, appears to correlate if only weakly with economic development. It was statistically verified in Segev Shalom that those who were involved in polygynous relationships were more likely to live in a permanent standard house than in a tent, shack, or temporary house, and were employed, albeit in low-income positions. While age helped explain participation in polygamous marriages for women, men regardless of age had a potentially equal chance of being involved in such a marriage.

Table 11.2
Percentage of Segev Shalom Residents in 1993 Stating Satisfaction with Public Service Provision

Service	Percent Satisfied with Service
Water Service	85%
Sanitation	74%
Trash Removal	60%
Cleanliness of Public Areas	60%
Health Services	60%
Electricity (citing "no problems")	50%

Source: Dinero 1996a:114.

Although it might be assumed that with social development would come lessened polygamous activity, this assumption fails to acknowledge the deep-rooted functions that multiple wives play in bedouin society. Wives always served central roles in Negev bedouin society; they helped to build the tent and kept it in order, brought water, fetched wood, prepared food, and carried out a variety of domestic activities. Most importantly, they bore children to add to the labor pool of the settlement, directly contributing to the reproduction of the community.

While men's lives increasingly were impacted by external interactions in the towns, women's roles remained controlled and defined largely by their male relatives such as fathers, brothers, and husbands. The state of concealment of women (*harem*) to ensure marriage with other agnates is particularly strong in urbanized bedouin society, where it seeks to further a continuity of traditional gender roles and the perpetuation of family alliances through marriage ties (Kressel 1992).

Given that the social desire and prestige of having multiple wives (and thereby, numerous children) persist, gains brought on by wage labor occupations have appeared to lend to the further economic ability to maintain more than one household. As a result, even young formally-educated men raised within a modern context, as well as some who are financially less able to support these families, are taking on multiple wives, especially women hailing from the now increasingly accessible Palestinian Territories and Jordan (Rehes, July 14, 1996, *personal communication*).

EDUCATION SERVICES IN SEGEV SHALOM

Access to formal education for bedouin families in the planned towns is a crucial component of the State's social development initiative and a major attraction for resettlers. Only in the 1950s when Israel's Arab citizens were offered citizenship was compulsory education required of bedouin children, and only with the provision and development of the planned towns in the late 1960s was the requirement that bedouin families send their children to school effectively facilitated. That said, there is a direct correlation between age and the likelihood of having ever received any formal education, with those under age forty far more likely to have attended school than those over forty. However, for females there is no relationship between age and literacy.

The level of education of the respondents in the survey was largely consistent from 1993 to 1996. What was clear, however, was that with time more bedouin have been exposed to the State education system, although males are more likely than females to be educated.

While about 8 percent of female respondents were high school graduates according to the previous survey, about 11 percent were found to have graduated from high school in the 1996 results. Perhaps even more significant, less than 9 percent of males had graduated from high school in the 1993 survey, but 25 percent of those surveyed in 1996 had graduated from high school.

Although these statistics are low when compared to those in the Jewish Israeli population, the improvement is impressive for males and females alike. This is particularly true given that nearly all survey respondents who were age eighteen or older, by definition, spent most or all of their youth outside of the bedouin towns and only moved there as adults. By looking at the percentages of graduates now growing up and being educated *inside* the towns, some conclusions may be drawn concerning the effective provision of educational facilities found there.

Table 11.3 Demographic Breakdown of Those Interviewed (in percent) 1993, N=81; 1996, N=102		
	1993	**1996**
GENDER		
Women	43%	45%
Men	57%	55%
AGE		
40 or Younger	65%	58%
Over 40	34%	38%
Not Available	1%	4%
MARITAL STATUS		
Married (one wife)	64.0%	64.7%
Multiple Wives	18.5%	28.4%
Widowed	5.0%	1.0%
Divorced	2.5%	1.0%
Never Married	10.0%	2.9%
Unidentified	0.0%	2.0%
CHILDREN		
Percent of Households with Children	89.0%	92.0%
Average Number of Children in Households with Kids	5.5	5.3

There was one primary school and one secondary school in Segev Shalom in 1993. The primary school (grades 1–6) was created in 1983. The secondary school (grades 7–12) was created in 1988. In addition to math, science, and similar basic subjects, students study Arabic beginning in the first grade, Hebrew beginning in the third grade, and English beginning in the fourth grade.

Not long after the 1993 survey was completed, another secondary school was built on the distant southern edge of the town and the original secondary school was converted into another primary school. This, in part, was in response to the far greater percentage of elementary level children in the town as compared to older

Table 11.4
Percentage Breakdown of Segev Shalom Monthly Salaries
in 1996 New Israeli Shekels
(1 NIS = $0.30)

Salary (in NIS)	Percent of People Earning This Amount
Less that 3,000	40.2%
Between 3,000 and 5,000	31.4%
More than 5,000	2.9%
Don't Know/Not Available	16.7%
Receive Social Security Payments	8.8%

children; a reflection of the fact that most of the town's families are relatively young. Although in use in 1996, the secondary school was not totally completed. Moreover, it was feared that the school was not built large enough to accommodate present needs, let alone future spatial demands (El-Hamamdi, July 2, 1996, *personal communication*).

Overall, there is a marked increase in the demand for educational services among the younger generation of town residents. Ninety-four percent of the children of respondents, ages five through thirteen, attend one of the Segev Shalom primary schools, and 92 percent of respondents' children, ages fourteen through seventeen, attend the secondary school. Although bedouin schools have long experienced high drop-out rates in comparison with schools for Jewish Israelis (Abu-Saad 1991), these recent statistics suggest an increasing awareness of the importance of education as a vehicle for economic success in the competitive Israeli economy.

Calls for needed changes in educational provision and use still exist. Many survey respondents complained, for example, that the town's schools remain overcrowded, with an unacceptably poor teacher/student ratio. Some criticized the content of the courses taught, seeking more lessons dealing with bedouin culture and related topics. Several respondents, young and old alike, called for the provision of a trade school in the town,[5] to assist in acquiring the tools necessary for obtaining ever-elusive wage labor employment.

OCCUPATION AND EMPLOYMENT IN SEGEV SHALOM

The male survey respondents' employment status correlated highly with their levels of education, with those having more education more likely to be employed. This was not true of the women, however. Regardless of their levels of education, women were typically held back from wage labor participation for cultural reasons.

Economic opportunity usually associated with education continued to be extremely problematic even for the men of the bedouin community, according to the 1996 data.

Unemployment and the financial strains it brings was recognized as an acute problem in the bedouin community in the early 1990s, "significantly higher among bedouin Arabs than any other group in the Negev, and nearly double the Israeli average" (Lewando-Hundt et al 1991). A study conducted at that time (1991) placed the overall unemployment rate in the male bedouin community at about 12 percent, or even higher "as many job-seekers are not registered" (cited in Meir and Ben-David 1993). In Tel Sheva, for example, 23 percent of 460 household heads surveyed in 1991 were identified as unemployed. In the 1993 Segev Shalom study, 28 percent of the men were categorized as unemployed, retired, or otherwise incapable of working in wage labor (Dinero 1996a).

The 1996 survey employment figures were consistent with the figures noted in Segev Shalom and other bedouin towns in the early 1990s. The survey found that 28 percent of male respondents were not working in wage labor. Of these, 19 percent were able-bodied males between the ages of eighteen and fifty-five years identified in the survey as "unemployed," and an additional 9 percent identified themselves as either retired or incapacitated. Approximately 94 percent of the women surveyed do not work outside the home. The rest work primarily in small businesses and childcare. Though admittedly small in number, these working women may be indicative of a significant change in the status of at least some bedouin females.

Overall, the top occupations represented by male survey respondents were nonskilled and blue-collar, with only five percent working in "professional" occupations. Salary levels are, of course, impacted by the nature of the wage-labor occupations that bedouin typically fill. Given that the Israeli poverty line begins at 2,083 NIS/month (where 2.99 NIS = $1.00; that is about $700/month) for a family of four (*The Jerusalem Report*, Apr. 7, 1994), it is clear that a substantial percentage of even those town residents who are employed are still barely making it financially.

A high unemployment rate combined with low salaries continues to contribute to a sense of frustration and economic hardship. Indeed, many suggest that they have experienced little change since moving to the town, other than that they are now "poor" and dependent, proletarianized into the lower ranks of society as they shift to wage-labor economic activity. As one twenty-five-year-old female respondent in the 1996 survey stated: "I pay for electricity, live in a shack, and get nothing for it. And yet, we have to pay *arnonah*" (the tax placed upon all state-provided utilities and provisions). Adds another Segev Shalom resident: "The economic situation is like a balloon. There's no more room for air; there's a maximum. When you reach beyond it, it simply explodes...this is why it is so pressing that these economic needs be addressed now for the good of the State and for bedouin society as a whole" (Abu-Mu'amar, July 9, 1996, *personal communication*).

Given the ongoing financial difficulties in the urban bedouin community, it is understandable that animal husbandry and agricultural production persist as an important economic supplement. The percentage of those who undertake some form of agricultural production (vegetable gardens, olive/fruit trees), about 25 percent, remained consistent from 1993 to 1996.

Animal husbandry dropped substantially, however, from 38 percent in 1993 to about 22 percent in 1996.[6] This drop is likely due to a number of factors, including the ongoing shift from traditional pastoralism to wage labor, and the logistical difficulties of raising wide-ranging animals in a confined space.

Finally, in addition to unemployment and low-wage concerns, most of the complaints voiced in the 1993 survey results centered on the lack of employment within Segev Shalom. At the time the town served as a bedroom community with 88 percent of employed residents working in a Jewish city and only 12 percent working in Segev Shalom or a neighboring bedouin area. The 1996 results showed limited improvement in this regard, with 84 percent of those who worked holding positions outside of town, and only 16 percent working within the town. "After 15 years, we still have no economic infrastructure *in* the town," states Secondary School Headmaster Muhammed El-Hamamdi. "There is much discussion about this and a few people perform some agricultural activity, but it's just not enough for most residents" (El-Hamamdi, July 2, 1996, *personal communication*). Unless, and until, an effort is made on the part of town planners to alter the status quo, the lack of local employment is not likely to change to any measurable degree.

HOUSING IN SEGEV SHALOM

Economic difficulties are also reflected in the town's housing pattern. While many bedouin have been anxious to purchase lots in town, they have proven less capable of building and completing houses upon these lots. About 70 percent of those surveyed in 1993 lived in permanent standard dwellings (stone houses), while 30 percent lived in nonstandard dwellings including shacks, tents, and other temporary buildings. The results of the 1996 survey show 75 percent living in houses and 25 percent living in temporary dwellings; that is, the percentage has improved, but only minimally.

A more significant development is that far fewer lots had only one dwelling in 1996 than was the case previously. Those who owned a house plus a temporary dwelling, for example, comprised only 12.3 percent of respondents in 1993; in 1996 this percentage had risen to 30.4 percent, and the number of residents who owned only a house dropped from 57 percent to 45 percent.

This change is likely due to an increase in family size and the inability to house everyone in a single dwelling on one lot. It may also be an indication that the town is entering into a second stage of settlement. Those who have lived in town for some years are further improving their lots while those who are relative newcomers continue to strive toward completion of the construction of at least one permanent dwelling.

EVALUATION OF OTHER SERVICE USE

Given that the bedouins' traditional nomadic lifestyle was dependent upon access to water resources, the attraction of running water continued to be a particularly alluring provision in the town, and is the most well-utilized and well-regarded service. One of the greatest difficulties cited by the bedouin living outside of the planned towns is the unavailability of electric service. Some utilize unreliable yet costly mobile generators, and still others simply go without the service altogether. It was therefore significant to note that in 1993 only half of those residents surveyed were hooked up to the formal electrical system, a statistic that remained largely unchanged in 1996. Still, the percentage of those lacking electricity altogether had dropped from 10 percent in 1993 to only 2 percent in 1996. There also has been a dramatic increase in the number of those utilizing the "wire-hooked-to-the-neighbor's-house" option. Not only is this practice illegal, but these low-hanging and ground-level wires pose a real danger to the town's youth, who are known to play everywhere throughout the town—except, it seems, for the poorly maintained, designated play areas.

Whether acquired formally or informally, the availability of electricity has contributed substantially to ownership of electrical appliances including refrigerators and washing machines (see Table 11.5). More than any other item, however, is the ubiquitous television set, found in nearly all of the households surveyed. Television use is now so universal among the bedouin that one Segev Shalom entrepreneur has established a small UHF station with a range and programming content specifically oriented to the bedouin community.

Table 11.5 Percentage Ownership of Electronic Goods in Segev Shalom 1993 and 1996		
Item	1993	1996
Refrigerator	67%	69%
Washer	26%	49%
Television	86%	91%
VCR	14%	18%

Health services in Segev shalom include a *tipat halav* (pediatric clinic) and a *kupat holim* (public health clinic). The *tipat halav* clinic provides general pediatric care, as well as care for the health needs of some adults in the area. In particular, women frequent the clinics for basic health care, as they can walk to either easily and do not have to be dependent upon rides from male relatives.[7]

The 1993 survey found that residents' views of the town's health services were generally positive, but by 1996 less than half expressed satisfaction with the town's health services. This sharpened criticism for these facilities was the greatest change found concerning any service provision addressed in the updated survey. This change is significant, too, in that Segev's health facilities are the only services that were identified as being utilized by everyone who was surveyed.

There are a number of possible explanations for the drop in satisfaction with the town's health services. First, the vast majority of the clinics' patients in the past were town residents. Those from the spontaneous settlements utilized Be'er Sheva's clinics as they did before Segev Shalom was built because the city is more accessible by public transport. Since 1993, however, the clinics have become increasingly attractive to nonresidents, as well as to an additional influx of new Segev Shalom residents. As a result, the clinics are viewed as crowded, with an inadequate number of doctors to care for the patients, too few office hours, and, as a result, long waiting periods.

Second, the quality of the town doctors is also a topic of concern. In the 1993 survey, a major complaint was that none of the doctors spoke Arabic. After the survey was completed, and before its results were publicized, this problem was remedied with the addition of a new physician to the *kapat holim* staff. But a non-Arabic-speaking Russian immigrant is still the primary care doctor at the facility today. Moreover, many respondents criticized him and his Arabic-speaking colleague for their lack of medical knowledge, and for being insensitive to patients' needs.

Last, an essential area of public services that continued to lack recognition among town residents in 1996 is the Masos Office of Social Welfare, located in the old section of Be'er Sheva. In Segev Shalom a major improvement in social welfare service access was made since 1993 with the provision of office space in the town itself, housed within a caravan (mobile home) located near the new secondary school. Though in the town only part-time, the staff's physical presence and availability is a major advancement over the previous system in which residents were required to travel to Be'er Sheva whenever they needed some form of assistance.

In addition to the three Masos towns, the Office is responsible for the concerns of almost all of those living in spontaneous settlements excluding the Rahat periphery, a population totaling over 60,000 people or one-half of the entire Negev bedouin community. The Office's budget and number of staff have risen sharply in the last few years as a result of government's recognition of the variety of necessary functions the Office fulfills.

Nonetheless, the majority of the social workers are Jews (10), while only four are bedouin, and one is a Galilee Arab. Though this is a substantial quantitative improvement in coverage, residents remain resistant to use—if not simply unaware of the existence—of planned social welfare services now available to them. Moreover, an increase in the number of bedouin social workers in the future, particularly females, will certainly improve social welfare coverage in the community.

CHANGING IDENTITIES AS A RESULT OF RESETTLEMENT

The concept of Middle Eastern bedouinism in the final years of the twentieth century looks increasingly less like the traditional model that is so often perpetuated in the media today. "Traditional," "genuine" bedouin society, as defined by pastoral nomadic lifestyles or structures, is on the decline throughout the region. This is being replaced by a model that is yet difficult to demarcate geographically, socially, or economically. As a result, it has been determined that in the Negev, as elsewhere, bedouin identity is also in transition, no longer limited to specific housing types of geographic environments, or defined by particular social or economic activities.

In the case of the bedouin of the Negev, identity similarly is undergoing transition primarily as a result of planned resettlement, but the community is experiencing additional contextual issues that impact the reconstructed sense of bedouin identity in ways that differentiate the community from other Middle Eastern bedouin populations. Chief among these is the fact that *bedouin* identity in Israel has been shown to correlate not with housing type (tent versus stone villa), occupation type (shepherding versus wage-labor), or activity in growing crops or carrying out animal husbandry, but rather with political attitudes, ideals, and concerns that make them increasingly similar to, and at times indistinguishable from, other Arab/Muslim minorities in Israel.

The sense of exclusion from the mainstream dominant society continues in some sectors, or is even on the increase as the peace process serves to distract attention away from bedouin concerns and toward global interests. Indeed, post-nomadic bedouin identity, though long expressed in distinction from the nonbedouin, increasingly is expressed *in opposition* to the nonbedouin; that is, in terms of who the bedouin *are not* and cannot be —the Jews—as well as who they are and always will be—Arabs and Muslims. While physically the planned towns were designed to help ease some divisions *within* bedouin society (Fenster 1991), divisions *between* the bedouin community and the outside world remain as strong—or perhaps stronger—than ever before.

Thus, it is clear that the bedouin have been cut off from their traditional spatial connections with the ongoing resettlement and social development initiative. Rather than aligning with and assimilating into Jewish Israeli society, however, the bedouin have been drawn to the Arab and Muslim communities around them.

The outcome is predictable. A late-1997 report by Israeli's security services suggested that the bedouin community is like a "time bomb," and warned that a trend of anger and hostility is rapidly growing (*Jerusalem Post*, October 30, 1997). The report suggests that it is the clash of "traditional" and "modern" that is at the heart of bedouin anger—failing to mention the role of poor planning in this development.

Indeed, so long as the State continues to strive to separate the bedouin from the land, to treat the bedouins' interest as secondary to Jewish Israeli interests, and to treat the bedouin in a manner that distinguishes them from those around them, the sense of the community's bedouinism being increasingly equated with political Arabism and Islam is sure to grow. It remains to be seen if and when new planning policies of inclusion will be developed in Israel in order to preclude what will otherwise almost certainly be a future of political resistance and social chaos between the Negev bedouin minority and the dominant Jewish Israeli society at large.

CONCLUSIONS AND RECOMMENDATIONS

Several planning improvements have taken place throughout the Negev bedouin towns during the 1990s. During this period the town of Segev Shalom and indeed the entire bedouin community experienced increased budgetary commitments from the State, seen by some leaders as a direct outcome of the Labour victory in the 1992 elections (Sagie, July 31, 1996, *personal communication*). This trend has continued under the Likud government in the late 1990s, perhaps due to policies encouraged by Minister of Infrastructure Ariel Sharon (*Jerusalem Post,* Dec. 2, 1997). This change not only signaled an increasing State commitment to this minority sector, but saw real results in terms of an ever-increasing number of urbanized, healthy, formally educated bedouin community members.

These changes were not necessarily recognized or acknowledged by town residents. While new facilities and infrastructure have been added and existing services improved, user attitudes toward these services remained either the same, or in some cases, even worsened. Along with these communal improvements have also come an increased awareness among the bedouin of their rights as Israeli citizens, and with it increased expectations of what social and economic development needs are still lacking in the community.

In part, unmet expectations are also related to the inability to see a connection between the government's planning efforts and the quality of life improvements that families have accomplished. One senses when speaking with residents that they believe they have made progress *in spite* of the Regional Council's planning, rather than because of it. One forty-eight-year-old male summarized this sentiment well, stating: "Masos is terrible, they have done nothing. The roads are a mess, the kids have nothing to do. There are teachers in the schools who never got past 8th grade—that's Masos I pay *arnonah* (utility tax)—I want the town clean. But here there's garbage everywhere. All I have here is a house, that's all. The government does everything for the Jews. A Russian comes here yesterday, and today has more rights than we who were born here have" (Personal interview).

To complicate matters, a Local Council was created to govern Segev Shalom on August 1, 1996, to replace the Regional Council that governed the town since the late 1980s. The Council was to be comprised of nine men, three of whom are bedouin and six of whom are Jews. Minister of the Interior and Shas Party Knesset

Member Eli Suisse, a designate of the Netanyahu Government, appointed a Shas Party member to serve as town mayor for five years. Significantly, the Shas party constituency is comprised primarily of Orthodox Jews originating in the Arabian peninsula and North Africa, with little, if any, connection to the bedouin community and who have little understanding or appreciation for bedouin concerns.

It appears then that the top-down planning process, which has typified the bedouin resettlement program since its inception, will continue in Segev Shalom until at least 2002. Just a few bedouin have had any say in how the town initially was planned. Still fewer are now able to enjoy the democratic process of self-governance. Therefore, despite clear improvements in infrastructure facilities in the resettlement community, not everyone will have access to the services available.

Although from a planning perspective, conditions appear to be far more promising than they were in the early 1990s when Segev Shalom was yet a small, depressed, undeveloped village, town residents today are also more skeptical of the government's initiatives than ever before. As they became increasingly more educated and sophisticated in their understanding of the workings of government, they are also that much more aware of how their role in addressing their own development has been virtually ignored since the outset of the resettlement initiative.

A number of planning changes, additions, and improvements in Segev may potentially improve the town and make it a more attractive and viable resettlement center. Possible additions to the Segev Shalom's present planning agenda as suggested by town residents, officials, and the 1996 survey results include the following:

First, job training, technical skill development, and an emphasis upon appropriate education at the high school level, if not earlier, are needed to help the bedouin compete more effectively in the Jewish Israeli labor market. In addition, development of economic and commercial infrastructure in Segev Shalom (including a marketplace, bank, post office, cages, and other basic essentials) would provide jobs for at least some town residents, especially women whose movement far from their homes remains limited.

Second, the initiation and completion of standard houses in Segev remains a major difficulty for many residents. People who have succeeded in completing homes are now increasingly supplanting insufficient space in their homes with shacks, tents, additions, and other nonstandard structures. Potential home builders should receive assistance in choosing an architectural plan that is both appropriate to family needs and is financially affordable.

Third, resistance to formally connecting to the town's electricity system remains particularly strong. A campaign must be initiated to encourage those not yet hooked up formally to the electric system to do so, particularly for safety reasons.

Fourth, the town's health services must be expanded and improved. Segev Shalom needs a larger health facility and significantly more physicians than exist at the present time. Such physicians should be both fluent in Arabic and well qualified to provide quality care in a culturally sensitive, nonpatronizing manner.

Fifth, the town government offices should be relocated from Be'er Sheva to the town itself, giving residents a greater sense of access to, and participation in, the future of the town's planning and development.

Sixth, the town's social welfare planners should take a more direct and active approach in engaging more new residents to use their programs and initiatives. A "resettlement committee" should be available to help prepare families for moving, as well as provide follow-up services following their relocation.

In the final analysis, what continues to be most lacking in Segev Shalom and the other bedouin towns is a foundation for the establishment of communal-led civil institutions. Such a foundation, which might include the creation of formal or informal brotherhoods, religious associations, cooperatives, women's groups, or other community organizations that exist independently of the State-controlled superstructure, is lacking in the Negev bedouin case. That there are few such structures is emblematic of the community's current lack of a civil power base. Together such components are essential in helping form a basis for development through self-help, which can only further assist minority groups such as the bedouin in achieving self-determination and control heretofore absent from traditionally undertaken top-down planning initiatives.

It may be concluded, then, that further research on the development of bedouin civil society, including an emphasis upon how to help the bedouin community to help itself, is essential in ultimately furthering the social and economic development capacity of the resettlement initiative as a whole. A greater appreciation on the part of Israel's planners of how such civil entities can be developed may in turn facilitate the empowerment of the community. Such planning can benefit planners and residents alike, so that one day community members might run their own affairs, direct their own planning and development, and ultimately determine their own (hopefully) bright future.

NOTES

1. Throughout the chapter, the Hebrew name of the town, Segev Shalom, will be used rather than the Arabic name, Shqeb. This is done both for the purposes of consistency with published town plans and documents, as well as the recognition that the name Shqeb also denotes a large spontaneous area of settlement that extends well beyond the town limits.

2. These are Rahat, Tel Sheva, K'seifa, Aroer, Hura, Laqia, and Segev Shalom.

3. Reliable population statistics regarding the Negev Bedouin are not easily acquired. A more modest estimate places the 1995 population at 90,000; 55,000 in towns and 35,000 in the periphery (Fenster 1996:48–49).

4. One recent study found an even higher rate, with as many as 40 percent of an urban school's pupils coming from polygynous marriages (Jerusalem Report, May 15, 1997).

5. Previous calls for this provision, such as those noted in the 1993 survey analysis results that were submitted to the Masos Regional Council (Dinero 1996a:115), have gone unheeded.

6. Despite this drop, the town is now home to a new type of resident in addition to its chickens, geese, sheep, goats, donkeys, horses, cows and especially camels—creatures that were entirely lacking in the town in 1993.

7. In general, bedouin women do not drive.

REFERENCES

Publications

Abu-Saad, I. "Towards an Understanding of Minority Education in Israel: The Case of the Bedouin Arabs of the Negev," *Comparative Education*, vol. 27, no. 2, 1991:235–42.

Bailey, K D. *Methods of Social Research.* New York: The Free Press. 1987.

Berger, T.R. *Village Journey: The Report of the Alaska Native Review Commission.* New York: Hill & Wang. 1985.

Boneh, D. *Facing Uncertainty: The Social Consequences of Forced Sedentarization Among the Jaraween Bedouin, Negev, Israel.* Doctoral Dissertation, Brandeis University, Waltham, MA. 1983.

Brennen, E.C. and G. Berman. "Service Utilization and Alaskan Natives: Some Theoretical Applications," in *Human Services in the Rural Environment,* vol. 12, no. 1, 1988:11–16.

Dinero, S.C. "Resettlement and Modernization in Post-Nomadic Bedouin Society: The Case of Segev Shalom, Israel," in *The Journal of Planning Education and Research,* vol. 15, no. 2, 1996a:105–16.

Dinero, S.C. "Observation, Advocacy or Interference? Under-taking Research in a 'Fourth World' Community," in *Humanity & Society,* August. 20, no. 3, 1996b:111–32.

Falah, G. "The Development of the 'Planned Bedouin Settlement' in Israel 1964–1982: Evaluation and Characteristics," in *Geoforum,* vol. 14, no. 3, 1983:311–23.

Falah, G. "How Israel Controls the Bedouin," in the *Journal of Palestine Studies,* vol. xiv, no. 2, 1985:35–51.

Falah, G. "Israeli State Policy Toward Bedouin Sedentarization in the Negev," in the *Journal of Palestine Studies,* vol. xviii, no. 2, 1989:71–91.

Fenster, T. *Participation in the Settlement Planning Process: The Case of the Bedouin in the Israeli Negev.* Doctoral dissertation, London School of Economics, London. 1991.

Horner, D.F. "Planning for Bedouin," in *Third World Planning Review,* vol. 4, no. 2, 1982:159–76.

Jerusalem Post. Various issues.

Jerusalem Report. Various issues.

Kressel, G. "Shame and Gender." *Anthropological Quarterly,* vol. 65, no. 1, 1992:34–46.

Lewando-Hundt, G.; I. Abu-Saad & K. Frederick-Abu Saad. "The Health and Health Care of Negev Bedouin Arab Infants in the 1980's." Unpublished booklet, Galilee Society for Health Research and Services, Rama, Israel. 1991.

Maddrell, P. *Bedouin of the Negev.* London: Minority Rights Group Publications. 1990.

Marx, E. In Weissleder, Wolfgang (ed.) *The Nomadic Alternative.* The Hague: Mouton Publishers. 1978.

Massam, B.H. "Servicing Indigenous Persons in a Frontier Area: The Nunavut Experiment." A paper presented at the Negev Centre for Regional Development Conference on Regional Development: The Challenge of the Frontier, Ein Boqeq, Israel. 1993.

Meir, A. "Territoriality Among the Negev Bedouin From Nomadism to Semi-Urbanism." Paper presented at the Conference on Tribal and Peasant Pastoralism - The Dialectics of Cohesion and Fragmentation, by the commission on Nomadic Peoples of the International Union of Anthropological and Ethnological Sciences, Pavia, Italy. 1992.

Meir, A. and Y. Ben-David. "Welfare Support for Israeli Negev Bedouin Elderly Men: Adaptation During Spatioecological Transformation," in *The Gerontologist*, vol. 33, no. 3, 1993:308–14.

Stern, E. and A. Meir. *The Negev Atlas, Part A.* Be'er Sheva: Ben-Gurion University. 1981.

Tel Sheva Survey. Unpublished report by the Office of Social Welfare, Tel Sheva Regional Council (Hebrew). 1991.

Interviews/Personal Communications

Abu-Gardod, S. Agriculturalist and herder. November 20, 1992.

Abu-Mu'amar, A. Eldest son of El-Azazma Sheikh Abu-Mu'amar; Board Member, Masos Regional Council. July 9, 1996.

El-Hamamdi, M. Headmaster, Segev Shalom Secondary School and Regional Council Board Member. July 2, 1996.

Gur, Yochanan. Regional Planner (Southern Region), the State Ministry of the Interior. November 17, 1992.

Masos Regional Council. Information and Statistics. 1993, 1996.

Rahat City Council. Information and Statistics. 1996.

Rehes, H. Social worker, Masos Regional Council. July 14, 1996.

Sagie, I. Mayor of Masos Regional Council (comprised of Segev Shalom, Aroer, and K'seifa). July 1, 1996; July 31, 1996.

Shapira, Yehoshua. Land Inspector for the Israel Lands Authority. November 24, 1992.

Institutional Responses to Planning in a Multicultural Society

CHAPTER 12

The Higher Duty of Local Planning Commissions in a Multicultural Society

David Allor & J. T. Spence

Within the larger processes of American urban planning, the deliberations of local planning commissions will increasingly reveal the continuing emergence of America as a multicultural society in three related dimensions. First, in their efforts to construct a value consensus by which to guide public decision-making, local planning commissions will seek to reweave the tapestry of American culture. This will require a continuing acceptance of, accommodation to, and integration with very diverse immigrant cultures. The current dominant culture, one largely Northern European-American, will give way to an expanding constellation of cultures within which it is one significant minority. In turn, the current minority cultures, most notably the Native American, Appalachian, African American, and Hispanic American, will have to reassess their position, contribution, and visibility within that expanding tapestry.

Second and in consequence, there will be recurrent cross-pressures toward cultural homogenization and cultural pluralism. The deliberations of local planning commissions will center on four critical aspects of culture: religion, family, property, and aesthetics.

The third dimension is the character of the planning commission itself. Local planning commissions will struggle to reconstitute themselves as representative bodies in both formal and substantive aspects. Here, cultural cross-pressures will place great stress upon planning commissions to be more responsive to value diversity while assuring continuity and effectiveness of process. The success of local planning commissions will rest upon the ability of each of its members to attain a multicultural mentality as an essential component of conscientious service to an increasingly multicultural society.

REWEAVING THE TAPESTRY OF AMERICAN CULTURE

There is an ongoing cultural revolution occurring in America. It is beginning to change the way Americans do business, affecting their social interactions and the political institutions of their democracy. The demographic changes that are occurring in America's population will have, by the year 2050, created a dramatic cultural and ethnic transformation of the nation. Non-Hispanic, White Americans will no longer be a majority of the population that comprises the American cultural tapestry, but instead, a significant minority within a diverse set of minorities. Comprising 80 percent of the American population in 1980, non-Hispanic Whites are projected to be just 53 percent by the year 2050.[1] As a corollary, the Hispanic population is expected to rise to 25 percent and Asians will make up 8 percent of America's future population. The impact of this demographic change is significant because the dominant cultural norms that have framed American society for the past 300 years are beginning to be modified to reflect the impact of other ethnicities and other cultural norms.

The assumptions that have provided the pattern for the design of the current American cultural tapestry are beginning to fray. The signs are already evident throughout America, not only in the coastal cities, but in its very heartland. Hindu temples are rising in the cornfields of Ohio; diversity and cultural awareness training programs are commonplace in industrial settings in Kentucky; police officers in Lincoln, Nebraska are being assigned as liaisons to the city's Asian, Hispanic, Native-American, and African American community centers; and Spanish-language television broadcasting is now widely available.[2] America's growing cultural diversity has come to mean more than learning the names of ethnic holidays and sampling from the diverse menu of the world cafeteria. America's dominant cultural paradigms, those basic assumptions rooted in the nation's Anglo-European national heritage, are becoming dramatically altered.

America today is predominantly composed of immigrants and their descendants. Although many immigrants came to this country unwillingly, most entered into American culture to gain freedom and opportunity. Specifically, there were four primary reasons immigrants came to America: to secure religious freedom, to assure political rights, to protect human rights, and to enjoy economic opportunity. These immigrants viewed America as value tolerant, where all people, regardless of creed, religion, or self-identity, had an opportunity to better themselves while still preserving aspects of their cultural identities.

America became known as a "melting pot" where many different cultures were united in their similar distaste for prejudice and tyranny. Although it has typically regarded itself as a nation based upon a pluralist ideal where compromise reigns, America has not been a nation that has blended ethnic groups. America has been a nation with one dominant culture. It has not been an American culture created out of the amalgam of diversity, but a predominantly English culture, transplanted to America, that has imposed its own cultural values, language, and religion upon all minority cultures. "Thus," describes Benjamin Schwarz, "long before the United States' founding, and until probably the 1960s, the unity of the American people derived not from their warm welcoming of and accommodation to nationalist, ethnic, and linguistic differences but from the ability and willingness of an Anglo elite to stamp its image on other peoples coming to this country" (Schwartz 1995:56–67).

Despite the influx of immigrants from other cultures, there was no confusion about the national identity: it was Anglo-European. Willingly, as well as forcibly, the national culture was adopted by the majority of immigrants. Its adoption provided the means to achieve acceptance in American society as well as the ticket to participation in the economic and political life of the country. In a series of wars with other cultures, America expanded westward during the 1800s, converting whatever society existed in those vast lands to one where the American cultural ideal held sway. There was no discussion about accomodation—the process was one of absorption. America was built by the dominance of one culture over all others. It is not possible to realistically consider what America would be like today had cultural compromise been the national strategy.

Despite the pervasive influence of Anglo-American culture, the threads of other cultures remained faintly visible, particularly in small-town, agrarian America. Perhaps it was the civil rights movement that first motivated America to adopt a more conciliatory attitude toward the idea of multiculturalism. It may also be argued that the education America received as a result of its involvement in international wars brought a new understanding and respect for cultural diversity. More realistically however, the cultural revolution of the 1960s happened to have coincided with American minorities' gaining sufficient economic, social, and political influence that they began to be considered a significant element of the nation's economic and political life. This, in turn, has led to a grudging acknowledgment and (arguably superficial) acceptance by America's dominant Anglo-European culture that the nation's minorities practice their beliefs, live their lives, and invest their assets in ways different from those prescribed by the dominant culture.

Thirty years later the realization is dawning that the American prototypical nuclear family practicing Anglo-European cultural values, habits, and religion is soon to be, in another fifty years, another minority within the larger population. Comprehending this fact is critical because what Americans determine to do during the next few decades to prepare for the shift from a paradigm of one dominant culture to one much more open to being influenced by a vast array of cultural values, may well determine the fate of the democracy. Anglo-Americans, indeed all Americans of Western European background, will need to learn how to live among compounding minorities within the larger American culture.

Learning to live as a minority within American culture will not be easy for Anglo-Americans. The country can expect friction as power is dispersed, compromises are made, and institutions are modified to reflect other people's cultural values. To preserve American democracy, the majority culture will be forced to divest itself of powers that it has long held. Not just political decision-making powers, but also those that establish social, economic, and cultural norms will have to be shared. That this shifting of power will result in conflict is inevitable, for a democracy is a system of government that encourages conflict. America's challenge will be to ensure that its culture and its political institutions remain flexible and able to adapt to changing circumstances by adopting elements of the new national multiculturalism, while still continuing to have the confidence and support of the current majority. The reweaving of the American cultural tapestry will stress the very structure of the democracy.

America, as defined by its dominant culture, has been expecting its citizens to shape their behavior, attitudes, and beliefs within a set of very narrowly defined values. The dominant Anglo-European culture has been using one process, one set of values, to define what is appropriate, correct, and acceptable. It is true that the nation's governmental processes and institutions have often provided security and direction for immigrants. Yet these same processes and institutions have also controlled and shaped the behavior, attitudes, and values of immigrants, making their own cultural associations secondary to those of the larger and more powerful dominant culture. The "melting pot" was actually a process of homogenization where differing cultural values were transmogrified and where distinctiveness was no longer recognized. More recently, however, America is becoming a salad, where differences are valued and where diverse cultures make a distinct representative contribution to the whole. Within the rewoven tapestry of the future American culture, there will be no dominant color.

If one of America's primary goals as a nation is to protect and preserve its democracy, then it is imperative that all Americans understand the potential impacts of the oncoming demographic change. The entire society, as a people, must begin to adapt to ensure that the transition will not destroy the government and the people for which it serves. The key feature of American democracy, and one that has repeatedly preserved the union, has been the flexibility of the nation's governmental institutions to adapt to changing circumstances. Just as the past forty years of racial conflict have impacted the nation's priorities, policies, and institutions, so, too, will the radically changing demographic profile of the next fifty years impact America's cultural paradigms. The oncoming demographic changes are inevitable. If Americans prepare for the changes, they may well be able to preserve the overall stability of the society, even while they are engaged in the process of reweaving its cultural elements.

While all aspects of American culture will be affected by changing demographics, it is especially important to consider how democratic governmental institutions will be impacted. In the future the American people may rely more upon a belief in, and adherence to, the processes of these institutions to determine what constitutes an American than any other aspect of the nation's culture.

THE CRUCIAL POSITION OF THE LOCAL PLANNING COMMISSION

As the millennium approaches, the turbulence of America's adjusting to a new cultural milieu will be mirrored within its democratic institutions. One dramatic example is the local planning commission that typically holds responsibility for preparing a local community's planning guidelines and zoning codes. The planning commission then interprets these guidelines and codes in order to make decisions regarding land development and to determine what constitutes appropriate design, mixes of uses, and modifications to the existing physical landscape.   Planning commissions wrestle to pragmatically integrate diverse thought and opinion into the standards the commission uses to determine appropriate planning goals and objectives. For those who will sit on the planning commissions of the future, an increasing awareness and responsiveness to ethnic and cultural diversity will play a central role in their institution's ability to continue to represent democratic values and community norms. The integration of diverse cultural values will modify a community's criteria for decision-making and what in the past was deemed appropriate, correct, and acceptable will be questioned. The main challenges to prevailing thought and practice will be centered upon certain fundamental issues such as religion, family, aesthetics, and property.[3]

Religion and Culture

Among the most difficult decisions made by a planning commission are those tied to issues of religion and culture. There is growing evidence that American society is placing an enhanced emphasis on religious values, and not only tolerating, but valuing, cultural pluralism. Planning commissions, in step with the planning profession, have long found safe ground in promoting functional values; that is, improvements in a community's physical quality of life loosely associated with the common good, general welfare, or public interest. Though no doubt sensitive to the constitutional guarantees of freedom of religion, speech, and assembly, planning commissions have maintained the separation of church and state mostly by pursuing secular, usually material, values. In so doing, they have promoted cultural homogeneity. There are now indications that this strategy must be modified. Assertions of varied religious preferences and diverse claims for cultural recognition have brought new stress to planning commission decisions. In this context two points require the patient attention of planning commissions.

First, the historical perspective shows the nation to have dedicated itself to an abstract monotheism. This is demonstrated by the imprint on its legal tender and expressed in this century in the Pledge of Allegiance. The founders of the nation were acutely aware, however, of Europe's history of unrelenting, violent, and selective suppression of religious faiths. They were also aware that many of the nation's initial settlers were driven by a search for religious freedom. Tolerance of religious diversity led to a cultural tolerance that was necessary for a nation begun and built by successive waves of immigrants. In actuality, though, the dominant religious note in American public life since the early 1900s might be said to have been a mild Protestantism, tempered by the gradual acceptance of Catholicism and Judaism, but on less than equal terms. Neither this descriptive history, however, nor the nonspecific monotheism expressed by the founders defines the United States as an exclusively Christian nation, although adherents of some Christian groups are vocal with that claim. Their insistence that American society and polity give precedence to particular sectarian beliefs is an unfortunate misrepresentation of the constitutional framework that the nation's founders hoped would keep America free of religious imperatives. When such claims are forwarded in local politics, planning commissions may find it difficult to maintain neutrality. It is critical in a democracy, however, that its institutions identify the common values that give continuity and direction to American communities.

The increasing cultural pluralism of America also complicates, in other ways, the effort to deliberate within a framework of common values. Until recently, the nation's historical record has not included approval of either the religious preferences or the broad cultural values of, for example, Native Americans, African Americans, Appalachian Americans, or Hispanic Americans. These cultures, now resurgent, demand recognition as partners in the American democracy, and some an apology for historical insult and compensation for discrimination. The adamant public expression of such claims is not always comfortable to encounter. These current forms of turbulence may well make it more challenging for planning commissions to conduct public hearings or even their deliberative sessions, as they consider decisions with implications for deeply held religious and cultural values.

Second, identifying the commonly held values in American communities will become more complex. Even with a national monotheistic and Anglo-European cultural tradition, the increasing necessity to accommodate, for example, adherents of Islam, who themselves are composed of very diverse ethnic groups, is likely to be a disconcerting experience for many Americans. New residents of American communities, such as the adherents to Sunnite, Shiite, or perhaps Black Muslim traditions, may be from among ethnic groups who have migrated from anywhere along the broad band stretching from the Straits of Gilbraltar, across all of North Africa, the Middle East, India, Southeast Asia, to the Philippines. Even more unfamiliar are the polytheistic, spiritualistic, ancestral, or animistic religions of Africa, India, China, Southeast Asia, Japan, northern Brazil, and the Caribbean. It is not farfetched to consider that, at some time in the near future, a religious group will seek to open a "church" in a community that is not familiar with animistic practices. Such a church seeking to locate in an urban residential neighborhood and wishing to continue its theistic tradition of sacrificing animals could prove more than difficult for the local community to accept, yet these are possible religious preferences for many of those who will in the future be American. Planning commissions will have to "internationalize" themselves, not only by broadening their composition but also, and more critically, by broadening their individual and collective minds. Defining what is a church, for instance, and what constitutes appropriate religious conventions may require developing a new context for decision-making. Members of the local planning commission will have to understand they are critical players in efforts to successfully reweave the local cultural tapestry.

Family and Community

The American nuclear family, while widely recognized, was an artificial construction of post–World War II economic policy, planning process, and Hollywood stereotyping. Throughout the history of the nation, the descendants of new arrivals sought to maintain extended family structure, multi-generational kinship, and ethnic identity. The deprivations of the Great Depression and World War II undoubtedly constrained the occupational, residential, and educational opportunities of at least one generation, but that generation's pent-up demand to enjoy the bounty of peacetime (albeit Cold War) America profoundly changed the urban landscape. Economic development policy, strongly supported by the processes of local comprehensive physical planning, greatly accelerated the suburbanization of America, scattering the population at so low a density across so vast a continent segregating American society not only by economic class and race, but also by generation.

The inordinate and sustained effort to create the American nuclear family (Ozzie and Harriet and David and Rickie, living in a single-family residence in an R-1 zone) was a compounding disaster. By dividing society intergenerationally, often abandoning grandparents in either the central city or the rural countryside, the new nuclear family pattern distanced kinship ties and weakened ethnic tradition. Today many families and individuals require alternative living arrangements such as the traditional mother-daughter residence or single-room occupancy (SRO). In many communities, however, the current response is to segregate the needy, viewing their situational needs as unsuited for single family zoning. Whereas extended families once cared for the old, the ill, and the dying, planners now find it a struggle to place congregate-living residences, elder apartments, granny flats, nursing homes, and hospice facilities in nuclear-family residential areas, as if such uses were inherent nuisances. The oncoming demographic changes will not allow such thinking to go unchallenged.

As the population cohorts that provided the impetus for the construction of vast tracts of single-family residences age and begin to adopt more varied patterns of living, the sanctity of single-family residential developments will be tested. The changing cultural demographics of the marketplace, and the smaller size of future population cohorts, will not provide for the consumption of single-family dwelling units in the same manner as in the past. Single-family residences will be subdivided within families that need to live in multi-generational households, or between families seeking to find a better market return on an investment that they will not occupy themselves. The planning commissions who worked to protect and preserve communities composed of single-family housing will be forced to deal with the difficult pressures of the marketplace of the future and the changing demands of their citizens.

The segregation of American society by income, by ethnicity, by race, by generation, and by land use has been horrifyingly successful in producing both social isolation and cultural banality. Entire cities have been exceedingly stratified according to use, and on Sunday afternoons they often resemble Planet Earth after some terrifying disease has removed the human population.   If contemporary planning commissions must battle to reconstruct a traditional sense of community in America (an unpasturized version where economic, ethnic, generational, cultural, and land-use diversity is not seen as a plague), it is because antecedent planning commissions shared complicity in the homogenization of the nation, rendering the traditional American community an endangered species.

Future planning commissions must not only accommodate the alternative definitions of "family" honored by the diverse cultures making their homes in America, but must also take into account the longer life expectancies of present generations.   An increasing proportion of the current and future members of American communities will live two decades or more beyond retirement. They will become the senior members of a society stretching across four, possibly five, generations. Providing for their continued residence and, more importantly, their active participation in the democracy is essential to the continuity and the vitality of the nation and its communities.

Aesthetics and Community Design

In many American communities planning commissions have sought to strengthen the physical imagery of their communities through architectural conservation of existing structures and design regulations for new construction. Although these programs (which are often enacted as overlay zones to existing zoning ordinances) may be administered by an architectural review board or design review commission, they should serve the larger purposes of community planning. In some communities there is a significant historic and architectural heritage meriting special protective regulation. In other communities, however, style-based design regulations serve simply to wrap modern construction with a pseudo-historical veneer. The current popularity of "neotraditional" planning (and its concomitant reliance upon a locally relevant historical architecture) reflects a perceived failure of modern design to express community in a meaningful way, yet neotraditional planning often is no more than a random assemblage of conventional design details. Neither the local planning commission nor members of the community are able to discern any underlying "tradition."

Planning commissions should be especially careful in adopting style-related design regulations, whether honestly seeking to conserve a design heritage or, more modestly, to borrow one. Architectural styles carry connotations of the parent culture's attributes. While certain of those attributes may be seen as worthy of commemoration and perhaps of emulation, others can be problematic. In adopting style-dependent design regulations, a planning commission should examine which of the underlying cultural values it is promoting.

There are two troublesome problems with community design criteria. The first is that the choice of style expresses an underlying exclusiveness based on cultural ethnocentrism. Persons seeking to enter such a "designed" community are expected not only to live behind compatible facades, but also to subscribe to compatible values and behave in a compatible manner. Those unable or unwilling to do so are dissuaded from community membership. The effect is not to build the community as a whole, reflecting the larger society, but to fragment it.

The second, equally dangerous possibility is that the intention of community design is disingenuous in the sense that architectural conservation and design standards are imposed to raise economic barriers to community membership. Community design regulations can serve to implement economic discrimination.

In the future planning commissions should rely more on design regulations that do not specifically limit style. Guidelines that offer options in siting, form, signage, construction methods, materials, and colors will need to be more expansive in the culturally pluralistic communities that lie ahead. Where design regulations are imposed, the rationale for doing so should be honestly acknowledged and publicly accepted, and the economic costs associated with compliance should not be so severe as to raise cultural barriers or the suspicion of discrimination.

Property and Community

Planning commissions recurrently confront a central dilemma of the American polity. Modern citizenship in America's democracy is predicated upon the guarantee of certain rights that attach to a person. Historically, however, effective citizenship has been defined in terms of property ownership, and in some communities continues to be so. For some, property ownership is the material proof that one holds an interest in the community. Conversely, persons who do not own property in the community are not accepted by some as real members. A number of prejudices about the meaning of property ownership are frequently demonstrated in the hearings and deliberations of planning commissions: renters are inferior to home owners; apartment living is morally objectionable; prefabricated housing is inferior to "real" homes; the out-of-town developer is dishonest, while the local contractor is reliable. While a planning commission does have the responsibility to assess the differential impacts of development upon the land, ownership of property, or the lack of it, does not alter the responsibility of the planning commission to treat all persons appearing before it with fairness, reasonableness, and objectivity.

In the future full ownership of land will become less important in American society. As the economy shifts toward rapidly advancing, technologically oriented service and information-based industries, disposable income will move away from property investment to human resource investment. The adult working population will have to commit income to recurrently upgrading skills, or retraining for career changes. Similarly, for their children, far more income will have to be committed to carry them through advanced technical training or graduate professional degrees. With the "Baby Boom" generation aging and anxious to dispose of their family homes, and with much smaller numbers of "Generation X" and "Baby Boomlet" families in the market to buy such homes, real estate values will stabilize. Persons planning for retirement will choose more flexible investments with a higher and faster growth capacity than real estate to support their continued quality of life.

Communities that have dedicated themselves narrowly to "up-scale" residential development may soon find themselves doubly restrained; they will be unable to provide for their maturing populations and unable to attract buyers from the newer generations. The transition to the service economy will bring salary levels below those of the previously dominant manufacturing sector. The younger working population will have to postpone home ownership to secure their training and career paths. They will find it much harder to save enough for the down payment, or may not choose to commit their earning to large and long-term mortgage debts even at relatively low interest rates. Moreover, occupational ascent will require geographic mobility, further diminishing investment in real property. At the other end of the age scale, the elderly may seek to divest themselves of property, thereby eliminating tax and maintenance costs and reducing expenses while conserving capital assets. Retired and elderly residents may have to move from communities that have not encouraged a range of residential options even in the absence of immediate buyers for the housing.

Although providing "affordable housing" within communities is now discussed at length, local planning commissions have generally resisted approval of housing not only for low-income families, but also for young people and the elderly with limited incomes. In consequence, a community committed to stringent guidelines for single-family residential land use may find itself unable to provide for its mature residents and unable to attract the rising generation.

PREPARING THE PLANNING COMMISSION FOR DIVERSITY

If planning commissions are to successfully meet the challenges of a multicultural, democratic political environment, they must expand the definition of their own representativeness and look to more broadly define what constitutes the larger community. The processes needed to accomplish these tasks may result in the planning commission undergoing social-structural change. By "incorporating different people into the same structure, or incorporating the same people into different structures," the planning commission needs to be more representative of the larger community. Ethnic and racial prejudice, whether intended or not, may never be fully addressed until people of different cultural backgrounds, representative of the community-at-large, share community decision-making in a political arrangement where all are equals.[4]

Local planning commissions, in order to maintain their institutional impartiality and thus the community's support, must avoid acquiring labels. A planning commission that allows itself to exhibit prejudicial decision-making or to maintain policies supporting outcomes that increase cultural segregation will be seen as having lost its impartiality. Communities where this occurs will be accused of controlling admission into the local democracy. Planning commissions must understand that neither longevity of residence nor extent of property ownership confers special privileges on residents.   The last person to have entered a democracy does not have the right to close the door to those who follow. Promoting community character may be a subtle method for exclusion. Large-lot subdivision regulations, low-density residential zoning, and style-based design standards may not work so much to "improve the quality of the community" as to exclude some persons from the opportunity to enjoy it.

To protect the institutional integrity of the planning commission, policies should be adopted that relate community decisions to the actual circumstances of its residents and that consider what the future of a diverse cultural community will be. For issues of economic development, those policies should consider market viability, occupational diversity, and employment stratification. Residential policies should be flexible, providing for a range of density, style, and tenancy options appropriate for diverse income levels, family situations, and family values. Planning commissions should have policies on a wide range of issues related to the community's quality of life, incorporating the values of the community-at-large and establishing reasonable and equitable processes by which these values may be realized.

A planning commission's policies should also be based upon formally adopted, regularly updated, long-range, comprehensive plans that have been developed with meaningful citizen participation. All aspects of the community's plan should be open for discussion, questioned, and analyzed based upon the changing demographic and cultural milieu in which planning takes place.   The challenge posed to the planning commission is to find the balance between making modifications to a plan based upon immediate political pressures and holding on to existing planning goals long after public skirmishes have indicated that the plan no longer meets the needs of the evolving community. Local planning commissions that narrowly tinker with the land-use pattern through zoning regulation condemn themselves to recurrent, confrontational land-use disputes. Those commissions that fail to find the right mix of flexibility in their zoning to reflect the diversity of their community stand to subject themselves to courtroom confrontations and a loss of public confidence.

If a local planning commission truly desires to reflect its community, then it must clearly and consistently signal to those who come before it, and to the citizens-at-large, that a community-based comprehensive plan, and formally adopted public policies, guide its decision-making process.   The central responsibility of the planning commission is to provide collective sound judgement and intelligent direction in service to the future of the community. The commission must challenge itself to consider the impact of the changing cultural setting in which it works and to incorporate this knowledge into the community's plan.

The decisions of the local planning commission have a tremendous impact upon the life of its community, irrevocably altering people's lives through the shaping, not only of the physical landscape, but also of the patterns of social interaction: residence, work, education, worship, and play. Local planning commissions cannot be allowed to escape their responsibility to maintain the larger view of society and do their duty to represent the entire community. The members of the commission must understand that they are making judgments that should reflect the values of their community. Whether those values are based upon the ideas of a single culture or on the community's cultural diversity will, ultimately, be the responsibility of each individual member of the commission.

The next century poses a unique challenge to America's democracy: "Can we live in a truly multicultural society?" The nation's history is replete with admirable episodes during which society expanded to create political opportunity, fought to assure equal rights, and promoted religious and cultural tolerance. The conflicts that will arise as a result of the changing cultural dynamics in our society will certainly test America's ability to continue to call itself a democracy. Nowhere will change be as necessary as in its political institutions and, because of its close fundamental community decision-making role, nowhere will the conflict be more personal than in the local planning commission. It is in the local community that Americans must begin now to prepare themselves and their collective society for a multicultural future.

NOTES

The authors would particularly like to acknowledge the assistance of Colleen K. O'Toole, Ph.D. for her editing and valuable critique of this chapter.

1. Demographic data obtained from the U.S. Census Bureau report, "Population Projections of the United States by Age, Sex, Race, and Hispanic Origin: 1995 to 2050," published in 1996.

2. *Community Policing Exchange*, September/October 1997. Published by Community Policing Consortium, 1726 M. Street, N.W., Suite 801, Washington, D.C., 20036. The Community Policing Consortium recently dedicated an entire issue of its publication to issues of cultural diversity. The publication is sent to police departments and community policing organizations throughout the United States.

3. Much of the following was originally discussed in David J. Allor's article "Toward a Longer and Higher Duty for Local Planning Commissions," published in the *Journal of the American Planning Association,* Vol. 60, No. 4, Autumn 1994:437–43.

4. Mayer, Robert R. "Social Planning and Social Change." Prentice-Hall, Inc. Englewood Cliffs, N.J., 1972, p. 41. Mayer presents an analytical approach to answering questions related to social problems and structural interventions. In particular, chapter 3 presents a case study of interracial housing that, even though somewhat dated, has broad implications for finding solutions to living successfully in a multicultural democracy.

REFERENCES

Allor, David J. "Toward a Longer View and Higher Duty for Local Planning Commissions." *Journal of the American Planning Association,* vol. 60, no. 4, Autumn 1994:437–43.

Allor, David J. "Concensus and Dissensus in Decision-Making By Urban Planning Commissions: Some Reflections on a Sociology of Rationality." Paper presented at the North Central Sociological Association, Indianapolis, Indiana, April 1984.

Community Policing Consortium. *Community Policing Exchange*. 1726 M. Street, N.W., Suite 801, Washington, D.C. 20036. September/October 1997.

Mayer, Robert R. *Social Planning and Social Change*. Prentice-Hall, Inc. Englewood Cliffs, N.J., 1972:41.

Sanders, Welford and Judith Getzels. *The Planning Commission: Its Composition and Function.* Planning Advisory Service Report, no. 400. American Planning Association. 1987.

Schwarz, Benjamin. "The Diversity Myth." *The Atlantic Monthly*, vol. 275, no. 5, May 1995:57–67.

U.S. Census Bureau. *Population Projections of the United States by Age, Sex, Race, and Hispanic Origin: 1995 to 2050.* 1996.

CHAPTER 13

Some Thoughts on Incorporating Multiculturalism in Urban Design Education

Siddhartha Sen

Incorporating issues of multiculturalism in planning curriculums have become an important goal for planning educators in recent times (Friedmann and Kuester 1994; Thomas 1996). Multicultural issues can be broadly defined as ones that deal with race, gender, ethnicity, and internationalism.[1] The origins of multiculturalism date back to the late 1960s and early 1970s in the field of education, when the term primarily referred to introduction of diverse cultures that had been underrepresented or omitted in school curricula (Banks 1984). The term has since then been broadened to refer to ethnic, racial, social, and gender groups as well as groups with special needs (Hernandez 1989). The concept also includes empowerment of students from diverse cultures and classes (Banks 1994).

The concept of multiculturalism in planning is comparatively new. Until the 1960s "monocultural" physical planning was the bulwark of planning education. Although one cannot deny that concerns with race, justice, advocacy, and equality did enter planning education since the 1960s (Davidoff 1965; Davidoff, Davidoff, and Gold 1970), serious challenge to the monocultural planning pedagogy was first posed in the mid-1980s by the group of scholars who questioned the relevancy of U.S. planning education for students from developing nations (Banerjee 1985; Quadeer 1986). Later on other internationalists (Amirahmadi 1993; Sanyal 1989, 1990), interjected fresh thinking into the issue by proposing a "one world approach to planning education." This approach to planning education emphasized mutual learning process by bringing together students from the first and third world on common problems. With global restructuring, the first world could learn from the problems that were typically associated with the third world (e.g., homelessness and the informal sector). Such a perspective called for incorporation of an interdisciplinary multicultural and global outlook in planning education that would allow for better local practice and cultural diversity.

Others have challenged the monocultural perspective from the viewpoint of race and gender (Ritzdorf 1992; Sandercock and Forsyth 1992; Thomas 1996). These scholars have argued that "diversity" not only implies changing the curriculum and course content, but also understanding variation in teaching styles that diversity brings. Ritzdorf (1993), for instance, points out that to gain optimum effect in a classroom that is diverse in its racial, ethnic, and gender composition, planning academicians need to employ teaching tools that are not just technical and task oriented. A diverse classroom can benefit from assignments that allow students to interpret their own life experiences within a larger social or political context and relate them to the task at hand. According to these scholars, students would benefit from receiving strong overt and covert messages that all races and cultures are valuable as are both genders. From such a perspective diversity is a strength that should be nurtured rather than a requirement to be tolerated.

Today, even the Planning Accreditation Board (PAB) requires that such issues be incorporated as an integral part of the curriculum.[2] "Diversity training"[3] is gaining popularity even in the "real world of planning" (Knack 1997a). The planning director of Norfolk, Virginia, for example, stated that diversity training is fundamental to what planners do. To cite another example, the director of community development in Huntington Park, California, set up Ethnopolis Inc., a nonprofit organization dedicated to increasing awareness of ethnic diversity and its implications for contemporary urban life (Wong 1997). This particular director also believes that as a planner, one must recognize that racial and ethnic tensions threaten to tear apart our communities. It is up to planners to ensure that all voices are heard and everyone has a chance to build livable communities.

The planning faculty is still grappling with the issues of multiculturalism, however (Forsyth 1995; Thomas 1996). Most progress on pedagogy seems to have been made in sub-fields of international planning and race- and gender-oriented approaches to planning (Burayidi 1993; Ritzdorf 1993; Sanyal 1990; Thomas 1996). On the surface, very little progress seems to have been made on urban design pedagogy that incorporates multiculturalism. Some may even question the validity of the debate given urban design's traditional association with aesthetics or more recent preoccupation with technology. This chapter, however, argues that it is possible to forget this "unholy alliance" of multiculturalism and urban design.

The chapter draws from literature: on urban design, feminist critiques of space and built environment, cultural landscapes, cross-cultural studies on form and use of space, cultural aspects and spatial aspects of globalization and colonization, and the author's personal experience of teaching at a Historically Black College/University (HBCU)[4] and personal search for what should constitute the field of urban design. The chapter begins with a review of the origins of urban design in the Uniited States and traces the existence of multicultural thought in the field. This is followed by a discussion on the pragmatic needs for incorporating multiculturalism in urban design. I then present my own endeavors in incorporating multiculturalism in urban design and reflect on how an HBCU setting and my personal search has led to incorporation of such issues in my courses on urban design. This is followed by synthesis and concluding remarks.

THE ORIGINS OF URBAN DESIGN AND THE PRESENCE OF MULTICULTURALISM IN THE DISCIPLINE

Although "modern urban design" emerged sometime in the 1960s (Moudon 1992), "city design" (simply defined as the art and science of designing or laying out of cities) can be traced back to ancient civilizations of Mesopotamia, Egypt, China, and India. Such early examples of city design include the great bath in Mahenjodaro and Harappa (now in Pakistan) or hanging gardens in Mesopotamia. Most history textbooks classify early efforts of city design in the seventeenth- and eighteenth-century United States as city planning (Eisner, Gallion, and Eisner 1993; Levy 1997; Scott 1969). Such efforts of "city planning" was, in reality, "city design" when early settlers or surveyors laid out cities (e.g., Williamsburg, Philadelphia, and Savannah) with formal axes and grid iron street systems interspersed with squares. A slight variant of this form was the radial plan adopted in such cities as Annapolis. Diagonal avenues and circles were the primary design features of this radial plan.

The influence of design in the historical development of city planning has been well documented by Burgess (1997). As pointed out by Burgess, the planning profession had its roots in the nineteenth century in landscape architect Frederick Law Olmsted's work and the Chicago's World Fair of 1893, which were both inspired by design. Distressed with the monotonous streets, erect buildings, dirt, and squalor of the contemporary American city, Olmsted sought to rehumanize them through design. Daniel Hudson Burnham's vision was very similar. Burnham, an architect, was an official advisor to the Chicago's World Fair, which was held to commemorate the 400th anniversary of Columbus's voyage to America. Burnham assembled a team of architects, landscape architects (including Olmsted), and built a number of elegant buildings, sculptures, and gardens on the fair's site to show what a city could look like (Hines 1979).

The subsequent city beautiful movement encompassed both Olmsted's idealistic parks and Burnham's grandiose schemes. Its advocates believed that redesigning the city could solve its problems. Thus, at the turn of the twentieth century, city planning in the United States was guided by a strong concern for urban aesthetics (Banerjee 1990; Burgess 1997). The predominant belief was that cities could not only be designed but that they should be designed. The power of aesthetic and orderly environments were seen as essential, too, for the health and well being of the public. The living testimonies to such belief are civic landscapes and city designs created by architects and landscape architect planners such as Daniel Burnham, Frederick Law Olmsted, Frederick Law Olmsted Jr., and John Nolen. As pointed out by Burgess (1997), the term "urban design" best describes the city plans developed by these early planning consultants.

Utopian visions of the city, with an emphasis on aesthetics, continued to dominate city planning in the first half of the twentieth century. Englishman Ebenezer Howard's concept of the Garden City had a significant influence in the United States. This grand vision called for a system of small self-sufficient cities surrounded by a greenbelt and sought to combine the best of city and country.

Hundreds of communities ranging from early Radburn (begun in late 1920s) to the later day Columbia (begun in early 1960s) were influenced by the movement.

The design influence continued in the 1920s with the formation of Regional Planning Association of America (RPAA) (Birch 1980; Burgess 1997; Hall 1988). RPAA was joined by architects, designers, and urban critiques such as Lewis Mumford, Clarence Stein, Henry Wright, and Clarence Perry, who believed that good design could restore the sense of loss of community. Some of the design elements of the RPAA garden city movement were also implemented in the Greenbelt towns of the 1930s, while design elements of the Perry's "neighborhood unit" has left a lasting mark in residential design all over the United States.

Well-known design-oriented solutions to ills of the city were forwarded by architects, such as Le Corbusier and Frank Llyod Wright. In 1922 Le Corbusier presented his vision of La Ville Contemporaine. Aesthetics was the primary guiding principle of this vision, which consisted of a city of skyscrapers surrounded by sweeping open space. Le Corbusier followed this by other aesthetically oriented visions of the city, such as Ville Radieuse. Other architects such as Frank Lloyd Wright also proposed aesthetic visions of city design, such as the Broad Acre city. According to this utopian city design, industry, commerce, housing, and social and agricultural facilities were distributed along a railroad artery with access to highways. Each family would own an acre of lot in this city.

In the mid-1940s the International Congress of Modern Architecture (CIAM) produced the Charter of Athens, which became the "manifesto for urban design" (Jacobs and Appleyard 1987). Its emphasis was still on aesthetics, since it intended to rectify the ills of the industrial cities with healthy, humane, and beautiful environments for people.

The design element was lessened but not eliminated from the 1920s through the 1960s as planning evolved as a profession (Burgess 1997). However, except for the very early courses in city planning offered in the 1920s, from landscape architecture and architecture programs, we can hardly classify even earlier preoccupation with physical planning as city design. The physical planning paradigm, which was predominant until 1945, was concerned more with land-use planning than design (Guttenberg and Wetmore 1987; Weiss 1988). As pointed out by Guttenberg and Wetmore (1987), in the case of University of Illinois at Urbana-Champaign, the aesthetic concept of landscape was replaced by the pragmatic concept of land-use management. The meteoric rise of zoning contributed to the demise of aesthetics as a guiding principle for city planning.

The Chicago Program, which became the benchmark of planning education after its founding in the mid-1940s, further contributed to the demise of design in academia because of its social science orientation (Hemmens 1988; Kreditor 1990; Sarbib 1983). By the early 1960s the social science orientation of educators was well entrenched, banishing urban design to the back waters (Banerjee 1990; Kreditor 1990). As pointed out by Banerjee (1990), design was rejuvenated to a certain extent by Kevin Lynch and his followers, such as Donald Appleyard and Allan Jocobs, to the field of planning from the 1960s.

Lynch and his colleagues' effort can be broadly labeled as "contemporary urban design." The origins of contemporary urban design is coveted by many professions, such as architecture, landscape architecture, and urban planning. According to Oc and Tiesdell (1996), it constitutes the interface of architecture, urban planning, landscape architecture, surveying, property development, environmental management and protection, and a host of other disciplines.

Although the concern for multiculturalism is comparatively new and overshadowed by the search for aesthetics in the field of design, one may trace concerns with equity even in the early phase of its development. For example, Olmsted believed that a park was an antidote to the appalling conditions of the city. He further believed that the landscape architect could be a moral agent for reforming society (Burgess 1997). Other early designers such as Burnham, Le Corbusier, Lewis Mumford, Clarence Stein, Henry Wright, and Clarence Perry had similar visions. As discussed, they all thought that design could rectify the city and society's ills.

Concerns for justice, equity, and access can also be found in the writings of contemporary urban designers such as Lynch (1960) and Jacobs and Appleyard (1987). According to Lynch (1960) "good city form" has to deal with the above issues. Jacobs and Appleyard (1987) pointed out that good environment should be accessible to all citizens and that all citizens are entitled to minimal levels of identity, control, and opportunity. They continued that good urban design must be for the poor as well as the rich.

Banerjee (1985) was one of the first planning educators to voice the need for teaching urban design with a multicultural pedagogy. He was concerned about the appropriateness of urban design education for third-world students who came to universities in the United States. Banerjee argued that it was inappropriate to teach these students Western urban design values. There was little relevance of such education to the environmental problems of the developing world. He further argued that environmental design in the third world cannot be viewed separately from the political economy of development and underdevelopment. To treat it in the manner of urban design practices in the West would be inappropriate. Such design training would amount to a socialization to professional worldviews and values of the Western world.

Later Banerjee (1990) further developed the pedagogy of a design education for third-world students. Building on Lynch's work he pointed out that designers need three major types of knowledge: substantive, reflective, and instrumental. Substantive knowledge should focus on the interaction of people, places, place events, and institutions that manage them. The substantive core should include courses that deal with political economy of development and underdevelopment, spatial organization of society, urbanization in the third world, comparative urbanization, modernization, social and cultural change, and evolution of urban form. Reflective knowledge consists of the facility with design as a way of thinking and understanding theories, techniques, values, and models of design. Courses in this area should deal with such topics as history of city design, cultural context of built form, emergence of the design profession, and principles guiding urban design.   Instrumental knowledge deals with skills of observation, representation, expression, and communication. Courses dealing with environment or psychology and sociology, photography, cognitive mapping, and methods of visual anthropology should be taught in this area.

In recent times urban design has become more culture and socio-economic context oriented. As pointed out by Oc and Tiesdell (1996), urban design can be regarded as a re-emergent discipline. From an initial, predominantly aesthetic, concern with the distribution of building masses and space, it is now primarily concerned with the quality of urban public realm, which is both social and physical. Contemporary urban design is concerned with traditional aesthetics as well as cultural, social, economic, and spatial factors that make successful urban spaces.

Finally, we must recognize that other disciplines can make urban design more culturally, racially, ethnically, and gender informed. Most of these studies are "substantive" or "critically" descriptive as opposed to "normative" or "perspective" knowledge. Normative or perspective knowledge emphasizes what should be, while substantive or critically descriptive knowledge emphasizes what is and why it is so. In general, urban design is more concerned with the normative or perspective aspects of knowledge and urban designers are trained to design "good" cities and places.   While urban design research in general is associated with substantive information and understanding certain phenomenon, it   is expected to yield information that has normative dimension that will eventually lead to "good design" (Moudon 1992).[5]

Thus, substantive information on culture, race, ethnicity, and gender can lead to better design. Contributions to the study of physical space and its relationship with women made by feminist academicians in architecture, anthropology, environmental psychology, geography, and history since the early 1980s would be very useful (among others, see, Drucker and Gumpert 1997; Mackenzie and Rose 1983; Spain 1995; Stimpson et al. 1980; Weisman 1992).[6] Exposure to studies on cultural landscapes and indigenous architectural forms (Jackson 1980; Mattson 1992; Upton 1986) would also be useful knowledge for culturally sensitive urban design. Rapoport's (1969, 1984, 1987) cross-cultural studies on form and use of space and King's (1976, 1989, 1990) work on cultural and spatial aspects of globalization and colonization would also be helpful in this context. Finally, urban design could benefit from insights of postmodern geographers' conception of space (Soja 1989) and Foucault's (1977, 1986) treatise on space.

SOME PRAGMATIC REASONS FOR INCORPORATING MULTICULTURALISM IN URBAN DESIGN EDUCATION

Having discussed the progress made in terms of multiculturalism in urban design and potential sources for incorporating such pedagogy, let us now turn to pragmatic reasons for incorporating such issues in urban design. There are at least five pragmatic reasons for incorporating a multicultural pedagogy in urban design education today. First, thirty years of continuing immigration from Latin America, the Caribbean, and Asia has shifted demographics in the United States to make the country more multi-ethnic. Such a shift has resulted in different use of space or will require a different use of space in the near future. Second, there exist older ethnic neighborhoods and landscapes, which have different physical characteristics from predominant ones found all over the United States. We need to make students aware of such physical characteristics and landscapes, since redevelopment in these areas need to take these features into consideration. Third, there is an increasing awareness to preserve historic places that are non-White. This will require a different type of urban designer in the future. Fourth, there is an increasing need for designing spaces based on gender needs. Fifth, global restructuring has also resulted in deterioration of many urban spaces. Urban designers need to be aware of the effects of restructuring in order to "redesign" these spaces. The following paragraphs elaborate each of these aspects.

As stated, the ethnic composition of the United States is changing. About 13 percent of the nation's population is Black while about 10 percent or 25 million are Hispanic. Another 3.5 million are Chinese, Japanese, Koreans, Filipinos, and Vietnamese. In addition, there are hundreds and thousands of other types of non-Whites, such as Indians, Pakistanis, and Bangladeshis (Morganthau 1995). Immigration is not just limited to larger cities such as New York, Los Angeles, Chicago, Houston, or Miami; smaller urban centers are also receiving a share of these immigrants. For example, 38 percent of the population in Garden City, Kansas, are Hispanic, while 7 percent are Vietnamese (Andrews 1997).

Such immigration has led to diverse use of space or change in uses of spaces. The case of Huntington Park, a city on the edge of Los Angeles, is a good example of how a change in racial composition can lead to different use of space. This once Anglo-American city is almost 94 percent Hispanic now. As a result of this change in racial composition, the streets are now heavily used by pedestrians, and there are now taco shops, street vendors, mariachi music, colorful storefronts, and signs written in Spanish. Equally sweeping changes can be observed in many other cites in Los Angeles, such as the Chinese enclave in Monterey Park (Andrews 1997).

Significant changes can also be found in the use of other public spaces such as parks in ethnically diverse neighborhoods around Los Angeles (Loukaitou-Sideris 1995). As pointed out by Loukaitou-Sideris (1995) and by Ameyaw in chapter 7 of this volume, park design should be location specific in order to respond to cultural needs. The designer should avoid replicating the same standardized park design in all neighborhoods and pay attention to the type of park activities that better suit the cultural needs of ethnically diverse communities.

Thirty years of continuing immigration from Latin America, the Caribbean, and Asia is also likely to change the spatial needs of a large section of the population in inner cities. In fact, immigration has been a boon to depressed areas in New York and Los Angeles (Andrews 1997). More than 85 percent of the damage from the 1992 Rodney King riots in ethnic enclaves, such as Korea and the Latino Rico-Union district, has been rebuilt because of the enterprising activities of immigrants (see Weisman 1995). In the near future urban designers will work with these immigrant groups to regenerate their deteriorated inner city neighborhoods.

Thus, there will be a need for urban designers to identify the cultural needs of these communities to design safer streets and neighborhoods.

 Different uses of space or physical characteristics are not only limited to the newly ethnically transformed neighborhoods, but can be traced back to the earlier China towns in the United States (e.g., San Francisco or Portland) (Lai 1990) and other ethnic landscapes (Upton 1986). In China towns recessed balconies and facades covered with Chinese details are common features. Brilliant color schemes of gold, red, and yellow can be found in these towns. Uncommon decorative motifs such as dragons, phoenixes, lions, pagodas, Chinese lanterns, and decorative archways are integral parts of these neighborhoods. Other physical elements, such as signboards, telephone booths, and street lamps, are often more closely spaced than in other neighborhoods.   Pictures arcades, narrow alleys, and enclosed courtyards are also not uncommon.

 Studies on ethnic landscapes also show how various ethnic groups employed different architectural styles and landscaping (Mattson 1992; Upton 1986). To cite one example, during the early twentieth century, large African-American districts were formed in southern cities. The architectural and spatial forms of these cities were very different from the dominant features of the settlement patterns of the South. Among other features, the shotgun house and the uniquely landscaped gardens characterized such neighborhoods. Such unique features can also be found in Irish-American landscapes of Appalachia, German-American landscapes of Pennsylvania, and Japanese-American landscapes of Hawaii.

 Clearly, physical features and landscapes of these neighborhoods are different from the predominant ones in the United States. Redevelopment in these areas needs to take these features into consideration. This is why we need to make students aware of such physical characteristics and landscapes. Critiques have argued that the dominant landscape in the United States is Anglo-American (Zelinsky 1990). According to this view, foreign or ethnic modification of the built environment is not tolerated to a great extent because serious deviation from the norm is too offensive to the collective eye. Colorful patterns, motifs, and yards are nothing but compromised structures and a blending of styles from different ethnic worlds. I maintain Hayden's (1990a) view, however, that these ethnic landscapes of the United States should be seen as a terrain where class, gender, and ethnicity provide different experiences, clearly indicating the need for a "design manifesto" that is sensitive to these issues.

 In recent times there has been an increasing awareness to preserve historic places that are non-White. Hayden (1990b), for example, points out that in Los Angeles, many African-American, Chinese-American, Japanese-American, Native-American and Latino nonprofit history groups are in search of their cultural heritage in urban spaces. This has brought forth several opportunities to save common places such as homes and workplaces, as well as public spaces linked to ethnic history. To cite another example, African-American historic sites are getting new respect as the tourism industry is beginning to realize that a large section of America is non-White (Knack 1997b). As a result, several projects have been undertaken to revitalize historic African-American neighborhoods across the nation. Auburn Avenue in

Atlanta, Astor Row in Harlem, and Bronzeville in Chicago are just a few examples of urban America where historic preservation of Black neighborhoods are under way. As such projects become increasingly popular, urban designers will certainly require a knowledge of the cultural heritage of African Americans.

There is also a pragmatic need for sensitizing urban designers on gender-based differences in the use of public spaces. A large body of literature exists on women and public spaces, among others (see, for example, Weisman 1992; and Drucker and Gumpert 1997). As pointed out by this literature, safety is crucial in understanding gender-based differences in the use of public spaces. For example, fear of sexual harassment or rape often keeps women away from streets and public parks. Often women begin to realize that public streets and parks belong to men. Even suburban malls, which were created as secure environments, have now become unsafe for women with the increasing instances of robberies, rapes, and abduction of women. Design features contribute to the lack of safety in these public spaces. Toronto's METRAC (Metro Action Committee on Violence Against Women and Children) project has identified several design features that contribute to lack of safety for women. These include poor lighting, unpopulated places, lack of visibility to others, and access to help.

The fifth reason for incorporating multiculturalism in urban design is relatively unexplored in the literature. This is the physical manifestation of restructuring of the "post industrial city"—vacant warehouses, railroad stations, downtowns; derelict waterfronts; and so on.[7] For our purposes the post-industrial city is defined as those small- and medium-sized cities in the United States that came into existence because of industries such as fishing and manufacturing, or were dependent upon early modes of transportation such as the railroad. With global industrial restructuring, many of the industries that traditionally sustained these cities have now disappeared or shifted elsewhere, leaving a decreased economic base and a new demographic composition.

The long history of such cities and the very reason for which they came into existence gave them an image. They were known as fishing towns, mill towns, steel towns, textile towns, and so on. This association with a particular industry was an integral part of the town's image. The image was also associated with people's culture, the weather, the topography, architectural styles, and the town's layout. Sometimes the image or identity of the city was associated with a particular place in the town such as city square or the main street. There was often a strong relationship between the built form and the social, economic, and political reasons for which the city came into existence. With global industrial restructuring and changed circumstances, this strong relationship has disappeared. The traditional image of the city as a fishing town, clothing outlet town, mill town, steel town, and textile town can no longer be sustained. Students (as future urban designers) need to be exposed to these physical manifestations of global restructuring in order to restore the image of such cities.

INTRODUCING MULTICULTURAL DESIGN EDUCATION AT MORGAN

In this section I present some attempts that were made on incorporating multicultural issues in urban design at Morgan State University and reflect on the reasons for my limited success and attempt to introduce such concepts. Since my arrival at Morgan State University in the Fall of 1992, I have taught two interdisciplinary courses on urban design. The first is an introductory core course for architects and landscape architects. Planning students often take this course as an elective. The second is an elective course for all three disciplines.

With both courses I have experimented with introducing the concepts of multiculturalism through readings, discussion, written assignments, and graphic exercises. I have taught both classes in mixed format of seminar and studio. Although the majority of the readings are not on issues of multiculturalism in urban design,[8] I did incorporate some readings that dealt with the topic either directly or indirectly (Boyer 1990; Hayden 1990a; Loukaitou-Sidris 1996; Mattson 1992; Moudon 1992; Pivo et al 1990; Stoker 1987). Discussion of the readings have always led to good verbal debates on race, gender, ethnicity, and urban design. In addition to these discussions, students were urged to relate other topics covered in the course, to issues of race, gender, and ethnicity. They are also encouraged to relate current urban design topics in Baltimore to issues of multiculturalism.

Following Ritzdor's (1993) suggestion I also asked students to interpret their own life experiences within a larger social or political context and relate them to urban design through a written assignment. The purpose of this assignment was to write an essay about urban design from their own perspectives. I asked them to write a spontaneous essay arising from their undergraduate and graduate background/discipline, their cultural, racial, and ethnic background, and their gender.[9] Such an exercise has yielded interesting results. For example, an African-American female planning student wrote,

A combination of one's disciplinary background along with the cultural, ethnic, and racial background should play an important role in terms of defining urban design, but often it does not. Although the average person will define urban design in a way that is based on his/her own idea of what is acceptable, attractive and/or grand, often it is the dominant culture, ethic, or racial group who dictates what those ideas will consist of.

This type of essay gives the opportunity for minority students and foreign students to state how urban aesthetics is related to one's culture, race, gender, and ethnicity. This is, perhaps, a hidden feeling among many minorities and international students, and would never surface unless encouraged by the professor to express it.

The result of asking students to relate urban design to their own life experiences within a larger social or political context also produced interesting essays from the White students. It opened up the "fear of city" among White suburbanites, and perhaps even encouraged them to overcome this "fear" if they were to be good urban designers. A White male Architecture student wrote, "Until recently, I have had little experience in urban environments, along with limited understanding and appreciation of cities. This is mostly due to the fact that I have lived in middle class suburban communities all through my life. In addition to this, my parents rarely discussed cities and seldom traveled to them." He continued, "At home, my parents disliked cities and during my early upbringing, I learned from them that cities were places to be avoided because of the crime and the presence of poor minority groups."

Although this particular student had himself overcome this fear and realized that cities could be interesting places to work, play, and live, not many students may have this self realization. Thus, there is a need to expose future designers to the inner cities.

I have also used graphical assignments (mainly cognitive mapping) to expose students to inner city neighborhoods and to discuss the design features of the predominantly Black parts of Baltimore. In particular, I have asked students to use the concept of "cracks in the city" developed by Loukaitou-Sideris (1996) and Boyer's (1990) concept of "utopia" and "heteropianan" spaces to look at the city.

Among other spaces, Loukaitou-Sideris (1996) sees cracks in: the urban core where corporate towers assert their dominance over the skies, but turn their back to the city; inner city where parks and playgrounds have been left to decay; public housing developments that are fenced islands of poverty; abandoned and deteriorated vacant places filled with trash and human wastes; and walled or gated communities that assert their privateness by defying the surrounding landscape. According to Boyer (1990), utopian spaces are unreal spaces existing in the fantasy and untroubled, consoling, perfected regions of the city. In contrast, heterotopian spaces are places of deviation from the normal; they are the pathological or diseased part of the city.

Finally, I was also very fortunate to be able to introduce my students to the insights of the physical manifestation of industrial restructuring in small- to medium-sized towns of the Northeastern and Southern United States from the joint grant that I have held with the School of Architecture at the University of Maryland since 1993. This National Endowment for the Arts Grant sponsors the Mayor's Institute on City Design, Northeast.[10] The Mayor's Institute was set up by the National Endowment for the Arts in 1986 to develop a multi-disciplinary dialogue by encouraging constructive debate to improve the understanding of the design of American cities and the mayor's role in the design process. It consists of a series of small forums where participation is limited to twenty people: half are mayors and half are urban design experts. Each mayor presents a design problem from his or her city. Each case is analyzed by the mayors and design professionals, who, working together, discuss how an appropriate design process can help solve the problem. I have structured urban design classes around these institutes. Students help collect the data and in two particular semesters they also formulated urban design plans for two cities. In this way they were exposed to the physical manifestation of the industrial restructuring in small and medium-sized cities.

My attempt and limited success in introducing multiculturalism in urban design is facilitated by institutional characteristics and context of the university where I teach. My own personal search for "what should constitute the field of urban design" has also prompted me to introduce these issues. I teach at the oldest accredited planning program[11] at an HBCU, which is also one of the nation's oldest such institutions.[12] Morgan's planning program, which had more than 200 graduates as of Spring 1997, has certain unique features because of its HBCU home. One of its unique characteristic lies in its emphasis on the interests, needs, and concerns of African-American planning students. Such an emphasis naturally leads to discussions on gender, race, ethnicity, and class in almost all classes, including urban design. The program follows the traditional advocacy approach to planning education because of the HBCU advocacy role for the disadvantaged (see Davidoff 1965; Davidoff, Davidoff, and Gould 1970). Such an approach to planning education also leads to discussion of gender, race, ethnicity, and classroom in almost all classes.

Another unique feature of the program that helps incorporate multiculturalism is its focus on Baltimore. This is in part dictated by Morgan's urban mission, which carves out for it a major role in the development and study of Baltimore as a major urban metropolis. The 1975 legislation that created Morgan State University stated, in part, that Morgan State should emphasize urban-oriented education. It also stated that Morgan is expected to become the State's primary public institution dealing with programs that address specific social, political, and economic concern of urban areas. The mission was defined by the State Legislature and the State Board for Higher Education and reiterated by Morgan's Board of Regents and the Morgan administration. Morgan's self-study reports from the late 1980s and 1990s also reiterate the mission. These documents emphasize that the university should be an integral part of the resource base used by planners and developers and promoters within the Baltimore city. Furthermore, the university should make every endeavor to inculcate in its student body an understanding of urban America and a sense of social responsibility for improving the quality of life in urban areas. Morgan's mission clearly carves out for it a major role in the development and study of Baltimore as a major urban metropolis.

As a part of the University's urban mission of dealing with programs that address specific social, political, and economic concern of urban areas, the planning program utilizes Baltimore as a laboratory for most of its courses. Projects on disadvantaged sections of Baltimore are an integral part of Morgan's curriculum. In addition, the program frequently responds to requests for projects from disadvantaged communities from Baltimore. As an HBCU Morgan's historic role of reaching out to the disadvantaged further facilitates classroom projects on poor African-American segments of Baltimore. Furthermore, students are often concerned with community development by virtue of residence, ethnic background, or social concern. This in turn leads to incorporation of multicultural issues even in urban design.

My personal search for what should constitute the field of urban design has also led to incorporation of multicultural issues. My entry into urban design was by default. I earned both of my jobs because of my background in architecture. I have a bachelors' degree in architecture from India and a masters in architecture from Rensselaer Polytechnic Institute. Both of my jobs at California State

Polytechnic University, Pomona, and at Morgan State University required me to teach urban design and graphics. Yet my dissertation was far from being a physical planning one. It examined the role of nongovernmental organizations (NGOs) in housing and development in India from a political economy perspective. As one of my Professors, David Sawicki (Sawicki 1988) had correctly stated some years back, I was at that time like many young scholars captivated by romantic notions of political and social reform. Urban design, which had come under severe critique because of its "physical determinism" and "normative orientation," was far from being attractive to me as an area of study.

After a few years of teaching urban design both at California Sate Polytechnic University and Morgan, I began to realize that one cannot teach a subject without conducting research in the area. In particular, I was struggling to see how I could incorporate my romantic notions of political and social reform in teaching with that of conducting research on urban design. Literature on the study of physical space and its relationship with women made by feminist academicians in architecture, anthropology, environmental psychology, geography, and history; cultural landscapes and indigenous architectural forms; cross-cultural studies on form and use of space; cultural and spatial aspects of globalization and colonization; postmodern geographers' conception of space; and Foucault's treatise on space helped me to develop my teaching and research paradigm. Given such an outlook, I was able to incorporate multiculturalism into urban design.

CONCLUDING REMARKS

The discussion suggests that incorporating multiculturalism into urban design is, after all, not an unholy alliance. As discussed, the concern for multiculturalism in urban design may be comparatively new, but one may trace concerns with equity even in the early phase of its development in the visions of early designers such as Olmsted, Burnham, Le Corbusier, Lewis Mumford, Clarence Stein, Henry Wright, and Clarence Perry. Concerns for justice, equity, and access can also be found in the writings of contemporary urban designers such as Kevin Lynch.

In today's multicultural and global society, incorporating multiculturalism into urban design education is more than a "wish-list" of progressive academicians. As discussed, there are at least five pragmatic reasons for incorporating a multicultural pedagogy in urban design education today. To reiterate, first, thirty years of continuing immigration from Latin America, the Caribbean, and Asia has shifted demographics in the United States, which has resulted in different use of space or will require a different use of space in the near future. Second, redevelopment in older ethnic neighborhoods will require an understanding of the physical features and landscapes of these neighborhoods. Third, the increasing need to preserve historic places that are non-White will require a different type of urban designer in the future. Fourth, there is an increasing need for designing spaces based on gender needs. Fifth, urban designers need to be aware of the physical manifestation of global restructuring in order to "redesign" these derelict spaces.

In order to make future urban designers culturally, racially, ethnically, and gender informed, planning educators need to expose students to literature on physical space and its relationship to women, studies on cultural landscapes and indigenous architectural form, cross-cultural studies on form and use of space, cultural and spatial aspects of globalization and colonization, postmodern geographers' conception of space, and Foucault's treatise on space.

Educators should not only introduce the concepts of multiculturalism through readings and discussion, but should also use written assignments and graphic exercises. Following Ritzdorf's (1993) suggestion, students could be asked to interpret their own life experiences within a larger social or political context and relate them to urban design through written assignments. Graphical assignments, such as cognitive mapping, could be used to expose students to inner city neighborhoods and cities that have endured the brunt of industrial restructuring.

Despite my plea for a multicultural urban design pedagogy, I would like to end my discussion with two words of caution. First, we need not abandon traditional ways of teaching urban design or progress that has been made in terms of technology (see, for example, George 1995; Lynch 1990; Moudon 1992 and 1995). The task is to relate multiculturalism to the existing knowledge on urban design. Second, my relative success in incorporating multicultural issues may, in part, be attributed to my institutional setting at an HBCU, the department's and university's urban mission, and the availability of a city as a laboratory. Whether such an approach to teaching urban design will be successful at other institutions remains a matter of conjecture. Nonetheless, design educators could try to modify some of the suggestions presented here if we are to produce urban designers for the twenty-first century.

NOTES

1. In urban design diversity can also include designing for people with disabilities. This particular aspect of diversity is not discussed in this chapter. For a detailed discussion, see, for example, Imrie (1996).

2. The new criteria for accreditation was incorporated as a result of several commissions sponsored by the Association of Collegiate Schools of Planning (ACSP) to explore diversity in planning education. See Thomas (1996) for a detailed discussion.

3. "Diversity training" is simply defined as educating and consciousness raising on ethnic, racial, and gender differences.

4. HBCUs are generally defined as Black institutions of higher learning established prior to 1964 with the primary goal of educating African Americans. HBCUs must be accredited by a nationally recognized accrediting agency or must be making an effort to get the accreditation. For a detailed discussion, see Myers (1987, 1992).

5. Kevin Lynch's work is a well-known example of a designer who "researched" better ways of designing cities (Lynch 1960, 1981).

6. Some of these studies also provide normative perspectives.

7. The insights on the physical manifestation of industrial restructuring in small to medium- sized towns draw from a joint grant that I have with the School of Architecture at

the University of Maryland since 1993. The purpose of the grant is described in detail in a later section of the paper.

8. This is a function of the nature of the courses. The primary purpose of the courses is to introduce the "principles of urban design" to students. Thus, many of the readings are on these principles (among others, I employ such classic readings as Alexander, Ishikawa, and Silverstein 1977; Broadbent 1990; Lynch 1960, 1981; Trancik 1986).

9. Note that there was some flexibility in the assignment. The students were told that they did not have to write the essay keeping all the above-mentioned backgrounds in mind. For example, they could just write the essay from their educational background.

10. Until this year (Spring 1997) there had been four Regional Institutes and a National Institute. For the academic year 1996–97, the Southern Institute was combined with the Northeastern Institute. Hence, I could expose students to some southern cities also.

11. The seeds of the program were sown in the Urban Studies Institute in 1963. The Center for Urban Affairs came into existence in 1970 and the M.A. in Urban Planning and Policy Analysis was initiated. The program became the first planning program at an HBCU to get degree recognition—the forerunner of the accreditation process—from American Institute of Planners (AIP) in 1974. In 1975 the name of the degree was changed to Master of City and Regional Planning (MCRP). The program was first accredited by Planning Accreditation Board (PAB) in 1986. For a detailed discussion on the history of the program, see Sen (1997).

12. Morgan's history began in 1867 and can be characterized into four periods. Like most HBCUs, the first period (1867–90) consisted of an institution—the Centenary Biblical Institute—set up by missionaries for the sole mission of training African American men for the Methodist Ministry. Morgan College (1890–1939), the second period, saw a broadening of the mission to educate men and women for careers other than ministry. With the changing of the name to Morgan College, the primary mission was to prepare African Americans of good moral standing for careers in public school teaching. Morgan State College (1939–75) is the third period in the institute's evolution. It was created in 1939, when the institute was purchased from the Methodist Episcopal Church by the State of Maryland. Morgan's mission expanded from teacher training to a balanced liberal arts education in this epoch. The fourth period of the institute began in 1975, when Maryland General Assembly granted university status to Morgan. For a detailed discussion on the history of the University, see Sen (1997). For a good discussion on the evolution of HBCUs, see Roebuck and Murty (1993).

REFERENCES

Alexander, C., S. Ishikawa, and M. Silverstein. *A Pattern Language: Towns, Buildings, Construction.* New York: Oxford University Press. 1977.

Amirahmadi, H. Globalization and Planning Education. *Environment and Planning B*, vol. 20, 1993:537–55.

Andrews, J.H. The Newest Americans. *Planning*, vol. 63, 1997:4–9.

Banerjee, T. Environmental Design in the Developing World: Some Thoughts on Design Education. *Journal of Planning Education and Research*, vol. 5, 1985:28–38.

Banerjee, T. Third World City Design: Values, Models and Education in B. Sanyal (ed.), *Breaking Boundaries: A One World Approach to Planning Education.* New York: Plenum Press. 1990:173–89.

Banks, J.A. Multiethnic Education in USA: Practices and Promises in T. Corner (ed.), *Education in Multicultural Societies.* New York: St. Martin's Press. 1984:68–93.

Banks, J.A. *Multiethnic Education: Theory and Practice*. Boston: Allyn and Bacon. 1994.

Birch, E.L. Radburn and the American Planning Movement: The Persistence of an Idea. *Journal of the American Planning Association*, vol. 46, 1980:424–39.

Boyer, C.M. *Erected Against the City: The Contemporary Discourse of Architecture and Planning*. Center 6, 1990:36–43.

Broadbent, G. *Emerging Concepts in Urban Space Design*. London: Van Nostrand Reinhold. 1990.

Burayidi, M.A. Dualism and Universalism: Competing Paradigms in Planning Education? *Journal of Planning Education and Research*, vol. 12, 1993:223–29.

Burgess, P. The Expert's Vision: The Role of Design in the Historical Development of City Planning. *Journal of Architectural and Planning Research*, vol. 14, 1997:92–106.

Davidoff, P. Advocacy and Pluralism in Planning. *Journal of the American Institute of Planners*, vol. 36, 1965:12–21.

Davidoff, P., L. Davidoff, and N.N. Gold. Suburban Action: Advocate Planning for an Open Society. *Journal of American Institute of Planners*, vol. 36, 1970:12–21.

Drucker, S.J. and G. Gumpert. Shopping, Women, and Public Space in S.J. Drucker and G. Gumpert (eds.), *Voices in the Street: Explorations in Gender, Media, and Public Space*. Cresskill, New Jersey: Hampton Press Inc. 1997:119–35.

Eisner, S., A. Gallion, and S. Eisner. The Urban Pattern (6th ed). New York: Van Nostrand Reinhold. 1993.

Forsyth, A. Diversity Issues in a Professional Curriculum: Four Stories and Suggestions for a Change. *Journal of Planning Education and Research*, vol. 15, 1995:58–63.

Foucault, M. *Disciple and Punish*. New York: Pantheon Books. 1977.

Foucault, M. Of Other Spaces. Diacritics, vol. 18, 1986:22–27.

Friedmann, J. and C. Kuester. Planning Education for the Late Twentieth Century: An Initial Enquiry. *Journal of Planning Education and Research*, vol. 14, 1994:55–64.

George, R.V. Hyper Space: Communicating Ideas About the Quality of Urban Spaces. *Journal of Planning Education and Research*, vol. 17, 1995:63–70.

Guttenberg, A. and L. Wetmore. What's in a Name Change? City Planning and Landscape Architecture at the University of Illinois. *Journal of Planning Education and Research*, vol. 7, 1987:29–34.

Hall, P. *Cities of Tomorrow: An Intellectual History of Urban Planning and Design in the Twentieth Century*. Oxford: Basil Blackwell. 1988.

Hayden, D. Dolores Hayden Replies. *Places*, vol. 7, 1990a:36–37.

Hayden, D. Using Ethnic History to Understand Urban Landscapes. *Places*, vol. 7, 1990b:11–17.

Hines, T.S. *Burnham of Chicago: Architect and Planner*. Chicago: University of Chicago Press. 1979.

Hemmens, G.C. Thirty Years of Planning Education. *Journal of Planning Education and Research*, vol. 7, 1988: 85–91.

Hernadez, H. *Multicultural Education: A Teacher's Guide to Content and Process*. Columbus, Ohio: Merrrill. 1989.

Imrie, R. Equity, Social Justice, and Planning for Access and Disabled People: An International Perspective. *International Planning Studies*, vol. 1, 1996:17–34.

Jacobs, A. and D. Appleyard. Toward an Urban Design Manifesto. *Journal of the American Planning Association*, vol. 53, 1987:112–20.

Jackson, J.B. *The Necessity for Ruins*. Amherst: University of Massachusetts Press. 1980.

King, A.D. *Colonial Urban Development: Culture, Power, and Environment.* London: Routeledge and Keegan Paul. 1976.

King, A.D. *Urbanism, Colonialism, and World Economy.* London: Routeledge. 1989.

King, A.D. *Global Cities: Post-Imperialism and the Internalization of London.* London: Routeledge. 1990.

Knack, R. Vive la Difference. *Planning,* vol. 63, September 1997a:10–11.

Knack, R. Soul Cites. *Planning,* vol. 63, December 1997b:4–9.

Kreditor, A. The Neglect of Urban Design in the American Academic Succession. *Journal of Planning Education and Research,* vol. 9, 1990:155–63.

Levy, J. M. *Contemporary Urban Planning* (4th ed). Upper Saddle River, New Jersey: Prentice Hall. 1997.

Lai, D.C. The Visual Character of Chinatowns. *Places,* vol. 7, 1990:29–31.

Loukaitou-Sideris, A. Urban Form and Social Context: Cultural Differences in the Uses of Urban Parks. *Journal of Planning Education and Research,* vol. 14, 1995:89–102.

Loukaitou-Sideris, A. Cracks in the City: Addressing the Constraints and Potentials of Urban Design. *Journal of Urban Design,* vol. 1, 1996:91–103.

Lynch, K. *The Image of the City.* Cambridge, MA: MIT Press. 1960.

Lynch, K. *A Theory of Good City Form.* Cambridge, MA: MIT Press. 1981.

Lynch, K. City Design: What It Is and How It Might Be Taught (1980) in T. Banerjee and M. Southworth (eds.), *City Sense and City Design: Writing and Projects of Kevin Lynch.* Cambridge, Massachusetts: MIT Press. 1990:652–59.

Mackenzie, S. and D. Rose. Industrial Change, The Domestic Economy and Home Life in J. Anderson, S. Duncan, and R. Hudson (eds.), *Redundant Spaces in Cites and Regions?* London: Academic Press. 1983:155–200.

Mattson, R.L. Cultural Landscape of a Southern Black Community: East Wilson, North Carolina, 1890 to 1930. *Landscape Journal,* vol. 11, 1992:145–49.

Morganthau, T. What Color is Black? *Newsweek,* February 13, 1995:64–65.

Moudon, A.V. A Catholic Approach to Organizing What Urban Designers Should Know. *Journal of Planning Literature,* vol. 6, no. 4, 1992:331–49.

Moudon, A.V. Teaching Urban Form. *Journal of Planning Education and Research,* vol. 14, 1995:123–33.

Myers, S.L. What is a Black College? *NAFEO Inroads: The Bimonthly Newsletter of the National Association for Equal Opportunity in Higher Education,* vol. 1, 1987:1–24.

Myers, S.L. What is a Black College? NAFEO Inroads: The Bimonthly Newsletter of the National Association for Equal Opportunity in Higher Education, vol. 6, 1992:1–5.

Oc, T. and S. Tiesdell. Editorial: Re-Emergent Urban Design. *Journal of Urban Design,* vol. 1, 1996:5–6.

Pivo, G., C. Ellis, M. Leaf, and G. Magutu. Physical Planning Thought: Retrospect and Prospect. *Journal of Architectural and Planning Research,* vol. 7, 1990:53–70.

Qadeer, M. Comparative sSudies to Counteract Ethnocentric Urban Planning in I. Masser and R. Williams (eds.), *Learning From Other Countries.* London: Geo Books. 1986:77–88..

Rapoport, A. *House Form and Culture.* Englewood Cliffs, NJ: Prentice-Hall. 1969.

Rapoport, A. Culture and Urban Order in J.A. Agnew, J. Mercer and D. E. Sopher (eds.), *The City in Cultural Context.* Boston: Allen and Unwin. 1984:50–75.

Rapoport, A. Pedestrian Use—Culture and Perception in A. V. Moudon (ed.), *Public Streets for Public Use.* New York: Nostrand-Reinhold. 1987:80–92.

Ritzdorf, M. Feminist Thoughts on Theory and Practice of Planning. *Planning Theory Newsletter,* vol. 7-8, 1992:13–20.

Ritzdorf, M. The Fairy's Tale: Teaching Planning and Public Policy in a Different Voice. *Journal of Planning Education and Research*, vol. 12: 1993:99–106.

Roebuck, B. and K.S. Murty. *Historically Black Colleges and Universities: Their Place in Higher Education.* Westport, CT: Praeger. 1993.

Sandercock, L. and A. Forsyth. A Gender Agenda: New Directions for Planning Theory. *Journal of American Planning Association*, vol. 58, 1992:49–59.

Sanyal, B. Poor Countries' Students in Rich Countries Universities: Possibilities of Planning Education for the Twenty-First Century. *Journal of Planning Education and Research*, vol. 8, 1989:139–55.

Sanyal, B. Large Commitments to Large Objectives: Planning Education for theTwenty-First Century in B. Sanyal (ed.), *Breaking Boundaries: A One World Approach to Planning Education.* New York: Plenum Press. 1990:17–55.

Sarbib, J. The University of Chicago Program in Planning: A Retrospective Look. *Journal of Planning Education and Research*, vol. 2, 1983:77–81.

Sawicki, D. Planning education and planning practice: Can we plan for the next decade? *Journal of Planning Education and Research*, vol. 7, 1988:115–20.

Scott, M. *American City Planning Since 1890.* Berkeley: University of California Press. 1969.

Sen, S. The Status of Planning Education at Historically Black Colleges and Universities: The Case of Morgan State University in J. M. Thomas and M. Ritzdorf (eds.), *Urban Planning and the African American Community: In the Shadows.* Thousand Oaks, California: Sage Publications. 1997:239–57.

Soja, E.W. *Postmodern Geographies: The Reassertion of Space in Critical Social Theory.* New York: Verso. 1989.

Spain, D. *Gendered Spaces.* Chapel Hill: The University of North Carolina Press. 1995.

Stimpson, C., E. Dixler, M. Nelson, and K. Yatrakis (eds.). *Women and the American City.* Chicago: University of Chicago Press. 1980.

Stoker, R.P. Baltimore: The Self-Evaluating City? In C. N. Stone and H. Sanders (eds.), *The Politics of Urban Development.* Lawrence: University Press of Kansas. 1987:244–66.

Thomas, J.M. Educating Planners: Unified Diversity for Social Action. *Journal of Planning Education and Research*, vol. 15, 1996:171–82.

Trancik, R. *Finding Lost Space: Theories of Urban Design.* New York: Van Nostrand Reinhold. 1986.

Upton, D. (ed). *America's Architectural Roots: Ethnic Groups That Build America.* Washington, D.C.: The Preservation Press. 1986.

Weisman, L.K. *Discrimination by Design: A Feminist Critique of the Man-Made Environment.* Urbana: University of Illinois Press. 1992.

Weisman, L.K. Diversity by Design: Feminist Reflections on the Future of Architectural Education and Practice in Agrest, D., P. Conway, and L.K. Weisman (eds.), *The Sex of Architecture.* New York: Harry N. Abrams, Inc. 1995:273–86.

Weiss, M.A. Planning Education and Research. *Journal of Planning Education and Research*, vol. 7, 1988: 96–97.

Wong, J. Let's Not Stop Meeting Like This. Planning, vol. 63, 1997:12.

Zelinsky, W. Seeing Beyond the Dominant Culture. *Places*, vol. 7, 1990:32–35.

CHAPTER 14

Federal Urban Programs as Multicultural Planning: The Empowerment Zone Approach

Peter Marcuse

In the last two presidential elections, the Democratic Party made a deliberate decision not to confront urban issues as part of its platform. Minority voters, the strategists felt, had nowhere else to go, and proposing programs to meet their needs was likely to alienate more voters than it would attract. So, indeed, no major new initiatives were proposed, either during the election campaigns or thereafter. The federal department most obviously concerned with urban issues, the Department of Housing and Urban Development (HUD), spent most of its time reinventing itself in smaller and less controversial fashion, presumably to head off even greater Congressional attacks on its very existence. The only new initiative it proposed that related to multiracial/multicultural issues was the Empowerment Zone legislation of 1993. That proposal constituted (as many before it) an attempt to deal with problems that were essentially social and economic, that were inextricably connected to the development of the United States as a multicultural society, without making any reference at all to race, culture, or ethnicity. Empowerment zones are an attempt to deal, through spatial measures, with problems at the root.

Spatial arrangements, as a solution for social problems, have a long and checkered history. Protecting rulers behind walls, and creating a privileged and protected space for those at the top of the hierarchy of power and wealth, were classic patterns that continue to this day. Ghettoizing[1] the poor is the opposite side of the same coin. Confining the potentially troublesome at the bottom of the hierarchy, where they can be dominated and controlled, has an almost equally long history. But an apparently different approach tries to ameliorate, or even solve, social problems through spatially based policies. These have historically ranged from slum clearance to urban renewal to neighborhood improvement, and from neighborhood rehabilitation areas to poverty program target areas, and model cities districts. Their latest incarnation is Empowerment Zones. It is not an accident that, in a period when the mobility of capital and labor are at a historic high, the most developed capitalist country in the world should adopt a space-limited program to deal with the social consequences of that mobility.

The Empowerment Zone legislation adopted by the Clinton administration as a key part (if not indeed the whole) of its housing and community development program, and passed with little debate in the Congress in 1993, is a classic case of such policy. Concentrating public subsidies in limited "poverty" areas means something quite different in the Fordist city than it does in the post-Fordist city;[2] its net effect will be to increase ghettoization, if offering minor improvements to the ghetto's residents.

The Empowerment Zone legislation[3] is a classic case of change in meaning, while form remains the same, as its history will reveal. Its expansion is the centerpiece (and seems likely to be the only component) of an "urban program" promised by Clinton to the National Conference of Mayors in San Diego during his re-election campaign in 1996; nothing else has as yet been proposed by the Administration to Congress.

EMPOWERMENT ZONE DESIGNATION

Six urban empowerment zones have been designated in the United States. In each zone there will be $100 million available in social service funds from the federal government over a period of ten years, in addition to tax benefits for businesses within the zone that employ zone residents. Each zone may have no more than 200,000 residents, and all census tracts (statistical units of about 2,000 households each) must be in poverty, defined by a set of quantitative measures of income of residents. While poverty is, of course, not identical with minority status, the figures speak for themselves: in New York City's empowerment zone, 83 percent of the residents of the designated empowerment zone are either African American or Hispanic.

The local government (read: mayor) has to provide HUD with a "comprehensive plan" for the area to enter the highly competitive contest for these benefits.[4] Decisions as to programs must be made with citizen participation, but no specific form of decision-making structure is specified. In fact, the New York City application handled that requirement by simply having a number of public hearings, the results of which were largely ignored in the shaping of the plans submitted in the application for funding.

Assistance available in each zone is spelled out:

- tax credits to employees for full or part-time employees who are empowerment zone residents and perform substantially all of their services inside the zone. The tax credit is $3,000 a year for seven years;

- an increase in the deductibility of the cost of acquiring depreciable property up to $37,500, over seven years. Books, computers, trucks, and office equipment are eligible but buildings are not;
- tax exempt bond financing, up to $3 million per empowerment zone, is available for empowerment zone businesses to acquire property within the empowerment zone. Credit enhancement is expected to be needed in most cases;
- $100 million over ten years in Social Services Block Grants; and
- set-asides within existing federal programs for empowerment zone communities, from HUD, Treasury (the tax credits above), and Small Business Administration loans.

THE EMPOWERMENT ZONE STRATEGY IN NEW YORK CITY[5]

The strategy behind New York City's Empowerment Zone is to expand the range of economic opportunity available to Empowerment Zone residents through the following:

1. *Training programs.* Programmatically focusing on comprehensive assessment, training, basic skills education, and placement; job training for persons returning from prison; expansion of adult education; training for health care and construction workers; and linking training to the private sector.
2. *Stimulate more retail establishments.* Programmatically supporting business improvement districts (BIDS) and an incubator program, a vendors mall at Yankee Stadium, and a greenmarket.
3. *Improve access to capital* for individuals who want to be self-employed (the micro-enterprise strategy). Programmatically, a small business assistance program, a business development fund, a private community capital bank, and a community development corporation. There was also a requirement for a "community first" source procurement and hiring policy for all public and major private development projects in and near the empowerment zone.
4. *Provide capital and ties to an information network* for individuals of different cultures with ties to the global economy. Programmatically, culturally appropriate learning centers and support for the culture industry.

The idea of concentrating federal assistance in the areas of greatest need, which of course included the Black ghettos, was one very much espoused by progressive social activists, the civil rights movement, and the major Black organizations, in the 1960s. The history goes back to the attempts to make urban renewal legislation progressive in its social impacts through the creation of Urban Renewal Advisory Councils in the 1950s, the funding of General Neighborhood Renewal Plans in the late 1950s, and the adoption of a "Workable Program" requirement in the 1954 Act. Thereafter, this changed to a Community Renewal Program in 1959, was reincarnated as a Neighborhood Development Program in 1968, and a Community Action Program of the anti-poverty period in the mid-1960s, to the Model Cities Program with its Model Cities Neighborhoods in 1966. There is a large assortment (over two dozen listed in 1973) of rehabilitation programs based on the targeting of specific neighborhoods. In each case the program was linked to affirmative anti-discrimination policies and measures to open up exclusionary suburbs.

The death knell of geographic programs targeted to help the poor, without confining them, came with the dismantling of the Model Cities Program and the adoption of General Revenue Sharing by the Nixon administration in 1972, putting the allocation of funds not in the hands of the residents of the targeted neighborhoods, but in the hands of city-wide officials. Charles Haar, who had a major hand in shaping the Model Cities Program when he was Assistant Secretary of HUD, described the program in 1975 as "a Waterloo for 'urban planning' (implying neighborhood-controlled planning) . . . and a Pearl Harbor for local or neighborhood capacity" (Haar 1975:25). The Community Development Block Grant Program of 1974, and then, with an increasing twist away from social targeting, the Urban Development Action Grants provided for in 1977, and the Enterprise Zones, that were a great favorite of George Bush's conservative Secretary of the United States Department of Housing and Urban Development, Jack Kemp,[6] complete the lineage of today's empowerment zones.

THE OUTLOOK OF EMPOWERMENT ZONES

From an ideological point of view, Empowerment Zones are a bastard idea. Their mother of record is the concept of community empowerment, grass-roots democracy, an idea that was developed as part of the civil rights struggles of the 1960s, and picked up in the Kennedy and Johnson era anti-poverty and model cities legislation. The most conspicuous, however, was the proposal put forward by the Bush administration as a cheap answer to the Los Angeles riots two years earlier, and pushed by Kemp as a part of a conservative "get the government out of social policy" campaign. The godmother, surely, was fiscal bias: political leaders sense that they've got to cut taxes, and social program spending cuts was the easiest way to go. That's why the Kemp proposal was killed by a Bush veto when he decided, in an election year, it looked too much like "do good" spending, cheap as it was in comparison to the problem. Clinton adopted it as his own, his only bow to the reality of urban poverty, and a limited and noncontroversial one. Individual politicians who figured the idea could be a help to their districts supported it (half-heartedly, according to Nicholas Lemann) in New York City as doing some good and no harm. A good bit of log-rolling was involved, as is shown by the inclusion of the 50,000 population limit, for one zone also has the requirement that it cross a state line, which almost names the district that is supposed to get it.

While the essential form of all of these programs, targeting assistance to areas of poverty concentration, has remained the same, their impact has radically changed.

When the civil rights movement fought for such programs in the 1960s, it was with the hope, ultimately, of abolishing the ghettos and bringing their residents into the mainstream of economic, social, and political life in urban centers (Marcuse 1998). With what must now be recognized as the defeat of the progressive thrust of that movement in the 1970s, Nixon's re-election and the "fiscal crisis" being the signposts of that defeat,[7] attention devoted to poverty areas acquired a new content: the reinforcement of the walls of the ghetto. No longer is the hope to eliminate the ghettos, the movement of those now confined to them to any new location of their choice, but just the opposite. In order to qualify for tax benefits, an employer must be within the empowerment zone (substantially, the ghetto) and must hire individuals from within the ghetto.[8] Implicit state policy is thus to reinforce the ghetto, not dismantle it. If one takes John Logan and colleague's definition of the key characteristic of an enclave, "co-ethnicity of owners and their employees,"[9] one finds little in the legislation that promotes it, although the older concept cried out for it. In the pithy words of Paul Hoggett describing the parallel evolution in Great Britain; "our recent analysis of neighborhood participation in Islington and Tower Hamlets has convinced me that to speak of 'empowerment' in the context of fragmented city communities is plain daft"[10] (Hoggett 1994:14).

The argument against the empowerment zone approach may be simply summarized: the troubled neighborhoods to be designated are more likely to cumulate problems than strengths. At best, empowerment zone policies will move problems around, not solve them. What is needed is a redistribution of resources from those not living in such zones to those living in them. The call for "marshaling of resources" within such zones obscures this basic fact, in what is at bottom a "blaming the victim" approach to the new urban poverty. The only problem is that "the ghetto economic state is less affected by the operation of its local economy than it is by the larger metropolitan economy" (Rose 1971:47).

Thus, the genetic code running through this entire lineage is a diseased one. Zones are no way to deal with problems of unemployment, bad education, miserable health care, international competition and multi-national mergers, distorted public priorities, and greed-driven unproductive private investments. These are not problems created in a particular place, and certainly not in the ghettos of our cities. Pretending they can be addressed in particular places, let alone a trivial number of "zones," is pure deception; it distracts attention from where the real problems lie. And yet it is politically appealing, for those most victimized by the real causes of poverty can hardly turn down even the crumbs that may come their way in these zones. Congressman Rangel was serving his constituents when he pressed for the zones; how could he not? Yet he himself knows their limits.

Take only one element—a central one—economic development. There is a substantial market within the areas of minority concentration that constitute the empowerment zone; much of it is supplied outside the zone, with both profits and jobs going outside the zone. It makes sense to try to capture more of that market demand within the zone itself, for the benefit of its residents. Yet the lure of attracting big money to Harlem makes it very tempting to bring in a Disney enterprise, controlled outside the zone, profits flowing outside the zone, and cultural appeal created outside the zone (indeed, homogenizing the very idea of culture). And often what ends up being done demands support from public funds. Those responsible for the administration of the empowerment zone are aware of the point, as clearly as the residents themselves. Thus, when the fight about whether to permit a zone change for a major supermarket in the area came up, the settlement gave an equity interest to a local church-based development group. Although new jobs will be created, old jobs will be lost; in particular, the work of older, small shopkeepers who cannot compete with the bargaining power and mechanical efficiency of a modern supermarket. Even though the Empowerment Zone places great weight on fostering local enterprise, it may result in the support of small entrepreneurs who simply place the Empowerment Zone logo on mugs imported from Thailand and sell them at a profit.

It is not only that economic development within the zone is marginally advanced by its efforts, if at all; it is that the whole approach to economic development is more likely to reinforce the ghetto than to break down its walls. The legislation makes tax credits available only to employers *within the zone* who hire residents living *within the zone*. Its result is to confine those in the ghetto to the ghetto. People in the United States, by and large, do not work where they live. In an area like New York City, the large concentration of jobs and, even more, the places where good new jobs are likely to be found, are not in the ghetto, but downtown and/or in suburban-like areas insulated from inner city-type problems. For residents of New York City's empowerment zone, the figures from the United States Census are clear—only 7 percent walked to work in 1990 (presumably within the zone); 23 percent took the bus, of which we estimate less than half were to destinations within the zone; and the balance used the subway, of which only a very small number went to work places within the zone.

As Alan Okagaki, writing for the Center for Community Change, a group consistently and intelligently monitoring community economic development policies, put it: "the need is to expand low income people's access to jobs in the larger community, not just in a particular neighborhood. Unless they work at home, very few people today work in the neighborhood in which they live" (Okagaki 1997:4). One knowledgeable observer put it directly: "public officials would rather have low-income people in somebody else's jurisdiction" (Gramlich 1994:1). Taxes get public officials to do what the search for profits and social stability get economic leaders to do—to confine zone residents to work within the zones goes directly against the conception of entry into the economic mainstream, of promoting a just multi-cultural society.

There are some positives to the Empowerment Zone idea: they can fund some experiments; they can put some people to work; they can get a few limited things done. Their biggest weakness is their geographic formulation—they will support neither investment for new job creation nor new hiring for the residents of an area unless it is in the area itself. The much broader and more sensible provision in the original bill making support available for businesses and jobs, wherever located, for residents of a zone was struck out in conference committee, reportedly because it might cost too much money.

Within an Empowerment Zone the possibilities for new business investment are limited. The problems are already well known from experience in the Bronx.

Merely having empty land available is little help. Hospitals and educational institutions and perhaps some social service agencies and nonprofits are potentials; see who they are, give them some help if they really need it, but don't have illusions about what they can produce. Infrastructure investment is another story. Both in-zone construction and employment of in-zone residents on construction jobs qualify for support under the act, both have immediate and tangible benefits for a poor area, and both might, in the long run, stimulate economic development. That is where the focus should be placed. Looking at the legislation just as a way of increasing social services is, on the other hand, not the right way to go; they are generally remedial and not curative, and should not be even further concentrated in poor areas. Empowerment zones should be used to equalize—not to further ghettoize.

Empowerment Zones can be used to plan ahead. The legislation calls for economic development plans. Those plans needn't be limited to what the Empowerment Zones will pay for, nor to the area included in the zone. Communities can use this as an opportunity to do real economic planning. For the community boards only slowly getting under way with charter-authorized 197-A community plans, this can be an opportunity for getting that show on the road. So there are positive impacts possible from the Empowerment Zone legislation.

But it can also have negative impacts. Worse than failing and/or being trivial, it can co-opt, detour, and defang. There is incredible hype in the promotion of Empowerment Zones. The phrases all come from the official documents sent out to communities encouraging them to apply for empowerment zone designation, a few of which are given below:

You can address the future of your community comprehensively . . . engender new enterprises, expansion of existing firms . . . creation of new employment opportunities . . . engine of urban revitalization . . . innovative new means to empower zone residents . . . as key stakeholders . . . a common vision of the kind of economy and job opportunities that each community's future should hold . . . the social health of the community and the physical form of the community . . . integrate economic, physical, environmental, community, and human development.

The preliminary results in Harlem, however, suggest the limitations of the process. The major economic investments have gone into supporting a movie theater that is sponsored by the Magic Johnson chain,[11] and a Disney store, neither creating significant local employment nor generating profits for local owners. A piddling amount has been allocated for HUD's evaluation of the program, as if the agency were afraid of what might be found. Grass-roots participation has dropped to almost zero. Personal experience in New York City and Community Board 9, of which the author is a member, suggests that, while some who participated in the structuring of the empowerment zone tried making the application and governance process an empowering strategy, it instead became an end in itself. It has ended up concentrating power in the hands of a board not made up of community residents

(1/3 are appointed by the governor; 1/3 by the mayor; the local community plays a minor role) with a strong element of politically dependent technocracy.

The relationships that are established are not those that would be considered appropriate to a multicultural society committed to just treatment and democratic opportunity for its diverse members. It ends up, in spite of the efforts of some of those involved, as fostering a top-down approach whose objective is rather gilding the ghetto than eliminating its barriers. The prospects do not look good.

And what is promised is more of the same, but with even less behind it. In the balanced budget legislation, twenty more empowerment zones are to be created—fifteen urban and five rural. Whether they will be funded even at the limited level of the first round remains, however, in doubt.[12] The underlying approach, tackling the issues of a multicultural society by measures spatially designed and spatially limited, is not being questioned. Unless major changes are made in the program, it will not make much difference; it is as likely, in the long run, to hurt the cause of multicultural justice in the United States as to help it.

NOTES

1. I use the term "ghetto" here in the specific sense of an involuntary spatial concentration of members of a dominated group. For a detailed discussion, and the differentiation from an enclave or similar immigrant areas of concentration, see Marcuse, Peter "The Enclave, the Citadel, and the Ghetto: What Has Changed in the Post-Fordist U.S. City." *Urban Affairs Review*, vol. 33, no. 2, November 1997:228–64.

2. Among the best short critical discussions are those of Ed Gramlich, prepared for the Center for Community Change and the Coalition for Low Income Community Development, both in Washington, D.C. For my own comments on the New York City application and the politics behind it, see Marcuse, Peter "Empowering New York," *City Limits*, March 1994:20–21.

3. Part I of Title XIII, Chapter I, Subchapter C, of the Omnibus Budget Reconciliation Act of 1993: "Empowerment Zones, Enterprise Communities, and Rural Development Investment Areas."

4. The history of federal efforts to impose an effective planning requirement on municipalities goes back as far as the idea of geographically zoned assistance itself (see below) and with as few results. The lineage includes Workable Programs, H.A.P.s, C.H.A.S.s, and most recently Consolidated Plans.

5. From the New York City empowerment zone application, as submitted to HUD.

6. For a biased history of some of these programs that has attracted wide-spread attention, but which ignores the changes discussed in the next paragraph, see Lemman, Nicholas. "Rebuilding the Ghetto Doesn't Work." *The New York Times*, January 9, 1994:27.

7. For a more detailed discussion, see Marcuse, Peter "The Targeted Crisis: On the Ideology of the Urban Fiscal Crisis and Its Uses," in *International Journal of Urban and Regional Research*, vol. 5, no. 3, 1981:330.

8. Section 1398(d)(1)(A) and (B) of the Act.

9. Op. cit., 4.

10. The very term "empowerment" is ambiguous in its social impact if empowerment is defined as "a necessarily long-term process of adult learning and development" (Wright and

Roberts 1994:9). A study of "empowerment" policies in Puerto Rico concluded that "personal control was gained at the expense of critical consciousness; it accepts individual success at the expense of the social development, sustained inequality, individualism, and private over social property" (Wright and Roberts 1994:10). Wright and Roberts suggest a redefinition that uses the term "collective empowerment" to capture the original oppositional content of the term. Barbara Cruikshank goes further to argue that the whole concept of empowerment is a way of linking those "empowered" to the power holding them in subjection.

11. This is a proposal that, however, does not seem likely to become reality as of this writing.

12. The legislation in question is Public Law 105-33. In the arcane procedure used in adopting budgets in the United States, funds need to be first authorized, then appropriated. Thus far, only $25 million has been submitted as an appropriation in the House, and, in the words of the Community Development Digest, September 2, 1997:15, "The funding picture doesn't look so good."

REFERENCES

Gramlich, Ed. *Targeting Times*, vol. 5, no. 1, Winter 1994:1.

Haar, Charles M. *Between the Idea and the Reality: A Study in the Origin, Fate, and Legacy of the Model Cities Program.* Boston: Little, Brown. 1975.

Hoggett, Paul. "The Modernization of the United Kingdom Welfare State" in Burrows, Roger and Brian Loader, *Towards a Post-Fordist Welfare State.* London: Routledge. 1994.

Lemman, Nicholas. "Rebuilding the Ghetto Doesn't Work." *The New York Times*, January 9, 1994:27.

Marcuse, Peter. "The Targeted Crisis: On the Ideology of the Urban Fiscal Crisis and Its Uses," in *International Journal of Urban and Regional Research*, vol. 5, no. 3, 1981:330.

Marcuse, Peter. "Empowering New York," *City Limits*, March 1994:20–21.

Marcuse, Peter. "The Enclave, the Citadel, and the Ghetto: What Has changed in the Post-Fordist U.S. City." *Urban Affairs Review*, vol. 33, no. 2, November 1997:228–64.

Marcuse, Peter. "Space Over Time: The Changing Position of the Black Ghetto in the United States." *Netherland Journal of Housing and the Built Environment*, vol. 13, no. 1. 1998.

Okagaki, Alan. Editorial in *Community Change*, vol. 19, Fall 1997:4.

Rose, Harold. *The Black Ghetto.* New York: McGraw Hill. 1971.

Wright, Talmadge and Michael Roberts. "Homeless Collective Empowerment Strategies: San Hose, California vs. Chicago, Illinois." A paper presented at the XIII World Congress of Sociology. Bielefeld, German. July 1994.

CHAPTER 15

Measuring the Stability of Multi-Racial, Multicultural Neighborhoods

Richard A. Smith

Planning in a multicultural society requires planners to address issues concerning the multicultural use of space. This issue converts to one of planning for and accommodating racially and ethnically diverse neighborhoods. Unfortunately, much of the classical literature on neighborhood diversity suggests that it is difficult, if not impossible, to achieve. Mixed neighborhoods are viewed as inherently unstable (Aldrich 1975; Duncan and Duncan 1957; Molotch 1972; Schelling 1972), resulting from both housing market dynamics that make possible the separation of different racial and ethnic groups, as well as the protection of single race neighborhoods and communities from the entry of racial and ethnic minorities (Danielson 1976; Massey and Denton 1993; Turner, Struyk, and Yinger 1991). Thus, in the most common conception, neighborhoods are seen as changing from majority (White) to minority (Black) over time, and integration (or diversity)[1] is a temporary condition that exists only between the arrival of the first Black and the departure of the last White household.

Some evidence exists to contradict this conception of the instability of diverse places. An important component of this evidence is a series of studies of racially integrated communities, such as Shaker Heights, Ohio; Oak Park and Park Forest, Illinois; and others (DeMarco and Galster 1993; Goodwin 1979; Helper 1986; Keating 1994; Saltman 1990). Such places, however, have come to our attention because they are offered in contrast to models of neighborhood instability and transition. As such, they appear to be exceptions to the general conception of racial instability rather than as readily adaptable models; they suggest what *can* work under special circumstances rather than what *does* work under more usual conditions. Indeed, in one of the most comprehensive studies of integrated neighborhoods, Saltman suggests that such neighborhoods are "fragile," dependent on a series of critical conditions that will not always exist, and support from city administrations that will not always be forthcoming. Similar themes are suggested by Keating (1994) in his discussion of the integration programs of the Cleveland suburbs. Few jurisdictions, even where the formal authority exists, are able to maintain the level of effort required to maintain stable integration. It is, therefore, ironic that many of our best examples of stably integrated places serve to highlight the unusual nature of their condition.

If planning for multi-racial and multi-ethnic neighborhoods is to be a reality, then the development of stronger evidence about the existence and maintenance of diverse places than has heretofore been available from the case study literature is required. This evidence needs to take the form of locating places that are diverse and stable under conditions other than the massive infusion of energy and resources that characterize the case study exemplars. Indeed, we need to address the question of whether "ordinary" places can construct and maintain themselves as diverse and stable. Stating the argument in this way suggests that a reasonable research strategy is to identify and study diverse and stable neighborhoods in a broader context than the case study literature. This strategy rests on the assumption that a number of different models of diverse places do exist beyond the classical examples referenced above. Many of these assumed places may have developed subsequent to the racially tumultuous period of the 1960s and 1970s, under the protections of a series of federal, state, and local fair housing acts and increased enforcement of their nondiscrimination protections. Identifying such places and studying the potentially different conditions under which they operate will provide critical models for planners wishing to pursue these outcomes as a public policy goal.

A critical ingredient in this strategy is the development of appropriate methods for measuring stable diverse places. Without such methods, the wider incidence and distribution of these places remains unknown and we are unable to begin the process of description as a prelude to understanding. Unfortunately, most of the work done in this area to date is meager; we have concentrated our efforts on developing numerous indexes measuring segregation, with virtually no effort given to measures of integration. In what follows I briefly review some of the existing methods for measuring diversity and stability in urban neighborhoods and then propose a number of alternative methods for general use. Two methods, in particular, are developed and their use in a study of racially diverse places in the metropolitan counties of Florida, 1970–90, are demonstrated. Both methods rely on existing data such as is available from the Census of Population, and both methods respond to some of the criticisms of existing techniques in which the standards for identifying diversity and stability are not adequately defined. Even these new methods, however, are not without problems, as will be discussed in the conclusions.

MEASURING RACIAL AND ETHNIC DIVERSITY

Within the research and policy literature, there exists a number of standards to define neighborhood diversity and stability, most of which have been developed within the context of the literature on racial integration. These standards range from rather vague references, as when integration is seen as an increase in the number or proportion of minorities within previously all White neighborhoods, with no particular magnitudes specified (Smith 1991), to requiring specific proportions of each racial group in order to constitute integration. At issue in the latter context are the standards that are used to construct these proportions, and a variety of research offers neighborhood racial classifications by standards that are not well understood or documented (Duncan and Duncan 1957; Jargowsky 1994; Millen 1973; Obermanns 1980; Rosenbaum 1996; Taeuber and Taeuber 1965; Vernarelli 1986).

Most recently there have been a number of systematic attempts to measure and locate diverse and stable neighborhoods, where diversity is defined in terms of an extended range of proportions for minority representation within a census tract, and stability is operationalized as a change in these proportions within certain narrow limits. For example (Lee 1985; also, see Lee and Wood 1990, 1991; Wood and Lee 1991) defines diversity (more accurately, racial mixing) as a tract in which the proportion of Blacks ranges from 10 to 89 percent, and in which this proportion does not change by more than five percentage points over a decade. Similarly, Ellen defines integration as a proportion of Black population between 10 and 50 percent, with stability defined as change over time of 10 percent or less in either the White or Black population of a tract (Ellen 1998). Clark (1993) goes beyond the two-group model and tests a number of models of multi-ethnicity that involve equal proportions of two, three, and four groups within tracts, allowing variations around these ideal proportions of from 5 to 7.5 percentage points. Thus, in the two-group model, one race or ethnicity can comprise as much as 57.5 percent of the tract population, with the other at 42.5 percent. In none of these papers is a clear rationale provided for the standards for defining diversity and stability other than what the authors perceive as reasonable.

Clearly, however, because the methods used to measure diversity and stability differ widely, this research is difficult to both interpret and compare. Thus, Lee finds a substantial proportion of his study neighborhoods are both mixed and stable over time (29% between 1970 and 1980). In contrast, Ellen finds only 7.3 percent of the study tracts remain stably integrated over the same time period, and only 6.8 percent remain stably integrated over the longer period of 1970–90. However, the stability of the tracts first identified as integrated in 1980 and that remain integrated in 1990—approximately 75 percent of the 1980 integrated tracts remain integrated in 1990—causes her to conclude that the "figures hardly suggest relentless and inevitable succession." In still further contrast Clark finds few such instances of diversity and less reason to be optimistic. He suggests that the number of multi-ethnic/multi-racial tracts between 1960 and 1990 still represent only a small percentage of tracts and that the process of neighborhood transition is not creating mixed integrated tracts in very large numbers.

Because it is not clear that through the use of these standards, integration and stability are actually being measured, we cannot be certain that any of these studies actually deal with racially integrated places. This creates the context for consideration of alternative measures.

One alternative responds to the need to construct the definition of diversity on some commonly understood standard, and does this by grounding the definition in the racial proportions of the larger context within which the neighborhood exists, such as the county or metropolitan area. This is a *comparative* approach, in which a neighborhood is seen as diverse if it contains a proportion Black that is similar to that of a comparison group. For example, neighborhoods with 20 percent Black population, in a county that is 20 percent Black, may be considered diverse. Under this conception, diversity is generally seen as a continuum, where a neighborhood can be characterized as more or less diverse according to the degree to which it diverges from the racial proportions of the comparison area. An example of this comparative approach is provided by Saltman (1990), but the rationale for defining the stages of the scale, as well as the criteria for stability, are not given. Similarly, Nyden and colleagues (1996; also, see Maly and Nyden 1995) use a version of this comparative approach by defining a metric based on the index of dissimilarity in which the racial composition of the tract is compared to the proportional size of each racial group in the city. Three degrees of diversity are defined: diverse, moderately segregated, and segregated; although the rationale for establishing the boundaries of each type are unclear. Using this method to study Chicago, they identify ninety-three areas that are diverse in 1980, of which fifty-nine (63.4%) remain diverse and, therefore, stable in 1990.

Another conception of diversity that is suggested within the literature is based on the comparison of potential to actual demand for housing in an area by both White and Black households (DeMarco and Galster 1993). In its simplest form it corresponds to the view that the market for housing in an area that is undergoing racial transition from White to Black experiences a drying up of White demand and a corresponding increase in Black demand. In contrast, integration is characterized by the continued existence of an appropriate level of realized housing demand by both races. Expectations of the size of each group vary, however. Bradburn and colleagues (1971) and Moore and McKeown (1968) suggest no particular racial proportions, while Saltman operationalizes this concept as "relatively similar proportions . . . of Whites and Blacks . . . moving into a neighborhood" (1990:25). This concept is defined more critically in the integration maintenance programs of both Shaker Heights (DeMarco and Galster 1993) and Park Forest (Helper 1986) as in-movers that are roughly in proportion to the representation of each racial group in the income classes associated with the community's housing stock. This approach thus creates a different comparative standard; in areas in which owner-occupied housing is relatively expensive we would expect lower demand by Black households given the smaller proportion of Blacks at the upper end of the income distribution, and a smaller number of Black in-movers. Conversely, in areas with less expensive rental housing, potential demand by Black households will increase, leading to the expectation of a larger number of Black in-movers. In this sense racial diversity is clearly not economic diversity and, depending on the distribution of housing costs within the community, may represent large or small proportions of Black households.

The market approach has its roots in the study of the causes of segregation. Central to the debate on segregation has been the relative contribution of income to the creation and maintenance of segregated living patterns. Since Black household income is, on average, substantially lower than White household income, some amount of segregation will be associated with the differences in purchasing power of each racial group. The market approach seeks to understand the proportion of a segregated pattern that is created by these income differences alone by measuring the hypothetical amount of segregation that would exist if only the income factor were operating (Farley 1995; Hermalin and Farley 1973; Taeuber and Taeuber 1965). I am not aware of any instances, however, where the approach has been applied to the measurement of diversity.

Beyond the measure of diversity is that of stability. Stability is most easily defined as the persistence of racial proportions over time. Since much of the existing literature has used relatively wide ranges to define the proportions that constitute diversity, however, stability cannot be judged simply by remaining within this range. Thus, when change does occur it must be within certain prescribed limits, such as Lee's (1985) use of the five percentage point standard or Ellen's (1998) use of a ten percentage point standard. Alternatively, under both the comparative and market approaches, stability can be interpreted not as the persistence of racial proportions *per se,* but as the persistence of proportions relative to the standard on which the method is based. Thus, according to the comparative approach, tract proportions can change, but only in line with corresponding changes in the comparison place. For example, a tract proportion Black can rise from 20 percent to 25 percent over time when the same change has occurred in the county. Stability in conjunction with the market approach can be similarly interpreted; that is, persistence of racial proportions relative to affordability. Hence, if Black household income increases over time, there is the expectation of an increased demand and an increased proportion of Blacks in the neighborhood in-mover stream. Both methods, then, avoid having to specify an arbitrary standard for change.

A DEMONSTRATION

The demonstration reported herein operationalizes both the comparative and market approaches to measure the incidence and distribution of diverse places (relative to Whites and Blacks) in the metropolitan counties of Florida. For the comparative approach, the analysis is done primarily for the period 1980–90 and then extended, where possible, back to 1970. For the market approach, however, the necessary data are unavailable prior to 1990 and no analysis of stability over time is possible.

Twenty-six Florida counties are identified as belonging to eiighteen metropolitan areas in both 1980 and 1990. The counties are both urban (i.e., the central county of the respective metropolitan area) and suburban. County populations range from 33,000 to 1.6 million in 1980, and from 44,000 to 1.9 million in 1990. More important is the size of the Black population in each place. In 1980 the proportion of the county populations that are Black ranges from 2.1 percent to 24.7 percent, and from 1.9 percent to 24.4 percent in 1990. Comparable comparisons for the state as a whole show the Black population to be 13.8 percent in 1980 and 13.6 percent in 1990. The large variation in county location, size, and proportion Black provides a basis for observing the potentially varied conditions under which neighborhood diversity may occur.

The analysis for each of the twenty-six counties is done on the basis of census tracts. Tract boundaries are standardized on the 1980 boundaries to ensure comparability over time. The need for comparability between the 1980 and 1990 boundaries, however, will constrain the number of places that can be included for 1970. The analysis is conducted using the non-Hispanic White and non-Hispanic Black populations of these places.

THE COMPARATIVE APPROACH

For the comparative definition of diversity, I have used the county as the comparison area, although other comparison areas, such as the urbanized and metropolitan areas, are possible. The methodological issue here is establishing the degree to which neighborhoods (census tracts) may be diverse relative to the racial composition of the county, and defining the criteria by which the different degrees of diversity are recognized. The model developed here is based on seven stages of diversity defined along a continuum of neighborhoods ranging from mostly White to mostly Black. The stages are given as:

(1) substantially White;
(2) minimally diverse White;
(3) moderately diverse White;
(4) substantially diverse;
(5) moderately diverse Black;
(6) minimally diverse Black;
(7) substantially Black.

Type 4, substantially diverse, is defined as that stage of diversity in which the racial composition of the tract is comparable to that of the county, and is the stage that is the primary subject of the demonstration. As a tract declines in proportion Black and becomes increasingly White, it is characterized along the lower stages (types 1–3). Conversely, as the racial proportions of the tract diverge from those of the county in favor of an increasingly larger proportion of Black residents, the tract is characterized along the higher stages (types 5–7). The stages of the continuum thus allow us to recognize that neighborhood diversity is one of degree.

At issue is how these stages are to be defined. It is unreasonable to characterize a neighborhood as diverse only if it contains the exact proportion of Black residents that are contained in the comparison area; some range around the county proportion is needed. To establish this range I have divided the proportion Black in the county by four to correspond to the first four categories, and have used the dividend to define the upper and lower bounds of each of the lower stages numbered 1–4. Assuming a county percentage Black of 20 percent, the division by four yields an interval of five percentage points by which to separate each of the lower (1–4) categories. Hence, the substantially White category is defined as having between 0 and 5 percent Black population; the minimally diverse White category as having between 5 and 10 percent Black population, and so forth. The substantially diverse place, centered on the county proportion Black, is defined as containing between 15 and 25 percent Black population. In like fashion I have divided the range between the upper limits of the diverse category and 100 percent by three, to create three types of places with increasing proportions of Black population. Thus, the moderately diverse Black category will, in this example, be defined as between 25 and 50 percent Black; the minimally diverse Black will be defined as between 50 and 75 percent Black, and so forth. The ranges that define each stage are not equal around the middle diversity category and this was done in recognition of the need to center the distribution on the racial proportions of the comparison area. This, then, results in the need for smaller proportions of Blacks in predominantly White neighborhoods to constitute diversity, and larger proportions of Whites in predominantly Black areas to constitute diversity, and this appears to correspond to the ways in which we think about this issue.

Clearly, the actual boundaries of each of the seven categories will differ, depending on the actual proportion of Blacks in each county. Not having to specify *a priori* boundaries to each category and then imposing a universal definition of the categories across all cities is the major advantage of the approach. Nevertheless, the construction of the categories is open to question and other definitions, such as constructing five or nine categories of diversity, will yield different results, although there do not appear to be any generally agreed upon standards (Nyden, Maly, and Lukehart 1996; Saltman 1990).

Under this conception of diversity, stability is defined as the persistence of a tract's level of diversity over time; that is, substantially diverse in both 1980 and 1990. Again, however, because the proportions of Whites and Blacks within the comparison area (county) can change over time, the boundaries for the substantially diverse category will also change. Thus, stability is not interpreted as constant proportions within the tract or change only within some narrowly prescribed limits, but as a constant relationship to the racial composition of the county. The clear implication of this approach is that as a county becomes increasingly Black/White, the proportion of Blacks/Whites required at the neighborhood level for it to be classified as diverse will also increase.

THE MARKET APPROACH

The definition of diversity under the market approach is substantially more complex. The approach involves the construction of a housing allocation model in which households of each race are allocated to tracts in proportion to their representation in the income groups defined as the market for housing in this tract. Examples of this approach are provided by Taeuber and Taeuber (1965), Schnare (1977) and Farley (1995). Rental- and owner-occupied housing are treated separately, and the range of income required to afford housing of each type, at each cost level, is estimated according to the standards of 27 to 33 percent of gross household income allocated for rent, and housing purchased at a 2.2–2.8 multiplier to annual household income. These proportions are established around national benchmarks (Bogdon, Silver, and Turner 1993). In this instance the population considered as the potential market for housing in the tract is the population of the metropolitan area. However, only six of the eighteen metropolitan areas included in the study involve more than a single county.

Data for the market analysis are taken from the 1990 Census of Population and Housing (STF 3a). The census tract reports indicate the distribution of units by contract rent categories in the case of rental housing, and the distribution of owned units by categories of home value. The census reports also provide data on the distribution of household income by category for each race, but the income categories extend only to the terminal group of $150,000+, and this is inappropriate for estimating the households that can afford housing in the higher end of the value distribution. Housing value is reported up to $500,000+, for which a household income of approximately $179,000 - $227,000 would be needed at a multiplier of 2.8 and 2.3 respectively. Accordingly, the distribution of household income in the terminal category of $150,000+ was estimated across a number of subcategories, up to $250,000+, by use of a Pareto estimating procedure (Shyrock and Siegel 1971).

The output from the housing model consists of a series of racial proportions that constitute the *expected* population of households in each tract. These expected proportions can then be compared with the *actual* racial distribution of movers to the tract, as indicated in the census tract reports for the period 1985–90. These reports show the number of persons living elsewhere (in a different house) in 1985. Since the data are not reported by persons living in a different tract at the earlier date, all persons having changed houses are considered as (new) movers to the tract. While some of these movers are intra-tract only, it is reasonable to include all as one category of movers who have made a fresh decision to reside in the subject tract.

The basis for characterizing a tract as diverse is the comparison of the actual racial distribution of in-movers to the expected distribution. In this instance tracts that attract Black households in scale with these expectations are considered substantially diverse, while those that attract a lesser or greater amount are categorized accordingly. The schema for classifying tracts on this basis is the same as that used in the comparative approach; the expected proportion Black becomes the comparative standard and tracts are characterized along the continuum of substantially White to substantially Black according to the method detailed above.

Table 15.1 provides a simplified example of the housing allocation model. The example assumes a county population of 18,000 White households and 6,000 Black households with the income distribution as shown in line 1. Line 2 gives the distribution of rental units by rent levels for a single tract. Using the standards of 27 percent to 33 percent of gross income for rent, these rental levels are converted to minimum and maximum household incomes required to afford each level of rental housing (line 3). The number of households of each race that fall into each of these income ranges is computed (line 4) by proportioning the number of White and Black households that exist within each of the county income categories (line 1). Thus, for example, if income of up to $4,444 is required to afford units renting at under $100/month, this is 88.9 percent of the under $4,999 income category, producing 2,222 White households (.889 x 2,500 White households in the income category) and 1,333 Black households. In line 5 the number of White and Black households that create the market for rental units at this rental level are converted to proportions of Whites and Blacks expected in these units, and these proportions, multiplied by the number of rental units at this rent level, produce the expected number of households of each race in these units (line 6). The sum of expected households across line 6 yields the total number of White and Black households expected in all rental housing in this particular tract.

A parallel analysis is done for owner occupied units (lines 7–11) using the standards of 2.2 to 2.8 of gross household income to define the expected market for owner housing. The sum of these expectations in line 11 produces the total number of owner households by race. Lines 12–14 establish the total number of White and Black households that are expected (both renter and owner) and compare the proportions of expected households to the actual proportions of in-movers by race, 1985–90. The boundaries of the diversity categories are based on the expected proportion of Black households, and the tract is classified on the basis of the actual proportion. The procedure illustrated in this table is done for each tract within each of the counties included in the analysis.

RESULTS

Comparative Method

The first panel of Table 15.2 shows the distribution of tract types according to the comparative analysis for 1980 and 1990 across all 26 metropolitan counties. The total number of 1980–90 comparable tracts is 1,637, with substantially White tracts being the largest type in both 1980 (947; 57.8%) and 1990 (683; 41.7%), as expected. Diverse tracts, by the comparative criteria only, increase from ninety-one (5.6% of all tracts) to 146 (8.9% of all tracts) over the time period. Based on the perspective of a single date (1980 or 1990), substantially diverse places appear relatively frequent.

Table 15.3 reports the joint outcomes for both dates; that is, how 1980 tracts changed in 1990, again only by the comparative method. The pattern here is one of substantial instability; reading down the diagonal shows that only in the case of tracts classified as substantially Black in 1980 did the overwhelming majority remain in the category in 1990 (93%). Substantially White, moderately diverse Black, and minimally diverse Black tracts return a majority of their 1980 tracts to the same category in 1990. Minimally diverse White, moderately diverse White, and substantially diverse tracts show more varied patterns of change in which only a minor percentage of each type remains in its respective category in 1990. The central figure of Table 15.3 is the stability of 1980 substantially diverse tracts. Of the ninety-one such places in 1980, only twenty-four remain as diverse in 1990. This represents only 1.5 percent of the tracts that constitute the sample. Of those that changed, thirty-nine (42.9%) became more Black, and twenty-eight (30.8%) became more White.

The extension of the analysis to 1970 involves the twenty-four tracts shown as substantially diverse in both 1980 and 1990. Of these, only eight could be traced back, in their 1980–90 configuration, to 1970 (a substantial number of these tracts exist in counties that were not tracted in 1970). Considering these eight tracts, six were also classified as substantially diverse in 1970, with one as substantially White and one as minimally diverse White. Thus, while substantially diverse tracts represent a small percentage of all tracts in the analysis, there is sufficient evidence to suggest that such tracts can and do remain stable over extended periods of time.

The Market Approach

The second panel of Table 15.2 shows the distribution of diversity types for 1990 by the market method. I had initially expected that this approach would yield fewer diverse places than shown in the comparative method under the reasoning that in a discriminatory housing market, Black household income could not be used to secure housing simply on the basis of affordability to the same degree possible for Whites. The results show, however, that this is not the case; a greater number of tracts satisfy the market criteria for substantial diversity than satisfy the comparative criteria for substantial diversity in 1990 (195; 11.9% versus 146; 8.9%, respectively). Indeed, even more surprising is the finding that fewer tracts are classified as substantially White (462; 28.2%) compared to the 1990 results by the comparative approach (683; 41.7%). This suggests that the two methods are tapping different dimensions of diversity; to a degree Black households are gaining entry to tracts based on their income characteristics in relation to housing costs, but in many tracts this entry is not sufficient to raise the proportional representation of Blacks beyond the lowest levels. The relative inability of income to fully operate for Black households is shown, however, in the comparison of moderately diverse Black tracts identified by the two methods. Here, there is a large difference between the market and comparative findings (327; 20% versus 209; 12.8%, respectively), suggesting that in many Black tracts, Blacks are over represented relative to affordability beyond what would be considered on a comparative (i.e., proportional) basis.

Table 15.1 Illustration of Market Analysis							
(1) Income (county)		<4,999	5-9,999	10-19,999	20-29,999	30-39,999	40-49,999	Total
White		2500	3500	4500	4000	3000	500	18000
Black		1500	2000	1300	800	400	0	6000
(2) Tract 1: rental units								
rent		<100	100-299	300-499	500-699	700-999	1000+	
# units		100	150	75	60	10	0	395
(3) Affordable @								
high	0.27	4444	13333	22222	31111	44444		
low	0.33	0	3636	10909	18182	25455	36364	
(4) # HH in afford group								
White		2222	5682	4980	5151	5040	1591	
Black		1333	2842	1360	1081	764	145	
(5) % HH in afford group								
White		0.625	0.667	0.786	0.827	0.868	0.916	
Black		0.375	0.333	0.214	0.173	0.132	0.084	
(6) # HH expected								
White		63	100	59	50	9	0	280
Black		37	50	16	10	1	0	115
(7) Tract 1: owner units								
value		<25,000	25-49,999	50-74,999	75-99,999	100,000+		
# units		0	10	20	50	10		
(8) Affordable @								
high	2.2	11364	22727	34091	45455			
low	2.8	0	9259	18519	27778	37037		
(9) # HH in afford group								
White		6614	1757	5894	4162	1389		
Black		3677	411	1156	578	119		
(10) % HH in afford group								
White		0.643	0.811	0.836	0.878	0.921		
Black		0.357	0.189	0.164	0.122	0.079		
(11)# HH expected								
White		0	8	17	44	9		78
Black		0	2	3	6	1		12
(12) Total expected	#	%						
White	358	0.737						
Black	127	0.263						
(13) Diversity categories		Sub w	Min w	Mod w	Diverse	Mod b	Min b	Sub b
high		0.066	0.131	0.197	0.328	0.552	0.776	1.000
low		0.000	0.066	0.131	0.197	0.328	0.552	0.776
(14) Actual movers								
White		0.890						
Black		0.110	= minimally diverse White					

	1980		Comparative 1990		Market 1990	
Table 15.2 Distribution of Diverse Places by Level of Diversity Comparative and Market Methods						
	#	%	#	%	#	%
Substantially White	947	57.9%	683	41.7%	462	28.2%
Minimally diverse White	152	9.3%	232	14.2%	255	15.6%
Moderately diverse White	85	5.2%	138	8.4%	157	9.6%
Substantially diverse	91	5.6%	146	·8.9%	195	11.9%
Moderately diverse Black	166	10.1%	209	12.8%	327	20.0%
Minimally diverse Black	81	4.9%	101	6.2%	117	7.1%
Substantially Black	115	7.0%	128	7.8%	124	7.6%
	1637	100.0%	1637	100.0%	1637	100.0%

FURTHER TESTS OF DIVERSITY

What are the characteristics of the twenty-four tracts identified as stably diverse from 1980–90? These tracts are shown in Table 15.4 according to their metropolitan and county locations and their ecological position within their respective counties. Tracts are classified as located in either the central city (or cities) of the metropolis, in suburban cities, or in the unincorporated area of the county.[2] For ease of exposition the tracts are lettered A–X. Overwhelmingly, the diverse tracts are located in suburban/unincorporated areas (20 of the 24, or 83%). This is in contrast to much of the literature on the racial exclusivity of the suburbs (e.g., Danielson 1976), but is consistent with hypotheses that suggest that racial integration is more likely in newer suburban areas that have been developed in the context of increased enforcement of fair housing laws (Smith 1989; Wilger 1988). Indeed, of the twenty tracts shown to be in suburban or unincorporated areas, *all* have had a majority of their development since 1980.[3]

The suburban or unincorporated status of the diverse tracts raises two issues that bear on the quality of their diversity. First, all tracts, but especially large tracts (of which most are suburban), allow for the possibility that Blacks and Whites occupy separate geographical parts of the tract. Thus, even though the comparative analysis shows that both groups are represented in the appropriate proportions, internal tract segregation may exist, thereby compromising the characterization of diversity. Under these conditions, the apparent diversity may be only a reflection of the way in which tract boundaries are drawn.

Second, a hypothesis exists within the literature suggesting that racial integration may be greater in suburban tracts of southern cities due to the combination of historical patterns of segregation and current patterns of suburbanization (Logan and Schneider 1984; Stahura 1988). Under this reasoning Blacks traditionally

Table 15.3 Diversity Types by Comparative Method Change From 1980 to 1990								
	Sub White		Min div-White		Mod div-White		Sub diverse	
	#	%	#	%	#	%	#	%
Substantially White	661	69.8%	164	17.3%	64	6.8%	37	3.9%
Minimally diverse White	13	8.6%	40	26.3%	43	28.3%	29	19.1%
Moderately diverse White	5	5.9%	17	20.0%	12	14.1%	33	38.8%
Substantially diverse	3	3.3%	8	8.8%	17	18.7%	24	26.4%
Moderately diverse Black	1	0.6%	3	1.8%	2	1.2%	22	13.3%
Minimally diverse Black	0	0.0%	0	0.0%	0	0.0%	1	1.2%
Substantially Black	0	0.0%	0	0.0%	0	0.0%	0	0.0%
Total	**683**	**41.7%**	**232**	**14.2%**	**138**	**8.4%**	**146**	**8.9%**
	Mod div-Black		Min div-Black		Sub Black		Total	
	#	%	#	%	#	%	#	%
Substantially White	20	2.1%	1	0.1%	0	0/0%	**947**	**57.8%**
Minimally diverse-White	27	17.8%	0	0.0%	0	0.0%	**152**	**9.3%**
Moderately diverse-White	15	17.6%	3	3.5%	0	0.0%	**85**	**5.2%**
Substantially diverse	32	35.2%	6	6.6%	1	1.1%	**91**	**5.6%**
Moderately diverse-Black	102	61.4%	35	21.1%	1	0.6%	**166**	**10.1%**
Minimally diverse-Black	13	16.0%	48	59.3%	19	23.5%	**81**	**4.9%**
Substantially Black	0	0.0%	8	7.0%	107	93.0%	**115**	**7.0%**
Total	**209**	**12.8%**	**101**	**6.2%**	**128**	**7.8%**	**1637**	**100.0%**

resided in rural "agricultural" tracts outside of cities into which White suburbanites have recently located. Remnants of these types of tracts exist throughout the South, and are generally recognized by the juxtaposition of older rural Black communities and modern White suburban developments. At issue is whether the diverse suburban tracts identified above belong to this Black-to-White transitional model.

In order to measure the internal distribution of population by race, I have computed the index of dissimilarity for each tract based upon the distribution of population within census block groups.[4] Most of these purportedly diverse tracts contain between five and fourteen of these block groups, thereby providing a basis for judging the extent to which Whites and Blacks reside in the same areas. A few tracts, however, contain less than four such groups, so that conclusions are less reliable, and these have been omitted from the dissimilarity computations reported in Table 15.4.

Standards for the segregation of population within tracts generally do not exist and it is difficult to know what to expect. Some degree of internal tract segregation is likely, and separate White and Black settlement areas are characteristic of even the "classic" diverse places as reported by Goodwin (1979), Saltman (1990), and Keating (1994). Also, the index of dissimilarity is sensitive to the size of the spatial area on which it is computed so that, all other things being equal, larger index values will occur when smaller spatial units are employed (Farley 1993; Taeuber and Taeuber 1965). At the city level, using tracts as the basis for computing levels of segregation, experience shows that places with a dissimilarity index of below .3–.4 are considered to have low levels of segregation, and those with an index below .6 to be only moderately segregated (Farley 1993; Massey and Denton 1993). This standard is most likely overly rigorous for use with index values computed on the basis of the smaller block groups. Nevertheless, the values reported in Table 15.4 show that fifteen of the nineteen tracts for which dissimilarity has been computed have 1990 index values of .49 or less.

This evidence also suggests that the suburban transitional tract model is not appropriate for explaining these diverse tracts. If the transitional model applied, then it is unlikely that the tracts would show low levels of internal segregation as reflected in the dissimilarity scores, and there would not be a continuing growth of new Black households as shown in the market analysis. Nevertheless, in order to more fully test this possibility, I have computed proportions of households by race over time. These proportions are also shown in Table 15.4. Under the reasoning of the Black-to-White transitional suburban model, we would expect to see different settlement patterns over time for Whites and Blacks. For Blacks, large proportions of households should have first moved into their current residence prior to 1970, but small proportions to no Black households will have moved into their homes during the latest period, 1980–90. For Whites there should be small proportions prior to 1970 and large proportions for 1980–90. Contrary to these expectations, however, the patterns of settlement for Blacks and Whites over time are near similar. For each race, the largest proportions exist for the 1980–90 period, and in most instances these proportions are similar for both Whites and Blacks. While there does exist, in most instances, larger pre-1970 proportions for Blacks than Whites,

Table 15.4 Characteristics of Diverse Tracts				
		1970	**1990**	
MSA	**County/Tract**	**Status**	**Location**	**Dissimilarities**
Daytona Beach	Volusia			
	a*	-	unincorp	-
Ft. Walton Beach	Okaloosa			
	b	-	city	0.35
Gainesville	Alachua			
	c	-	unincorp	0.40
	d	-	unincorp	0.24
	e*	-	unincorp	-
Jacksonville	Duval			
	f	sub div	city	0.41
	Nassau			
	g	-	unincorp	0.28
Lakeland-Winter Haven	Polk			
	h	-	unincorp	0.62
	i*	-	unincorp	-
	j	-	unincorp	0.49
Melbourne-Titusville	Brevard			
	k	-	unincorp	0.44

		Year Moved into Present House (%)					
		White			**Blacks**		
MSA	**County/Tract**	**<1970**	**1970-79**	**1980-89**	**<1970**	**1970-79**	**1980-89**
Daytona Beach	Volusia						
	a*	-	-	-	-	-	-
Ft. Walton Beach	Okaloosa						
	b	17.9	21.5	60.6	18.7	13.9	67.4
Gainesville	Alachua						
	c	11.9	22.0	66.0	25.8	17.6	56.8
	d	9.4	20.1	70.2	26.8	20.8	52.5
	e*	0.1	7.3	86.8	26.3	0.0	73.7
Jacksonville	Duval						
	f	27.4	8.6	45.1	17.8	12.9	69.3
	Nassau						
	g	7.7	18.7	73.5	23.5	29.7	46.7
Lakeland-Winter Haven	Polk						
	h	11.0	13.9	75.1	23.9	23.3	52.8
	i*	-	-	-	-	-	-
	j	16.0	18.8	65.2	24.8	13.5	61.8
Melbourne-Titusville	Brevard						
	k	1.1	6.5	92.4	0.0	8.0	92.0

Table 15.4				
Characteristics of Diverse Tracts (continued)				
		1970	1990	
MSA	County/Tract	Status	Location	Dissimilarities
Miami-Hialeah	Dade			
	l	min div w	suburb	0.47
	m*	sub div	unincorp	-
	n	sub w	unincorp	0.59
	o	sub div	suburb	0.45
	p	sub div	suburb	0.43
	Seminole			
	r	sub div	unincorp	0.51
Panama City	Bay			
	s	-	city	0.49
Pensacola	Escambia			
	t	sub div	unincorp	0.69
	u	-	unincorp	0.29
Tampa	Hillsborough			
	v	-	unincorp	0.36
	w	sub div	suburb	0.41
	Pinellas			
	x	-	city	0.33

		Year Moved into Present House (%)					
		White			Blacks		
MSA	County/Tract	<1970	1970-79	1980-89	<1970	1970-79	1980-89
Miami-Hialeah	Dade						
	l	9.6	16.7	73.7	0.0	4.7	92.7
	m*	0.0	0.0	100.0	0.0	0.0	100.0
	n	3.1	29.4	67.6	0.0	15.8	84.2
	o	13.1	19.8	67.1	1.9	14.5	83.6
	p	4.5	9.6	85.9	9.5	25.7	64.8
	Seminole						
	r	-	-	-	-	-	-
Panama City	Bay						
	s	-	-	-	-	-	-
Pensacola	Escambia						
	t	7.5	16.4	76.2	27.2	8.9	63.9
	u	9.9	9.7	80.4	30.2	12.8	57.0
Tampa	Hillsborough						
	v	12.5	12.1	75.4	0.0	12.1	87.9
	w	17.5	21.1	61.4	22.8	20.9	56.3
	Pinellas						
	x	-	-	-	-	-	-

* Fewer than four block groups for the computation of 1990 dissimilarity index.

these proportions, in the context of continued large Black demand in the most recent period, do not appear sufficiently large to support the Black-to-White transition hypothesis.

No further tests of diversity have been performed for the tracts identified under the market criterion. Since these tracts are identified for 1990 only, it is unlikely that most will remain as stably diverse over time (e.g., only 26% of the 1980 diverse tracts under the comparative criterion remained diverse in 1990). Like the comparative tracts, however, 82 percent of the market tracts are located in the suburban or unincorporated areas of their counties, again, suggesting that diversity is increasingly a suburban phenomenon.

CONCLUSION

The main purpose of this chapter has been to explore methods for identifying stable diverse places. In contrast to measuring segregation, there exist few attempts within the literature for measuring integration. Most studies of integrated places have been selected specifically for their integrated qualities, and the few attempts that exist to measure integration more generally suffer from inadequate conceptualization and measurement. As a result, social scientists have little to no information about the incidence and distribution of racial diversity and have no basis for challenging the generally held perceptions that such places occur only as brief periods within the context of racial turnover.

Two separate methods for identifying stable diversity have been developed. The comparative approach rests on evaluating tract racial proportions relative to a comparison area, taken as the county. Diverse places should contain racial proportions that are both similar to, and change in conjunction with, these county patterns. This approach avoids having to define artificial standards for judging both diversity and stability. The market approach is a special instance of the comparative approach that rests on the correspondence between housing costs and the purchasing power of each racial group. Households are allocated to tracts in proportion to these concepts, producing an expected racial distribution within each tract that can be compared to the actual racial distribution of in-movers. Diversity is defined as a correspondence between these expected and actual distributions.

Ideally, both methods should be used separately since there is no proven relationship between places that are integrated by the comparative criterion and those integrated by the market criterion. Indeed, the independence of the two techniques is suggested by the outcomes; many tracts are identified as diverse by the market method but contain racial proportions that are inappropriate for diversity under the comparative method. Moreover, the overlap between the two sets of tracts is only modest; of the twenty-four tracts classified as diverse and stable by the comparative method, only about half (13 tracts) also satisfy the market definition of diversity (Smith 1998). Nevertheless, both types are more apt to occur within the suburban portions of their respective metropolitan areas.

The emphasis of this paper has been on a demonstration of the two methods for identifying diversity. While data limitations compromised the analysis of the market tracts, the evidence does suggest that the places identified as stably diverse by the comparative method are accurately portrayed; both Blacks and Whites appear to be distributed relatively evenly throughout most of the tracts, and most places seem to have maintained a housing market for both Blacks and Whites. Nevertheless, different results are possible with slight changes in some aspects of the methods. Perhaps the most sensitive issue is the criterion used to define the seven categories of diversity. While the particular method I used appears to be responsive to the distribution of the data, other choices are possible, resulting in both wider and narrower boundaries to the substantially diverse category. There are no clear guidelines on this issue, and the decision should be made and evaluated within the context of the particular research question and county racial proportions. For example, where the county proportion Black is either very large or very small, the particular divisions used here are less meaningful. Also at issue may be the relatively simple division of the range of proportions according to the selected number of diversity categories. An alternative may be to use categories based on standard deviation units, but this does not appear to offer much help; the number of categories and the division along the range of standard deviation units still remains an issue. In addition, the skewed distribution of Blacks across census tracts may result in the selection of a standard that reflects historical patterns of discrimination rather than expected outcomes.

A third issue concerns the choice of the larger area upon which the comparison standard is based and reasonable arguments can be made for each of a number of comparison areas. The county was chosen for the comparative method based on the reasoning that use of a larger area, such as the metropolitan area, would lead to unrealistically lower proportions of Blacks needed for a tract to be considered integrated in the central county (i.e., the boundaries of the integrated category would shift downward), and unrealistically higher percentages of Blacks needed for a tract to be considered integrated in the suburban counties. Alternatively, the population of the larger metropolitan area was used as the basis for computing the potential demand for housing in each tract under the market approach, and this was based on the reasoning that metropolitan housing markets generally extend beyond a single county. Given that the methods tap different dimensions of integration, there is no necessary reason to select the same spatial unit on which to define the comparative standard, but different choices are possible.

A number of issues surround the construction of the market method. One relatively minor issue concerns the proportions of income to be spent on housing that are used in the market housing allocation model. Slight changes in these proportions may affect the definition of households eligible for housing at each cost level, but sensitivity analysis with different proportions has shown that small changes have little to no impact on the final results.

Far more critical in the construction and use of the market method is the argument suggested by Galster (1998). Galster states that the use of a criterion based on the expected distribution of in-movers alone does not take into account the corresponding racial distribution of out-movers from the tract. Where the racial composition of out-movers is heavily skewed toward one group or another, the tract population will, over time, change in favor of the alternative group, independent of the racial composition of in-movers. Since the market criterion, as constructed here, has no basis in the existing racial proportions of a place, it can seriously misidentify places that are in the process of racial transition, irrespective of the characteristics of market demand.

Galster's criticisms are correct to a degree. The lack of a basis within the market method for monitoring racial proportions suggests that these proportions are unimportant relative to current racial demand and places that would otherwise not be considered as diverse can be categorized as such only on the basis of current in-movers. The rich, White suburb can claim to be diverse because a token number of minority households have moved in! Taking into account the distribution of out-movers, however, does not appear to be a realistic solution. Not only are these data not generally available, but it is highly unlikely that the distribution of out-movers would be so racially skewed while in-movers correspond to expected proportions. In the typical example the continued demand for housing in an area by a majority of Whites is not likely to be matched by excessive White out movement as well; this expectation contradicts the way in which we understand housing markets and the nature of racially based demand. The criticism does suggest, however, that both the comparative and market methods be employed jointly. Thus, diverse places are those that are composed of both Whites and Blacks in appropriate proportions and in which the market operates to secure the long-term stability of the place (Smith 1998).

Given the emphasis on demonstrating the methodology, I have refrained from a more involved analysis across groups other than non-Hispanic Whites and non-Hispanic Blacks. Clearly, however, the inclusion of Hispanics is warranted, and this is especially so in a state such as Florida where the Hispanic population reaches 13 percent in some counties (and 49% in Dade County). The two methods, however, are not designed to deal with multiple groups at the same time; thus, multiple group analysis must still involve successive two-group comparisons.

In sum, while issues continue to exist, some of them may be readily addressed within the context of a particular analysis. Some of the very thorny problems, however, such as that of constructing an appropriate standard for considering racial and ethnic diversity, may have been moved forward.

NOTES

1. "Integration" is the preferred term in the context of the literature on race, but "diversity" appears to be the preferred term when dealing with multi-racial and multi-ethnic places. In what follows I will use the latter term except where references to existing literature and techniques clearly argue for the use of integration as the most appropriate.

2. Split tracts, lying partially in one jurisdiction and partially in another, are classified on the basis of where a majority of the tract population is located.

3. Florida's fair housing law was first enacted in 1983.

4. These block groups are defined by the Bureau of the Census as aggregates of individual blocks, each of which contains between 250 and 550 housing units, with an ideal size of 400 units.

REFERENCES

Aldrich, Howard. "Ecological Succession in Racially Changing Neighborhoods." *Urban Affairs Quarterly*, vol. 10, March 1975:327–48.

Bogdon, Amy, Joshua Silver, and Margery Austin Turner. *National Analysis of Housing Affordability, Adequacy, and Availability: A Framework for Local Housing Strategies.* Washington, D.C.: U.S. Department of Housing and Urban Development, Office of Policy Development and Research. 1993.

Bradburn, Norman M., Seymour Sudman, and Galen L. Gockel. *Side by Side: Integrated Neighborhoods in America.* Chicago: Quadrangle Books. 1971.

Clark, W.A.V. "Neighborhood Transitions in Multiethnic/Racial Contexts." *Journal of Urban Affairs*, vol. 15, no. 2, 1993:161–72.

Danielson, Michael. *The Politics of Exclusion.* New York: Columbia University Press. 1976.

DeMarco, Donald L. and George. Galster. "Pro-Integrative Policy: Theory and Practice." *Journal of Urban Affairs*, vol. 15, no. 2, 1993:141–60.

Duncan, Otis D. and Beverly Duncan. *The Negro Population of Chicago: A Study of Residential Succession.* Chicago: University of Chicago Press. 1957.

Ellen, Ingrid G. "The State of Racial Integration in the United States: Revealing New Evidence from the 1970s and 1980s." *Journal of Urban Affairs*, vol. 20, no. 1, 1998:27–42.

Farley, John E. "Racial Housing Segregation in St. Louis, 1980-1990: Comparing Block and Census tract Levels." *Journal of Urban Affairs*, vol. 15, no. 6, 1993:515–27.

Farley, John E. "Race Still Matters: The Minimal Role of Income and Housing Cost as Causes of Housing Segregation in St. Louis, 1990." *Urban Affairs Review*, vol. 31, no. 2, 1995:244–54.

Galster, George. "A Stock/Flow Model for Defining Racially Integrated Neighborhoods." *Journal of Urban Affairs*, vol. 20, no. 1, 1998:43–51.

Goodwin, Carole. *The Oak Park Strategy: Community Control of Racial Change.* Chicago: University of Chicago Press. 1979.

Helper, Rose. "Success and Resistance Factors in the Maintenance of Racially Mixed Neighborhoods" in J. M. Goering (ed.) *Housing Desegregation and Federal Policy.* Chapel Hill: University of North Carolina Press. 1986:170–94.

Hermalin, Albert J. and Reynolds Farley. "The Potential for Residential Integration in Cities and Suburbs." *American Sociological Review*, vol. 38, October 1973:595–610.

Jargowsky, Paul. "Ghetto Poverty Among Blacks in the 1980s." *Journal of Policy Analysis and Management*, vol. 13, 1994:288–310.

Keating, W. Dennis. *The Suburban Racial Dilemma: Housing and Neighborhoods.* Philadelphia, PA: Temple University Press. 1994.

Lee, Barrett A. "Racially Mixed Neighborhoods during the 1970s: Change or Stability." *Social Science Quarterly,* vol. 66, June 1985:346–64.

Lee, Barrett A. and Peter B. Wood. "The Fate of Residential Integration in American Cities: Evidence from Racially Mixed Neighborhoods, 1970–1980." *Journal of Urban Affairs*, vol. 12, no. 4, 1990:425–36.

Lee, Barrett A. and Peter B. Wood. "Is Neighborhood Racial Succession Place Specific?" *Demography*, vol. 28, February 1991:21–39.

Logan, John and Mark Schneider. "Racial Segregation and Racial Change in American Suburbs, 1970-1980." *American Journal of Sociology*, vol. 89, no. 4, 1984:874–88.

Maly, Michael and Phillip Nyden. "Creating and Maintaining Stable Racial Diversity in Urban Neighborhoods: Public Policy for the 1990s." *Paper, Annual Meeting of the Urban Affairs Association, Portland, OR* . 1995.

Massey, Douglas S. and Nancy A. Denton. *American Apartheid: Segregation and the Making of the American Underclass*. Cambridge, MA: Harvard University Press. 1993.

Millen, James S. "Factors Affecting Racial Mixing in Residential Areas" in Hawley, A.H. and V.P. Rock (eds.), *Segregation in Residential Areas*. Washington, D.C.: National Academy of Sciences. 1973:148–71.

Molotch, Harvey L. *Managed Integration: The Dilemmas of Doing Good in the City*. Berkeley: University of California Press. 1972.

Moore, Maurice and James McKeown. *A Study of Integrated Living in Chicago*. Chicago: Community and Family Study Center, University of Chicago. 1968.

Nyden, Philip, Michael Maly, and John Lukehart. "The Emergence of Stable Racially and Ethnically Diverse Communities: A Case Study of Neighborhoods in Nine U.S. Cities." Paper presented at the Fannie Mae Foundation Annual Housing Conference, Washington, D.C. 1996.

Obermanns, Richard. "Stability and Change in Racially Diverse Suburbs, 1970-1978. Cleveland Heights, OH: Heights Community Congress. 1980.

Rosenbaum, Emily. "The Influence of Race on Hispanic Housing Choices: New York City, 1978–1987." *Urban Affairs Review*, vol. 32, November 1996:217–43.

Saltman, Juliet. *A Fragile Movement: The Struggle for Neighborhood Stabilization*. Westport, CT: Greenwood Press. 1990.

Schelling, Thomas. "A Process of Residential Segregation: Neighborhood Tipping." Anthony Pascal (ed). *Racial Discrimination in Economic Life*. Lexington: D.C. Heath. 1972.

Schnare, Ann B. *Residential Segregation by Race in U.S. Metropolitan Areas*. Washington, D.C.: Urban Institute, Report No. 246-2. 1977.

Shyrock, Henry S. and Jacob S. Siegal. *The Methods and Materials of Demography*. Washington, D.C.: U.S. Department of Commerce, Bureau of the Census. 1971.

Smith, Richard A. "The Effects of Local Fair Housing Ordinances on Housing Segregation." *American Journal of Economics and Sociology*, vol. 48, April 1989:219–30.

Smith, Richard A. "The Measurement of Segregation Change Through Integration and Deconcentration, 1970–1980." *Urban Affairs Quarterly*, vol. 26, 1991:477–96.

Smith, Richard A. "Discovering Stable Racial Integration." *Journal of Urban Affairs*, vol. 20, no. 1, 1998:1–25.

Stahura, John M. "Changing Patterns of Suburban Racial Composition, 1970–1980." *Urban Affairs Quarterly*, vol. 23, March 1988:448–60.

Taeuber, Karl E. and Alma Taeuber. *Negroes in Cities*. Chicago: Aldine. 1965.

Turner, Margery Austin, Raymond J. Struyk, and John Yinger. *Housing Discrimination Study: Synthesis*. Washington, D.C.: U.S. Department of Housing and Urban Development. 1991.

Vernarelli, Michael J. "Where Should HUD Locate Assisted Housing? The Evolution of Fair Housing Policy" in Goering, J. M. (ed.) Housing Desegregation and Federal Policy. Chapel Hill: University of North Carolina Press. 1986:214–34.

Wilger, Robert. "Enforcement of Fair Housing Laws: Indirect Estimates." Paper presented
    at the 20th Anniversary Conference of the Fair Housing Act of 1968. U.S. Department of
    Housing and Urban Development and Jackson State University. Jackson, Mississippi.
    1988.
Wood, Peter B. and Barrett A. Lee. "Is Neighborhood Racial Succession Inevitable? Forty
    Years of Evidence." *Urban Affairs Quarterly*, vol. 26, June 1991:610–20.

Index

About the Contributors

David Allor, AICP, is a professor in the School of Planning, and a fellow at the Center for the Study of Dispute Resolution, at the University of Cincinnati. He is the author of *The Planning Commissioner's Guide: Processes for Reasoning Together* (1984). He conducts planning commission training sessions nationwide and serves as a consultant to planning commissions. Dr. Allor received his Ph.D. from Syracuse University and his Master's in Planning from the University of Michigan.

Stephen Ameyaw, Ph.D. (Regional Planning and Resource Development, University of Waterloo, Ontario), is Research Associate at the Center for Community Economic Development, Simon Fraser University. Before coming to Simon Fraser University, he taught at the University of Calgary in Alberta. His research and writing has focused on women and socio-economic development, regional planning, sustainable and community development, and appreciative planning. He is the co-coordinator of the Ghana country study and contributed several articles in *Community Development Around the World: Practice, Theory, Research and Training* (H. Campfen ed., 1997). He acts as research and policy adviser to several women and indigenous organizations in Botswana, Tanzania, Burkina Faso, Ghana, and Canada. He has also served as Simon Fraser University's community economic development program coordinator for the Secwepemc Cultural Education Society.

Howell S. Baum is a Professor of Community Planning at the University of Maryland in College Park. He has conducted research and practiced in social planning, education, and community development. He is interested in problems of planning, governance, and development in communities, which he assumes to be multicultural. His most recent book, concerned with these issues, is *The Organization of Hope: Communities Planning Themselves* (1997).

Robert B. Beauregard is a Professor in the Milano Graduate School of Management and Urban Policy at the New School for Social Research in New York City. He writes on planning theory and urban theory.

Michael A. Burayidi is coordinator of the Urban and Regional Studies program at the University of Wisconsin Oshkosh. He is coauthor (with Alfred T. Kisubi) of *Race and Ethnic Relations in the First Person* (Praeger 1998), and editor and contributor to *Multiculturalism in a Cross National Perspective* (1996). His recent research work focuses on strategies for downtown revitalization in small urban communities.

Steven Dinero, Ph.D., is Assistant Professor of Middle East Studies at Philadelphia University in Philadelphia, Pennsylvania. He received his Ph.D. in Urban Planning & Policy Development from Rutgers–The State University of New Jersey in 1995, where he wrote his doctoral dissertation on the Negev bedouin resettlement project. His most recent research concerns the development of the bedouin community as an attraction for international tourism.

John Forester is Professor and Chair of the Department of City and Regional Planning at Cornell University. A Ph.D. from the University of California at Berkeley, his research interests include the micro-politics and ethics of planning practice, including the ways planners work in the face of power and conflict. For the past decade he has been producing first-person voice "profiles" of planners, mediators, and participatory action researchers in the United States and abroad. His previous work includes *Planning in the Face of Power* (1989) and (with Norman Krumholz) *Making Equity Planning Work: Leadership in the Public Sector* (1990). His most recent book is *The Deliberative Practitioner* (1999).

Thomas Harper is Associate Professor and Coordinator of the Planning Program, Faculty of Environmental Design, University of Calgary. In addition to planning theory, he has done research in several areas of public policy, management, and planning, and has been a consultant to all levels of government and to private clients on a variety of planning matters.

Alvin James currently serves as the Planning Director of Santa Cruz County, California. He has worked in the planning field for twenty-seven years, having begun his career as an assistant planner with Middlesex County in New Jersey. Mr. James has worked as a professional urban planner and public administrator at the regional, county, and municipal levels in various communities including: Pittsburgh, Pennsylvania; San Francisco, Oakland, and Pasadena, California. He has been a planning director for more than thirteen years, having served in that capacity, in addition to his current appointment, the cities of Oakland and Pasadena, California.

Mark Lapping is Professor in the Muskie School of Public Service and Provost/Vice President for Academic Affairs at the University of Southern Maine, Portland, Maine. Previously, he has served as founding Director of the School of Rural Planning and Development at the University of Guelph (Ontario, Canada), Dean of the College of Architecture, Planning, and Design at Kansas State University, and founding Dean of the Bloustein School of Planning and Public Policy at Rutgers University. He is the author of several books, including *Rural Planning and Development in the United States*, the *Small Town Planning Handbook*, *A Long, Deep Furrow: Three Centuries of Farming in New England*, *Rural America: Legacy and Change*, and *Contested Countryside: The Rural-Urban Fringe in North America*, as well as many chapters, articles, and monographs. He is a frequent consultant to local, state/regional/provincial, and national governments in the area of rural planning, rural and economic development.

Peter Marcuse, a lawyer and urban planner, teaches housing and comparative planning at Columbia University. He is now at work on a comparative study of the impact of public policy on the spatial patterns of cities under the pressure of globalization. He also has written widely, including work on housing policy, red-lining, racial segregation, urban divisions, New York City's planning history, property rights and privatization, and the history of housing.

Peter B. Meyer, Ph.D. (Economics, University of Wisconsin-Madison, 1970), is Director of the Center for Environmental Management and Professor of Urban Policy and Economics at the University of Louisville. He previously (1978–87) served as Director of the Local Economic Development Assistance Project at the Pennsylvania State University. He is the author of more than seventy-five articles, chapters, and reports on community and urban economic development, sustainable development, and urban brown fields. His most recent books include editing *Comparative Studies in Local Economic Development: Problems in Policy Implementation* (Greenwood Press, 1993) and coauthoring *Contaminated Land: Reclamation, Redevelopment and Reuse in the United States and the European Union* with Kristen Yount and R. H. Williams.

Christopher R. Reaves is a doctoral student in the Ph.D. program in Urban and Public Affairs at the University of Louisville. He is currently completing a dissertation on the problems of measuring environmental inequality, specifically looking at how differences in statistical definitions of "minority communities" and the geographic frames employed in the media can change findings. One major aspect of his work addresses the use of the percentage poor or minority in a defined geographic area, rather than an arbitrary cut off at some percentage defining a poor or minority area, and the resultant findings on environmental injustice problems.

Siddhartha Sen is an Associate professor and Coordinator of the graduate program in City and Regional Planning at Morgan State University. He has widely published in the areas of international planning and urban design.

Richard A. Smith is a professor of urban and regional planning at Florida State University. His general interests are in the area of urban growth dynamics and, within this context, the problems of population distributions by race and ethnicity. He has written numerous articles that appear in the planning and urban affairs journals on the subjects of racial segregation and racial integration.

J. T. Spence, AICP, holds a Master's of Community Planning from the University of Cincinnati School of Planning, and has held professional planning positions in both the public and private sectors. He is currently a City Commissioner in Covington, Kentucky, and a Teaching Assistant and Ph.D. student in the Political Science Department at the University of Cincinnati.

Stanley Stein is Resident Philosopher in the Faculty of Environmental Design, University of Calgary. In addition to planning theory, he is also interested in ethics, epistemology, aesthetics, and their application to design and planning.

ISBN 0-275-96125-7

90000>

EAN

9 780275 961251

HARDCOVER BAR CODE